Commissioned by the **CENTRAL CONFERENCE OF AMERICAN RABBIS** - New York 1972

Rabbi and Synagogue in Reform Judaism

THEODORE I. LENN, Ph.D. and ASSOCIATES

WEST HARTFORD, CONNECTICUT

"... Her
children
rise
up
and
call
her
blessed;

TO

NORMA LEHMAN LENN

her
husband
also,
and
he
praises
her..."

"A Rabbi is like Democracy. If all is well, we
take him for granted. If all is not well, we
blame him. Democracy, with all its faults, is
the bulwark for man's survival. The Rabbi, with
all his human failings, has been and shall continue to be the bulwark for the Jew's survival
as a Jew."

- Reform congregant -

FORWARD

The work leading to the following Study was initiated by Levi Olan and was authorized by the C.C.A.R. under his Presidency. Before the Study was undertaken, a number of preliminary procedures were adopted by the Committee responsible for the task. These included two task-force sessions with members of the HUC-JIR Faculty and U.A.H.C. representatives; conferences with Faculty and Board members of the HUC-JIR; conferences with U.A.H.C. lay and professional leaders; an all-day meeting with national congregational and youth leaders; and several meetings of the Committee itself.

It was decided that the Study itself should be descriptive rather than prescriptive and that evaluations and recommendations should emerge only after further deliberations by the Committee. Consequently, this Study represents the first aspect of our work. With the publication of the Study, the members of the C.C.A.R. will have an opportunity to evaluate and discuss it extensively. The Committee fells that this is an important part of the process of analysis, and it has chosen not to react until after our colleagues have responded first. We then propose to convene a meeting at which members of our entire movement will contribute their insights, after which the Committee will undertake to draw up its proposals.

It is apparent that the Study touches on all aspects of Reform Judaism including our own Conference, and offers an opportunity for each element to examine itself in the light of new opportunities now available to our movement. Self-examination and the new opportunities could well result in a great renewal for us all.

We thank Rabbi Olan and Rabbi Roland Gittelsohn during whose administrations the work of the Committee was encouraged and advanced.

David Polish, Chairman	Samuel Karff
Bernard Bemberger	Bernard Martin
Herman Blumberg	Lou Silberman
Leon Feuer	Daniel Silver

PREFACE AND ACKNOWLEDGMENTS

This study is not designed to <u>prove</u> anything. No hypothesis was formulated for the purpose of being tested.

All we have here is an inventory of findings. What one will want to prove or to disprove with any of these findings will be one's own concern.

Many questions were asked, and many answers were obtained. And it is these questions and these answers that constitute the heart of this study, - thus far. The rest is up to others.

Once having dispatched the objectives of the study, the Central Conference of American Rabbis respected the complete freedom of the researcher and assisted in all ways. For this, the writer is truly grateful.

Rabbi Roland B. Gittelsohn, then President, and Rabbi David Polish, then Chairman, <u>Committee on Rabbinic Training</u>,* and now President of the Central Conference of American Rabbis, gave of their minds and of their hearts, profoundly and unstintingly. Rabbi Sidney L. Regner, former Executive Vice-President and his successor, Rabbi Joseph B. Glaser, and Rabbi Malcolm Stern, Director of Placement, were most helpful at all times and gave good counsel.

---

*Name subsequently changed to <u>Committee on the Future of the Rabbinate and the Synagogue</u>.

Profound gratitude is herein acknowledged to professional colleagues and associates. Their names and contributions are noted on a subsequent page.

To Mrs. Elaine Martin and Miss Elizabeth Gabany, secretaries and research assistants, to whom <u>chuppa</u> is a very funny word, and <u>simcha</u> will always be a foreign car, but whose skills, trust, and devotion are a pleasure to behold, the writer is most sincerely grateful.

Most important are the many members of the rabbinate, - from pulpit, classroom, and administrative office, - and the many congregants, the rabbinical students, the rebbetzins, and the young people who responded to long questionnaires, submitted to (sometimes longer) interviews, and in many other ways shared of their knowledge and of their feelings of the Judaism that they are now living, and of the Judaism that they would hope to live in the years ahead. For their cooperation, their kindness, and for their contribution to this joint effort, genuine appreciation is herein tendered.

                               Theodore I. Lenn, Ph.D.

West Hartford, Connecticut
January 15, 1972

RESEARCH ASSOCIATES FOR THIS STUDY

Consultant	Consulting Capacity
1. Louis Gold, M.D. Psychiatrist, Hartford	Data analysis. Trend analysis.
2. David Komisar, Ph.D. Consulting Research Psychologist; Provost, University of Hartford	Research design. Refinement of questionnaire instruments. Data analysis.
3. James B. Mathews, Ph.D. Associate Professor of Psychology, University of Hartford	Technical consultant
4. Norman Miller, Ph.D. Chairman and Professor of Sociology, Trinity College, Hartford	Chief research associate.
5. Peter Park, Ph.D. Professor of Sociology, University of Massachusetts	Research design. Research procedures.
6. Seymour Warkov, Ph.D. Professor of Sociology, University of Connecticut	Research design. Refinement of questionnaire instruments.
7. May Weinstein, M.D. Psychiatrist, West Hartford	Data analysis.
8. Rabbi Harry Z. Zwelling Temple B'nai Israel (Conservative) New Britain, Connecticut	Rabbinical consultant. Trend analysis.

RABBI AND SYNAGOGUE

IN REFORM JUDAISM

T A B L E   O F   C O N T E N T S

PART IV: THE SEMINARY STUDENT

CHAPTER 20: (continued)

PART VII. CONCLUSION

x

G R A P H I C   P R E S E N T A T I O N S

F I G U R E S

G R A P H I C   P R E S E N T A T I O N S

T A B L E S

PART I

INTRODUCTION

CHAPTER 1: HOW IT CAME TO PASS . . .

At its 1969 convention, in Houston, Texas, the Central Conference of American Rabbis was presented with a report by Rabbi David Polish in his role as Chairman of the Committee on Rabbinic Training.

That report brought forth this study.

As happens with most committees who confront their tasks with zeal, sincerity and commitment, the initial formulations of the Committee on Rabbinic Training* espoused hopes and dreams, although realistic, that were nevertheless profoundly formidable bordering on lavish.**

Basically, the Committee put it this way:

> The area we hope to explore covers three questions:
> I. The role of the rabbi, present and future.
> II. What kind of training is needed for the American Rabbinate?
> III. The changing role of the Synagogue.

---

* The name was subsequently changed to Committee on the Future of the Rabbinate and the Synagogue.

**The full report is recorded in the Central Conference of American Rabbis Yearbook. New York: 1970, Vol. LXXXIX, pp. 106-108.

Each of the above "questions" was then reinforced by many equally
formidable "sub-questions," - each of which, if researched in
entirety, might very likely yield a major study in its own right.
And the plans called for a little more, - "a sociological projection
of the Jewish Community." Not unrealistic, but just a little too
much for one bite.

Approximately a month after the Houston Meetings, Rabbi David Polish,
while visiting a boyhood rabbi-friend of his in Connecticut, discussed the projected study with him, and upon the latter's suggestion, consulted with the writer.

Over the next month or so, the usual arrangements were completed.
Reformulations of basic plans, new research designs, contractual
agreements, and such, were consummated, and by the Fall of 1969
serious investigation got under way. By the Fall of 1971, the project
(sans write-up), was completed.

That is how it came to pass . . .

A few more words before we get into things.

This is "in-house" research. It means that the client commissioned a
researcher to investigate its "own house" for its own use. The
writer was not commissioned to produce a book for publication. The
findings belong to the client. The underlying assumption that jus-
tifies "in-house" research is that if the client's internal structure
and process derives benefit from the findings, it is presumed that
the results thereof will be transmitted, subsequently, to the
external world which it serves, and of which it is an integral part.
In the end, all knowledge that is to benefit society must be public

knowledge if society is to be served,- fully aware that society's values at a given time will dictate the use (or abuse) of such knowledge.

This is a sociological inquiry. As such, it is committed to the scientific method. Scientific inquiry deals with <u>what is</u>, not with <u>what ought or ought not to be</u>, or <u>should or should not be</u>. Values are dealt with as social facts, - as data, <u>per se</u>. This is the essence of the scientific canon of free inquiry. "The sociologist's chief duty is to build up the most accurate body of knowledge <u>about</u> human relationships that is possible. The use of this knowledge . . . remains largely for others to carry out."*

Thus the final <u>meaning</u> that is to be given to the data contained in this study, and the <u>use</u> thereof, are the responsibilities of The Central Conference of American Rabbis.

This study provides many answers, yet it provides no final answer. It provides answers to many specific questions. It usually provides few or no answers to questions that were not asked, and it provides few answers to that reader whose greater concern is for his own immediate professional needs, rather than for the needs of Reform Judaism as a social institution and a social process.

---

* John F. Cuber, <u>Sociology: Synopsis of Principles.</u>
    New York: Appleton-Century-Crofts, 1963, p. 5.

CHAPTER 2: PATHWAYS TO DATA: THE RESEARCH PROCESS

1. Formulation of Objectives.

Initial orientation of the research objectives involved in this study
was worked out with Rabbi David Polish, then Chairman of the Committee on Rabbinic Training of the Central Conference of American
Rabbis. Subsequently there were sessions with the Committee as a
whole and with Rabbi Roland B. Gittelsohn, then President of CCAR.

The discussions culminated in an overall objective that was formulated as a question:

> To the extent that any malaise exists in American Reform
> Judaism, how might it be identified and assessed by a
> study of the attitudes and behaviors of today's American
> Reform rabbinate?

2. Review of the Literature.

Fortunately there were primary sources which were immediately available to the researcher. A great number of Reform rabbis, at the
Committee's request, had submitted personal evaluations of the Reform
rabbinate and various other aspects of Reform Judaism. These ranged
from brief one- or two-page letters to twenty-page excellently prepared, well-thought-out statements. Many not only identified
specific inadequacies, but followed up with specific recommendations.
These evaluations had already been submitted to the Committee before
the present writer had come on the scene. Hence the immediate
availability of these documents provided the researcher with a very

meaningful orientation, in breadth and in depth, with the "big picture" that was to be investigated.

The plethora of <u>secondary</u> sources, those dealing with religion as a social institution which is presently enveloped in a massive confrontation with social change, would constitute a volume in itself. Most Reform rabbis are probably all too familiar with the majority of them. They comprise daily newspaper items, lead articles in the popular magazines, scholarly articles in both Jewish-sponsored and secular professional journals, as well as major monographs and books. The central theme of much of the current literature might properly be labelled as "crisis literature."

Almost all religious organizations which were flourishing (at least in terms of full pews), from World War II to about 1960, started to complain that they were beginning to experience something akin to the initial tremors of an earthquake, and by the time the second half of the decade was launched, the full force of the earthquake had already unleashed its fury in widely different sectors. God was dead. The pews were emptying. Roman Catholicism, the Protestant denominations, and Judaism (especially Reform and Conservative), began to identify dysfunctional apparatus, rebellious youth, recalcitrant clergy, and "lost" congregants and parishioners going every which way. By-products of traditional religious procedures began to crop up. Many Christian clergymen were moving some of their operations into the heart of the bedlam. Havurot came into being in Boston and New York. God was not always left behind in these forms, but God was beginning to have to share his authority and majesty with gurus, with some self-appointed and self-anointed deity figures, and with anyone else whose charisma "worked" for those who would follow.

Much of the secondary literature, at least as sampled by this writer, is hypercritical of the religious establishment, almost as though religion is a separate entity and not interwoven with the other major social institutions which constitute our total society. To be sure, Viet Nam, the environment, and the minorities are pulled in somewhere in the overall diagnoses, but not necessarily the <u>total social institutions</u> of education, the government, the economy, and the family. The latter, of course, have their own interpreters, evaluators, and breast-beaters. Religion, by many clergymen and laymen alike, has been dissected and diagnosed <u>as a failing social institution</u>. Unfortunately, it is rather uncommon to note in many of these writings the fact that social change in one major social institution is inextricably interwoven with the changes that are taking place in the other major social institutions. To focus one's attention on the changes that are manifesting themselves in <u>one</u> segment of society without regard for those changes and "happenings" in the other segments of society, makes possible the taking up of alarmist cries of "crisis."

It should be noted that not <u>all</u> the secondary sources yield this "gloom and doom" diagnosis. Not <u>all</u> pronounce the patient dead. Not <u>all</u> dissect and walk away without any prescription for at least some attempt at surgery. Not <u>all</u>, but <u>most</u>!

Piercing through the conglomeration of "gloom and doom" are a few writers who have harnessed themselves to "what is," and have then gone further to what might yet be, depending upon how we deal with

the "what is." The trees do not hide the forest from Professor
Nathan Glazer:*

> . . . the major problems facing Judaism and Jews today
> lie in the development of certain contradictions, cer-
> tain dilemmas, inherent in the effort to combine these
> two tendencies that make up modern American Judaism,
> the ethnic and the national on the one hand, and the
> liberal on the other, and in the development of these
> ideals themselves.
> . . . .
> . . . When Jews face an intellectual atmosphere in which
> to be a liberal is to be a sell-out, that is a crisis
> for American Judaism. For if it is not to be liberal,
> then what is it to be?

3. The Subjects of Our Study: The Samples.

The chief focus of this study is on the Reform rabbinate,- their
attitudes, and their behaviors. Supplementary to, and for the purposes of understanding the rabbi, his roles, his needs, his satisfactions and his frustrations in overall context, is an examination
of the Reform synagogue. Thus much of the data contained herein is
a comparative assessment of rabbis vis-à-vis their congregants, not
only as they see each other, but as each sees the world of Judaism.
As a major by-product, of course, we are now in possession of a
massive amount of data concerning Reform Jews in America. Further
supplementary samples to help in the assessment of the rabbi are
"inside" views of the attitudes and the behaviors of Reform rabbinical students, Reform youth (pre-college), and the rebbetzins.

---

*Nathan Glazer, "The Crisis in American Jewry," Midstream,
    November, 1970, pp. 6 and 8.

From the CCAR office an up-to-date directory of membership was
obtained. Selected from the total membership were all rabbis who
resided in the United States as of November, 1970. Included
also were Chaplains with A.P.O. addresses. The total number of
rabbis who were listed as living in the United States along with the
A.P.O. Chaplains was 942. Questionnaires were sent to these 942
Reform rabbis. The total usable questionnaires received prior to
the cut-off date was 620. The data tabulated and analyzed for this
study is based on 620 responses. This is a response rate of 66%.
Of the 620 usable responses, 506 were from full-time pulpit rabbis.
An additional 103 questionnaires were returned beyond the 620. Of
these, 33 were not usable for our research. They were invalid for a
variety of reasons, but mostly because they were not completed according to instructions, so that even after editing, they were unsuit-
able for key-punching. The balance of 70 could not be used because
they arrived beyond the cut-off date. Another 33 responses were received from rabbis' relatives or from their secretaries informing
us that the rabbis were not available to respond because of such
reasons as death, extended illness, vacations, or temporary non-
residence in the country. There were also 19 incorrect addresses.
When forwarding addresses were obtained, within the United States, a
questionnaire was sent to the new address. Only three forwarding
addresses yielded returns prior to the cut-off date.

The fact should be noted that if we deduct from the 942 figure, the
number of those who could not be reached because of a wrong address
(16) and the number of those who could not respond because of other
reasons (33), the total population sample reduces itself from 942 to
893, yielding a 69% return rate. Nevertheless our computations will
speak for a 66% return, because they are based on the 942 figure.
Reasonably similar circumstances prevail with all the other samples

which were queried, and this, of course, is good for survey research, and the response rates are more than acceptable in terms of validity.

We are obligated to take note of the fact that of the 942 rabbis who were asked to devote an hour or two of their time to complete the questionnaire, some 322 did not do it, for one reason or another. It is proper to deduct the total of 68 who could not do so for reasons of unavailability, which means 254 actually did not respond. It is a small percentage in most surveys, but one to be noted. Because the questionnaire was an exceeding long and demanding instrument, the researcher is happy to note nevertheless, that the actual returns exceed the projected expectations.

In an attempt to determine the amount of non-response bias to the mail questionnaire, a comparison was made between the distribution by length of service for those rabbis who returned the questionnaire, and the distribution of Reform rabbis ordained during the comparable periods. The comparison shows a very satisfactory concordance in at least this respect. While there are always additional sources of bias which may have crept in, one is greatly encouraged by the results of this test, particularly since many of the rabbis in the oldest group were deceased or for other reasons did not respond. This would serve to reduce even further the very small differences found.

The congregant sample was drawn not by households, since there is no nationwide mailing list available. It was drawn from the universe of Reform congregations. Eleven congregations were chosen on the basis of size, region, and date of founding. Considerable help in identifying the sample came from information that was supplied by Rabbi Malcolm Stern, CCAR Director of Placement, and by information

that was supplied by some Regional directors. Mailing lists from
each of the congregations selected were obtained from the congregations themselves, and the questionnaires were mailed directly to the
head of each household chosen. In the case of very large congregations,
a sample of households was drawn; in the case of the smaller ones,
every head of household was sent a questionnaire. The total of eleven
congregations and the number of congregants they represent was the
maximum manageable and needed for our purposes. The total number of
questionnaires mailed was 2498. The number returned after one follow-
up letter was 984 usable questionnaires, making for a return rate of
39%. More information on the congregant sample and its use will be
explained in the introduction to Part III: The Reform Congregations.

The seminarian sample was intended to reach all those currently in
residence at the three HUC-JIR centers. Only the California and
Cincinnati schools were able to respond. It was too late in the
semester for the New York school. It was arranged to accept the responses from New York in the Fall when classes would reconvene, but
these were not forthcoming. Hence all statistical data in this study
are based on Cincinnati and California responses only. Other data,
however, were obtained from New York, and this will be noted later.
Of the 192 questionnaires mailed to seminarians, 58 usable returns
were received, making for a return rate of 30%.

The youth sample is drawn from the same synagogues that provided the
adult congregant sample. In this manner we have information from
youth and adults who are exposed to the same rabbi, same religious
school, and same synagogue practices. And assuming there is an identifiable flavor to the overall Judaism that prevails in a given community or region, then this too will have been experienced (or be

available to be experienced), by both the youth and the adults who
were asked many of the same questions in their respective questionnaires. Furthermore there is the additional strong probability that
many of the respondents are parent-child combinations, so that our
comparative generational assessments represent an even closer "fit"
than required by the overall research objective. Of the 500 questionnaires for youth which were mailed to our synagogue sample, a
total of 264 usable returns from nine congregations came back, a 53%
return rate. One synagogue could not participate in the youth assessment because it was a reasonably new congregation and had no high
school department as yet. Another synagogue replied too late.

The construction of a sample for the rabbis' wives was an easy matter.
Since the rabbinate response had already revealed that virtually all
rabbis (94%) are married, it was decided to establish a wives' sample
by arbitrarily choosing every other rabbi's name and mailing a questionnaire to MRS. _____. To be sure this would be received by a small
number without a spouse, but it was still the least costly and completely random procedure that presented itself. Questionnaires were
mailed to 471 rebbetzins. The number of usable returns was 238, a
51% return rate.

Following is the summary of samples:

		Mailed	Usable Returns	Percentage Return Rate
1.	Rabbinate - - - - - -	942	620	66%
2.	Congregants - - - - -	2498	984	39%
3.	Seminarians - - - - -	192*	58	30%
4.	Temple youth - - - -	500	264	53%
5.	Rabbis' wives - - - -	471	238	51%

*The respective deans of the three HUC-JIR schools indicated the fol-
lowing numbers of students in residence: New York-45, Cincin-
nati-132, California-15. Inasmuch as no returns were received
from New York, the total seminarian response rate, if based on
Cincinnati and California only (147), could properly be viewed
as an almost 40% rate of return.

With the exception, then, of no questionnaire returns from the New
York school, the samples are fully acceptable by standard survey
research procedures.

4. Collecting the Data.

The data were obtained basically from five sources:

1) Primary (written) sources (letters, memoranda, minutes *162*
    of meetings, etc.).
2) Secondary sources (review of the literature).
3) Questionnaires. *160 open ended q 307*
4) Interviews. *155, 171*
5) Participant-observation. *14-15*
   Art of Soc. 152

We have already discussed the primary and secondary sources. The
questionnaire to the rabbinate consists of 60 pages, and 143 basic
questions. Many of the basic questions consist of several sub-
questions. Some questions ask for specific factual data, such as age
and income. Those questions which are designed to elicit attitudes
are usually scaled. This is a procedure wherein the respondent may
express himself, for instance, on a five-point scale such as "Strongly
agree," "Agree," "Uncertain," "Disagree," or "Strongly disagree." Thus
the respondent is not faced with a dichotomous situation wherein he
can only say "Yes" or "No." To be sure, certain key questions are
asked more than once, in different contexts, in order to assess
reliability and validity. For instance, after presenting the rabbinate
and seminarians with a proposed multi-university model, several scaled
questions are asked. The first question calls for a response to the
statement, " . . . it is a good proposal." The last question in the

same sequence calls for a response to the statement, "The whole proposal
is a dream." If equal thought is given in rendering these two responses,
ideally the same number who say yes to the first statement should say
no to the second statement. In a realistic context, it is hard to
assess something as "good," while simultaneously labelling it a "dream."
It so happens that 69% said "Yes" to the first statement, and 69% said
"No" to the second statement. Ideal reliability. Not all cases yield
such total consistency. As was stated, it was a long questionnaire.
It demanded from one to two hours to be completed. It is a tribute
indeed to the substantial number of rabbis who took the time and effort
to complete the instrument, and in the time allotted. After an initial
slow-up of returns, two follow-up letters, one from the then President
of the CCAR, and one from the researcher, brought forth 26% additional
returns.

The questionnaires to the remaining population samples were reasonably
similar to the rabbinate questionnaire in construction and format, but
not as long and not as demanding. In each case a small random sample
of subjects from each population universe was submitted a tentative
questionnaire for pilot study purposes. Aside from the basic rabbinate
questionnaire, by far the most incisive scrutiny, and the most helpful
assistance in the construction of a questionnaire instrument, came
from the eight rebbetzins who were consulted (via correspondence) for
this guidance. It was impossible to incorporate all their recommendations.

Interviews, over 85% of which were conducted by the writer himself,
consisted of "structured" and "unstructured" types. Many started off
as unstructured, but at points focused more sharply on specific concerns.

The interviews were conducted on a random basis, but were based always
on the availability of subjects wherever the interviewer happened to
be attending conferences, informal Synagogue meetings, conventions,
and Regional meetings. These ranged from Cape Cod, Massachusetts, to
Palm Springs, California. Where subjects could be reached on an individual basis, by virtue of the researcher's personal and professional
travels, they, too, would be subjected to interviews. Many were depth
interviews, others were of a briefer type.

The following categories were interviewed:

                Rabbis 101
                Congregants 260*
                Seminarians 18**
                Youth 62***
                Rabbis' wives 37

Throughout the two years of research, the researcher, as a Reform Jew,
fully participated in the many meetings and conferences that he attended. But it was more than mere participation. Notes were continually
taken on all that was observed. Verbal and non-verbal behavior were
noted and recorded. This is what the social anthropologist calls
participant-observation. It provides the researcher not only with
factual data, but also with the "feel" of things. During most of the
interviews, and during most of the participatory experiences, a tape

---

*These included 47 Board members from 41 different congregations.

**In addition, another 15 were interviewed in small group encounters.

***In addition, another 40 were interviewed in small group encounters.

recorder was employed. The participant-observation technique included
not only the formal experiences of meetings, conferences, and conventions, but also extended itself to various informal experiences that
are an integral part of formal meetings. These included the dinner
table, short walks between sessions, random conversations in the hotel
lobby, and informal evening "rap" sessions with small groups.

5. Processing the Data.

All the questionnaires were edited. This means that each questionnaire
was examined and prepared for transferring the data to punch cards.
Many respondents do not always follow instructions meticulously.
Although the answers are there, they aren't always in the right place,
and unless this is corrected, the key-punch technician cannot perform
her function. The editing process also extracted all written comments
which were included in the questionnaires, and these were many. Subsequently these were categorized, and random samples are included
into various sections of the report for the purpose of illustrating
the statistical data.

After the questionnaires were edited, the data were transferred to
punch cards and computer-processed. The two rabbinate and congregant
questionnaires, the two longest, were computer-processed at Columbia
University, Bureau of Applied Social Research. The seminarian, youth
and rebbetzin questionnaires were computer-processed by Eric Juhlin
Associates, Hartford.

The tapes and notes of all interviews and meetings were edited and
categorized in much the same way as were the written comments from the
questionnaires. Similarly all primary and secondary sources were also
prepared for inclusion in this report.

6. Presentation of the Findings.

Where possible, the data are formulated in terms of comparative assessments, and in terms of certain selected variables, such as length of service in the Rabbinate, age, religious belief, and several other attitudinal and behavioral components.

This report is divided into seven Parts. Allowing one part for the Introduction, and one part for the Conclusion, the remaining five parts are each devoted to the specific samples studied,- rabbinate, congregants, seminarians, youth, and rebbetzins.

The pertinent findings are presented in narrative form, often accompanied by some evaluative commentary, based on what the data tell us, not in terms of opinion or judgment.

Because of the voluminous amount of data, the reader is supplied with a number of graphic presentations. These are in the form of Tables and Figures. In some cases, the findings with regard to specific areas of investigation are so voluminous, that it would take pages and pages of narrative just to state them consecutively. This would be very demanding on the reader. In these cases, the findings have been codified in a manner where tabular presentation is substituted for narrative. But not all raw data will be presented in Tables or Figures. In many cases they will be treated in narrative form only.

The Figures are sufficiently illustrative, that no further comment need be made here. The Tables, on the other hand, may often be more demanding on the reader. Some Tables, to be sure, are a simple matter. One set of responses is recorded in one column of percentages. But other

Tables deal with <u>two or more variables</u>. These Tables can <u>not</u> be
<u>glanced</u> at, as the reader will soon find out. These multi-variable
Tables need to be approached by first asking oneself the following
questions:

1) What are the <u>questions</u> that this Table is trying to
    answer for us?
2) Who are the <u>respondents</u> involved in the answers?
3) What are we being told <u>about the respondents</u> who
    are involved in these <u>particular answers</u>?
4) <u>What do the responses really tell us?</u>

Many of these Tables have been composed from data that run across the
different population samples. And it is these <u>comparative assessments</u>
which may provide some of the most meaningful insights into what is
really going on in the Reform Movement.

Throughout the presentation, maximum effort is made to provide complete
anonymity for all questionnaire respondents, for all those interviewed,
for all other informants, as well as for all congregations. Only in
those cases where an item has appeared in <u>public</u> <u>print</u> is documentation
provided. Under the best of camouflage, it may be possible that one's
identification might show through. This would only happen when certain
readers might have some personal knowledge of specific conditions which
were unknown to the writer at the time of writing this account.

PART II

THE REFORM RABBINATE

CHAPTER 3: DEMOGRAPHIC PROFILE OF THE REFORM RABBINATE

1. Age Distribution.

The Reform rabbis in our sample range in age from 26 to 79, - a
span of 3 generations. Moreover, the very young and the old are
about evenly represented. As Figure 1 shows, 9% of our respondents are under 30, while 10% are 65 or over. On the whole,
however, the Reform rabbinate is a young group. One out of
four is less than 34 years old, and the majority (54%) are not
yet 45 years old.

The probable reasons for this are two-fold. Some older rabbis
are now retired and may have been disinclined to return the
questionnaire. The rapid growth of Reform Judaism since World
War II is probably even a more important explanation. It is
to be noted in this connection, however, that the number under
30 is about half the number in the next age group. We shall note
later that there has been a falling-off in the "holding" rate of
our seminarians during recent years. While by far the largest
single five-year category is the 30-34 year old group (17%), it
is significant to recognize that this has fallen off almost half

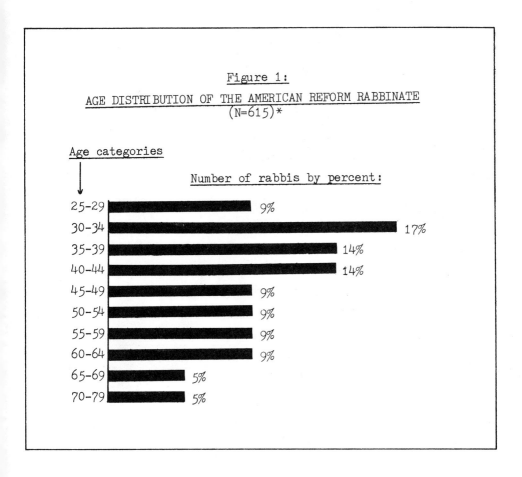

Figure 1:

AGE DISTRIBUTION OF THE AMERICAN REFORM RABBINATE
(N=615)*

Age categories

Number of rabbis by percent:

Age	Percent
25-29	9%
30-34	17%
35-39	14%
40-44	14%
45-49	9%
50-54	9%
55-59	9%
60-64	9%
65-69	5%
70-79	5%

(9%) with regard to the 25-29 year group, the latter being the most
recent five-year category of graduates. Virtually all (94%) Reform
rabbis are married and another 2% have been married in the past.
While 8% of the rabbis are not (yet?) fathers, 14% have 1 child,
42% have 2 children, and 26% have three. Some 10% have 4 or more
children. (Figure 31, Chapter 11, presents comparative figures
of family size of rabbis and congregants.)

---

*N indicates number of respondents to a particular question. This will
 apply to all graphic presentations.

		Table 1:		
		LENGTH OF SERVICE OF REFORM RABBIS		

Number of years since ordination	When ordained	Rabbis ordained (N=617)	In active rabbinate (N=608)	In present position (N=603)
		%	%	% *
0–4	1967–71	17	17	45
5–9	1962–66	17	18	17
10–14	1957–61	14	15	10
15–19	1952–56	11	10	9
20–24	1947–51	9	9	8
25–29	1942–45	6	6	4
30–34	1937–41	7	9	2
35–39	1932–36	10	8	2
40–44	1927–31	5	6	1
45–49	1922–26	3	1	1
50–54	1917–21	1	1	0

* Columns will not always equal 100% because of "rounding-off" process.

2. Length of Service and Tenure.

One out of six rabbis in our sample has been ordained for less than five years, and one out of every three has been ordained for

less than 10 years. At the other end of the continuum, one
out of four rabbis has been ordained for thirty or more years.

The findings, as shown in Table 1, thus reveal an interesting
story, - a large number of comparatively new rabbis, a steady
decline in the number of rabbis with experience, reaching a low
of 6% in the case of those in the 25-29 year bracket, followed
by an overwhelming 26% who have been ordained for thirty years
or more. This reflects the decline in the number of ordinations
during the late 1930's, a trend which continued throughout World
War II, and which began to reverse itself after 1946.

Tenure is another matter. Where 17% of all rabbis have been
ordained less than 5 years, only 45% of all rabbis have been in
their present positions during the past 5 years. More than six
out of every ten have held their present posts less than 10 years.
And at the other end of the range, where one out of four rabbis
has been ordained before 1942, one in ten is still occupying the
posts they held at that time. This is no surprise when one bears
in mind the rate of growth of the American Reform movement since
World War II. The data, in other words, do not necessarily suggest
an "abnormal" turnover rate. In fact, as we shall see later,
there appear to be no differences in satisfaction between those
who have held their positions a long time and those who have
recently changed posts.

3. The Employment Picture.

Almost all Reform rabbis are employed. Of our sample, one in

a hundred reports being unemployed. Another 6% are retired. The
rest have posts, and of these the overwhelming majority are
employed full-time (Table 2). As a matter of fact, 23%, almost
one in four, of those now employed full-time also have part-
time jobs.

Most full-time employed, 67% (Table 3), are full-time "senior"
rabbis, and an additional 11% are either associate or assistant
rabbis. Thus, almost four out of five are congregational
rabbis. An additional 7% are employed either as chaplains or
as Hillel directors. This brings the total of rabbis with some
sort of ministerial function up to the 85% mark. Of those who
do not occupy some form of pulpit, 8% teach or do administrative
work (many for HUC-JIR, CCAR, and UAHC), and the rest are involved in miscellaneous activities. In short, almost all Reform
rabbis are involved full time in some aspect of the Reform movement, either as pulpit rabbis, teachers, or administrators.

This is not the end of the employment story. As noted earlier,
a large number of rabbis hold two positions. Of those who
do, one in five is employed as a congregational rabbi as secondary employment, and another 12% serve as chaplains and Hillel
directors. Thus one in three have part-time pulpits in addition
to their regular posts. The most frequent part-time activity is
teaching. Some 41% of all Reform rabbis teach part-time as
secondary employment. It is interesting to note here that whereas
most full-time teacher-rabbis do their work in a Jewish setting,
by far the larger number of part-time teacher-rabbis do their
lecturing in non-Jewish colleges and universities. This is a
readily understandable pattern, of course. If one may assume
that most of those who teach in secular colleges do most of their

```
Table 2:
CURRENT EMPLOYMENT STATUS OF REFORM RABBIS
                 (N=609)


        Employed full time ———————— 89%
        Employed part time only —— 5%*
        Retired ———————————————————— 6%
        Unemployed ————————————————— 1%
        ────────────────────────────────

        *Most of these are in non-rabbinical
         full-time employment.
```

lecturing on Judaism or Jewish history, and if one reflects further on what the situation was in this regard a brief generation ago, then we have here a significant bit of evidence regarding the changing position of Jews and Judaism in American life. Certainly The Jewish Chautauqua Society, sponsored by the National Federation of Temple Brotherhoods, deserves its share of credit for this phenomenon.

Another employment factor to note is that approximately 80% of our Reform rabbis have served many congregations during the course of their active rabbinate. Figure 2 tells it briefly. Some 21% report being with only one congregation since ordination. The largest single group, some 30%, report service with two congregations. However, another 45% of our rabbinical respondents tell us that they are now serving their third to seventh congregation. A few have served more than seven congregations.

Table 3: *

CURRENT EMPLOYMENT PATTERN OF REFORM RABBIS

	Full-time employment. (N=595)	Part-time employment. (N=151)
	%	%
Senior Rabbi	67	15
Associate or Assistant Rabbi	11	5
Chaplain	4	9
Hillel	3	3
Faculty and/or Administrator	8	41
Other	8	28

4. Income.

Reform rabbis may not be the best compensated of professional groups, but neither are they at the bottom of the picture either (Figure 3). One out of three rabbis receives an annual base salary of $20,000 or more, and 5% are paid $30,000 or more. The middle third receives between $15,000 and $20,000. Finally, most of those in the lower third of the income distribution receive more than $10,000 a year. Compared with salaried professionals in business, industry, and academe, Reform rabbis do well. This becomes particularly evident when one compares their salaries with those of Protestant ministers. Where 7% of the rabbis receive less than $10,000 annually, the comparable figure for ministers is 75%, more than ten times as many. Where 35% of the rabbis earn

* Numbers show duplication because some rabbis hold two positions, one full-time and one part-time simultaneously. Such duplication may be expected in subsequent Tables and Figures.

less than $15,000, this is true of 98% of the ministers. Two
out of every hundred ministers have salaries comparable with those
of two out of every three rabbis. Stated another way, a Reform
rabbi is about 30 times more likely than a Protestant minister to
enjoy an income of $15,000 or higher. Figure 3 also provides us
with the incomes of Reform rabbis and ministers compared with
Reform congregants.

Four out of five rabbis report receiving additional income by

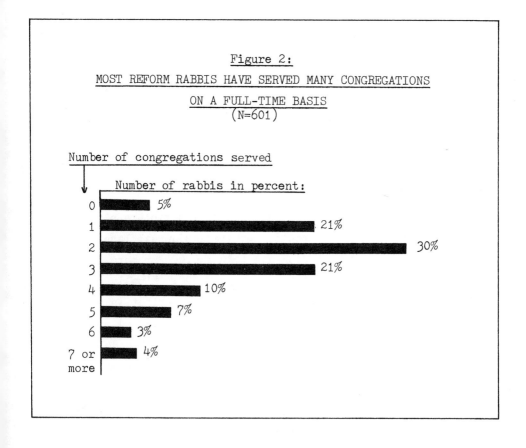

Figure 2:
MOST REFORM RABBIS HAVE SERVED MANY CONGREGATIONS
ON A FULL-TIME BASIS
(N=601)

Number of congregations served

Number of rabbis in percent:

0	5%
1	21%
2	30%
3	21%
4	10%
5	7%
6	3%
7 or more	4%

Figure 3:
REFORM RABBINATE ANNUAL INCOME COMPARED WITH
REFORM CONGREGANTS, AND WITH PROTESTANT MINISTERS

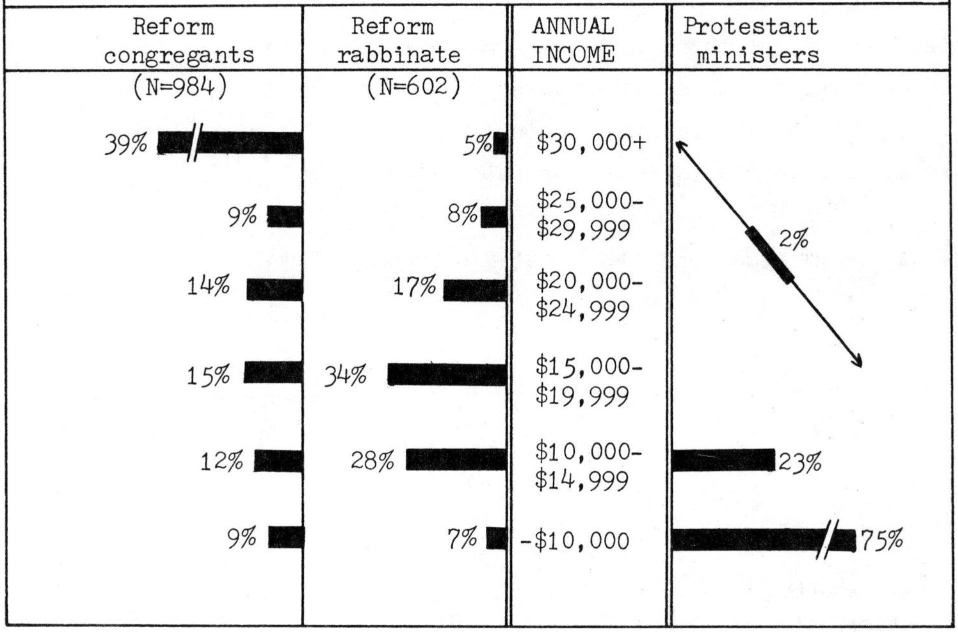

Reform congregants (N=984)	Reform rabbinate (N=602)	ANNUAL INCOME	Protestant ministers
39%	5%	$30,000+	
9%	8%	$25,000-$29,999	
14%	17%	$20,000-$24,999	2%
15%	34%	$15,000-$19,999	
12%	28%	$10,000-$14,999	23%
9%	7%	-$10,000	75%

virtue of their rabbinical roles. Here we need to note that in some congregations, monies received by rabbis from congregations as honoria for officiating at life-cycle events are deposited into a Rabbi's Discretionary Fund for the purposes of dispensing charity. These monies may or may not have been reported as additional income. For most, the additional income* is not very great, - less than $1,000; but for those earning additional income two thirds of the extra compensation amounts to at least $2,000 a year; and another 6% earn at least $5,000, and a few rabbis considerably more, in

---

* For rabbinical services.

addition to their regular salaries for services rendered <u>qua</u> rabbis.

In addition, fully half of the rabbinate report incomes from sources other than those already discussed. Royalties, lecture fees, and academic salaries probably account for most of this income (Figure 4). About half of those receiving income in this category earn less than $2,000. On the other hand, a substantial number (11% of all rabbis, and 21% of those receiving "non-rabbinical" income), earn $5,000 or more. In this latter category, 6% receive in excess of $15,000. Most of the rabbis in this last group, of course, have full-time positions outside of the rabbinate.

How does the Reform rabbi feel about his income? Only one out of

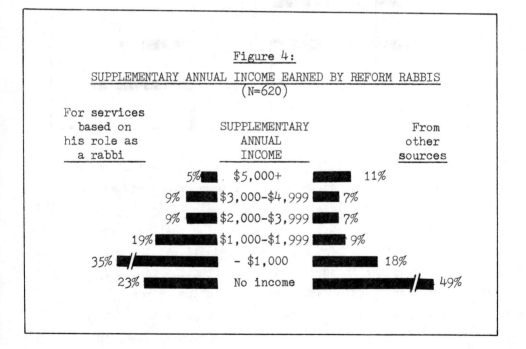

Figure 4:

SUPPLEMENTARY ANNUAL INCOME EARNED BY REFORM RABBIS
(N=620)

For services based on his role as a rabbi	SUPPLEMENTARY ANNUAL INCOME	From other sources
5%	$5,000+	11%
9%	$3,000-$4,999	7%
9%	$2,000-$3,999	7%
19%	$1,000-$1,999	9%
35%	- $1,000	18%
23%	No income	49%

four rabbis is "completely satisfied" with his rabbinical income,
while one out of ten is "very unhappy". On a closely related
matter, three rabbis out of ten express strong dissatisfaction
with the present system, or absence thereof, regarding salary
schedules, pay raises, and tenure, and more than half are at
least somewhat unhappy with the present situation. On the other
hand, there does not appear to be any particularly strong connection between amount of income and overall job satisfaction.

Here are some random comments from a few pulpit rabbis regarding
the SYSTEM:

> When the Rabbi was not paid a salary by a Congregation his
> influence, and prestige, were greater. Can we, in our
> time, work out a plan whereby members do not feel that
> they are giving a rabbi a living - or Boards wield
> power to such a degree that the effectiveness of
> rabbinic leadership is, at times, lost to them?

> One of the basic sources of dissatisfaction in my
> rabbinate is that there is no tenure. Rabbis are
> engaged to a term of years and may be dismissed even
> when these terms have been renewed.

> My great disappointment is with the Pulpit Committee.
> I have found it very difficult to make a decent change
> to another congregation. It appears as if the Committee
> is truly indifferent and unconcerned with my needs as
> a rabbi and human being.

> Congregations should not pay rabbis salaries. Should
> be CCAR - with congregations paying into a central fund.

> The rabbi, to be effective as a spokesman for 'spiritual
> ideals', must not be bound to his congregation by a con-
> tractual relationship whereby the congregation judges,
> evaluates, censors, and ultimately fires him!

5. Size of Congregations Served.

Almost exactly half of all Reform pulpit rabbis serve congregations with less than 300 families, and almost three out of four are in synagogues with less than 750 families (Figure 5). Only one in ten serves in congregations with 1,500 families or more.

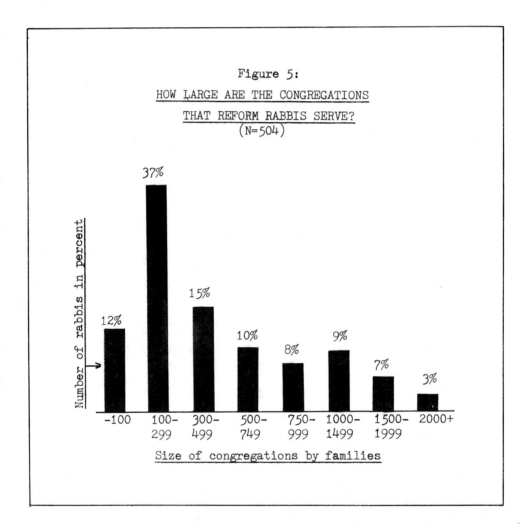

Figure 5:

HOW LARGE ARE THE CONGREGATIONS
THAT REFORM RABBIS SERVE?
(N=504)

This situation is somewhat new to Reform. Its once exclusively
urban membership has become dispersed in the vast suburban
tractlands, and some of the very substantial inner-city edifices
are in the transition of being replaced by smaller buildings that
serve a smaller population base. As with other religious groups,
this move to the New Diaspora (suburbanization) has had an enormous
impact on virtually every aspect of religious life, some of which
will be discussed at a later point. For the present, we will simply
consider the organizational implications. A large synagogue needs
and can more readily afford a large staff, not simply rabbis
and cantors, but ancillary personnel. The smaller congregation,
on the other hand, requires a multifunctionary rabbi. He must
preside over services, be his own cantor (if he can), be his own
Religious School director, act as an administrator, involve himself in his youth group, the auxiliaries, the Jewish community,
the non-Jewish community, etc., etc. What are the facts in the
case? Figure 6 suggests to us that Reform rabbis do a lot of
different kinds of things for lack of ancillary personnel.
Although only 6% are associated with congregations which do not
(yet?) have a full-time rabbi, 86% report no associate rabbis and
84% no assistant rabbi. Hence, most Reform rabbis are engaged
in sole practice.

As to full-time back-up personnel (Figure 6) some 66% of our
rabbis are in congregations without cantors (a substantial
number of rabbis and congregants had expressed the wish to
have a cantor), 58% without educators, and 62% without administrators. One may infer from this that a very large number of rabbis
not only perform all the normally required rabbinical duties
alone, but are required to perform additional duties which have
not always been associated with the rabbinate. To be sure,
Figure 6 covers only full-time personnel. Part-time personnel
undoubtedly take up some of the burdens that would otherwise

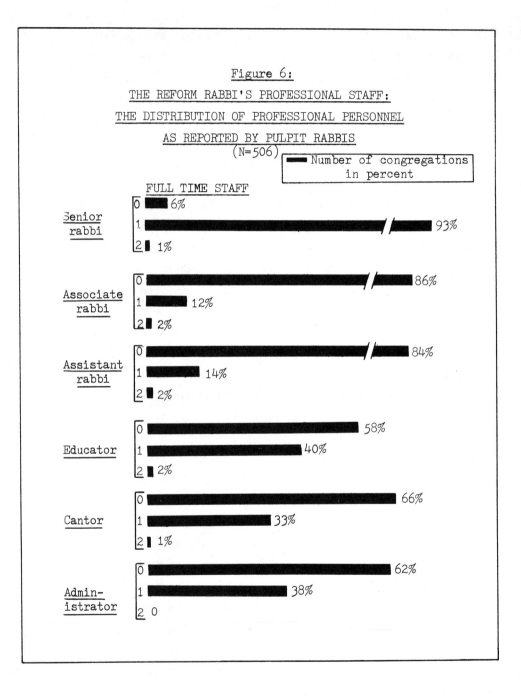

Figure 6:

THE REFORM RABBI'S PROFESSIONAL STAFF:

THE DISTRIBUTION OF PROFESSIONAL PERSONNEL

AS REPORTED BY PULPIT RABBIS
(N=506)

■ Number of congregations in percent

FULL TIME STAFF

Senior rabbi
0 — 6%
1 — 93%
2 — 1%

Associate rabbi
0 — 86%
1 — 12%
2 — 2%

Assistant rabbi
0 — 84%
1 — 14%
2 — 2%

Educator
0 — 58%
1 — 40%
2 — 2%

Cantor
0 — 66%
1 — 33%
2 — 1%

Administrator
0 — 62%
1 — 38%
2 — 0

descend on the rabbi's shoulders, but often the work to be accomplished with part-time personnel may still be very demanding on the rabbi.
In any event, rabbis appear to do more administrative work than they
think they should be doing or want to be doing. Where 6% think a
rabbi <u>ought</u> to do a great deal of administration, 38% report that
they <u>actually do</u> a great deal,- a six-fold increase. And three out
of ten report dissatisfaction with the failure of their rabbinical
training to prepare them for "dealing with many of the practical
aspects of a congregation". <u>Almost four out of ten complain of the
demands made on their time for things that they do not regard as
rabbinical</u>. In so many of the interviews, the Rabbi literally cringed
at the administrative detail that keeps him from being a rabbi.

Here are some comments:

> . . . nor do I mind the administrative responsibil-
> ities that involve me where I <u>should</u> be involved, like
> checking out the <u>religious</u> aspects of a creative ser-
> vice . . . (that the Youth Group is sponsoring), but
> when Sisterhood needs 500 copies of some rummage sale
> announcement to be sent out yesterday, or when the
> Religious School Committee wants me to keep an inven-
> tory of all books and school supplies . . . When do
> I read a book or do a little studying? Every Jew
> <u>ought to study</u>, a Rabbi <u>must</u>!

> Administrative work means <u>this</u> (pointing to his desk
> piled high with different memoranda, letters, etc.),
> . . . Do you see one book in all this? Believe me,
> when I want to read, to prepare a sermon, I must do
> it at home when the children are in school and the
> little one is asleep. Then sometimes it happens my
> wife has things for me to do . . . But this (point-
> ing to the desk again), has to be done. Here's a
> good case (holding up a letter). This young man -

he's now in college, - from junior high school, for every
part-time job and to maybe a half dozen colleges and for
financial scholarships, and I think one for camp I was
asked to write all these letters of reference . . . And
they're all different. You can't even use a _form_ letter
for these kids. Believe me I'm only too happy to do it.
But multiply this one item by hundreds like it, and believe me, it's _very_, _very_, _very_ time consuming . . .
Do you want to know what I do on my day off? _I_ _work_ _on_
_my_ _sermon_ _all_ _day_.

6. Summary Highlights (Reform Rabbinate: Demography).

1) On the whole, the Reform rabbinate is younger than 50. The
   majority are under 45.

2) Almost all are married and have two or three children.

3) Virtually all are employed. Some 25% also have part-time
   positions, mostly in academic teaching.

4) Four out of five are pulpit rabbis. The remainder are Hillel
   Directors, Chaplains, academicians, or administrators in
   Jewish agencies, many of which are part of the Reform move-
   ment.

5) Some 21% have served one congregation only; 30% have served
   two; 45% have served three to seven or more congregations.

6) Compared with other salaried professionals, incomes are good
   to excellent. Some 7% earn up to $10,000; 28% earn between
   $10,000 - $15,000; 34% between $15,000 - $20,000; 30% earn
   $20,000 to $30,000 and over.

7) Most are "satisfied" with their income; one in four is
not "completely satisfied". Three out of 10 are dissatisfied
with the mechanics of salary arrangements, tenure, etc.

8) Some 50% of the Reform rabbinate serve congregations with
less than 300 families; 25% serve 300-750 member congregations;
8% serve 750-1,000 member congregations; 19% serve congregations
of 1,000 families and over.

9) The large majority of pulpit rabbis perform almost all their
rabbinical duties without full-time professional help (ex-
cluding secretarial); 58% are without educators; 66% without
cantors; 62% without adminstrators.

10) Rabbis appear to be doing more administrative work than
they feel they should be doing. Three out of ten feel
they were inadequately prepared for this, and report real
discomfort in this area.

CHAPTER 4: SOCIAL ORIGINS OF THE REFORM RABBINATE

One of the most important sources of clues to a better understanding
of men's beliefs and behavior comes from an examination of their
pasts. Parent's birthplace, father's occupation, parent's religious
orientation, and the nature of the rabbi's early religious and
Jewish upbringing provide us with valuable insights in the interpretation of the data that we shall be examining later concerning
the Rabbi's present behaviors and attitudes.

It is even more helpful at times to compare some of these background factors of our rabbis with those of our congregants. Thus
throughout this section on the rabbinate, in order to gain greater
insight regarding the rabbi's world, we shall introduce some comparable data that pertain to congregants, seminarians, youth, and
the rebbetzins. These data will not be neglected in our subsequent analysis. It is only that their use, for comparative purposes
at this point, is designed to assist the rabbi in gaining insights
into the many intricate contexts within which he perceives others
in terms of his expectations of them, and how others perceive
him in terms of their expectations of him. This type of knowledge
constitutes the basic ingredients that one finds most useful if he
is to understand the dynamics of his interpersonal and intergroup
interactions.

1. Native and Foreign-born Origins of Rabbis, Their Congregants,
    and Their Respective Parents.

Let us begin with the parents of Reform rabbis (Tables 4 & 5). The
initial finding is that the majority of Reform rabbis are first-
generation Americans. One out of three has a native-born father.
Less than half of our rabbis have a native-born mother. This, of
course, varies with age. Of the older rabbis (those ordained prior

Table 4:

DISTRIBUTION OF NATIVE-BORN REFORM RABBIS,
CONGREGANTS, AND THEIR RESPECTIVE PARENTS

Rabbis: 83% (N=611)
Congregants: 92% (N=973)

	Rabbis	Congregants
Father:	35% (N=618)	46% (N=978)
Mother:	46% (N=618)	57% (N=975)

to 1941), some 11% have native-born fathers, a figure that increases
to 67% in the case of the youngest group (those ordained from 1967 -
1970). But it has only been in the last 10 years that newly-
ordained rabbis with native-born fathers have made up the
majority of their cohorts. The situation with respect to the
mothers of Reform rabbis is similar, except (perhaps because of
differences in age between husband and wife), there are more
native-born mothers for every age-group.

What of the sons (the rabbis)? (As of this writing there are still
no daughter-rabbis. But soon . . .) Here the findings are equally
striking. Approximately 83% of American Reform rabbis were born
in this country, and this figure is not subject to fluctuation due
to age. Where 90% of the youngest group is native-born, the same

Table 5:

NATIVE AND FOREIGN-BORN DISTRIBUTION

OF REFORM RABBIS, CONGREGANTS,

AND THEIR RESPECTIVE PARENTS
(N=611 rabbis)
(N=673 congregants)

	Have at least one native-born parent	Have two foreign-born parents
I. Native-born rabbis	50%	31%
Native-born congregants	58%	35%

II. Foreign-born rabbis —————————— 17%

Foreign-born congregants ————— 8%

is true for 85% of those ordained between 25 and 29 years ago
(Figure 7). Only those ordained more than 30 years ago have a
substantially larger number of foreign-born rabbis in their midst,
but even here, two out of three are native-born. These are
interesting facts, and one may draw equally interesting inferences
from them. Only in recent years has the Reform rabbinate stopped
recruiting first-generation Americans. Only in recent years has
there not been a discontinuity between the worlds in which rabbis
and their parents have grown up.

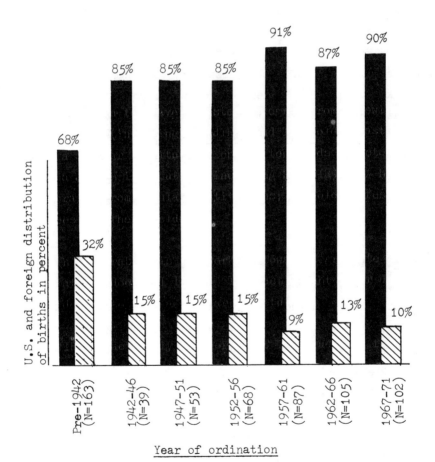

Figure 7:

U.S. AND FOREIGN DISTRIBUTION OF RABBI'S BIRTHPLACE

BY YEAR OF ORDINATION 1941-1971

(N=620)

= U.S.

= Foreign

2. Occupational Distribution of Rabbis' Fathers.

One out of every ten rabbis is the son of a rabbi, although not
necessarily from the ranks of Reform. This is a fairly substantial
degree of occupational inheritance, although it is less marked
than one finds in the case of physicians and lawyers. At any rate,
the number coming from rabbinical homes is far greater than chance
would suggest. As Table 6 tells us, an even larger number of
rabbis (15%) have fathers in other professions, resulting in an
overall figure of one in four coming from a professional ambiance.
The largest single group of rabbis, however, come from homes with
business backgrounds. The fathers of 38% are reported as merchants and another 8% as executives. Altogether, then, more than
seven out of ten rabbis come from solidly middle-class backgrounds.
Indeed, only 14% report fathers with blue-collar occupations.
The Reform rabbinate as presently constituted is clearly not being
recruited from the lower socio-economic ranks of American Jewry.

And it never was. While it can be argued that American Jews are
overwhelmingly middle-class, what is true in 1971 was certainly
not completely true in 1941. Yet the picture presented in
Figure 8 does not change when we introduce the age factor. With
one exception, there is no consistent pattern of change over
time with respect to the social class origins of rabbis. Older
rabbis and younger rabbis seem to have been recruited overwhelmingly (using occupations as an index), from the same source,
- the middle class. The only shift appears to be in the steadily
diminishing number whose fathers were retail merchants, but this
simply amounts to a redistribution of occupations within the
middle class.

Table 6:

OCCUPATIONAL COMPARISONS:

RABBIS' FATHERS AND CONGREGANTS' FATHERS

Father's occupation	Rabbis' fathers. (N-613) %	Congregants' fathers. (N=984) %
Professional	25	11
(Rabbi	10)	0)
(Other	15)	11)
Executive	8	17
Merchant	38	43
White Collar	15	13
Blue Collar	14	16

Moreover, as the aforementioned Table 6 suggests, Reform congregants come overwhelmingly from the same social stratum. While rabbis are somewhat more likely to have professional fathers, congregants are more often drawn from business families. The differences in overall life styles between the families from which most Reform rabbis and most Reform congregants come are probably not too great.

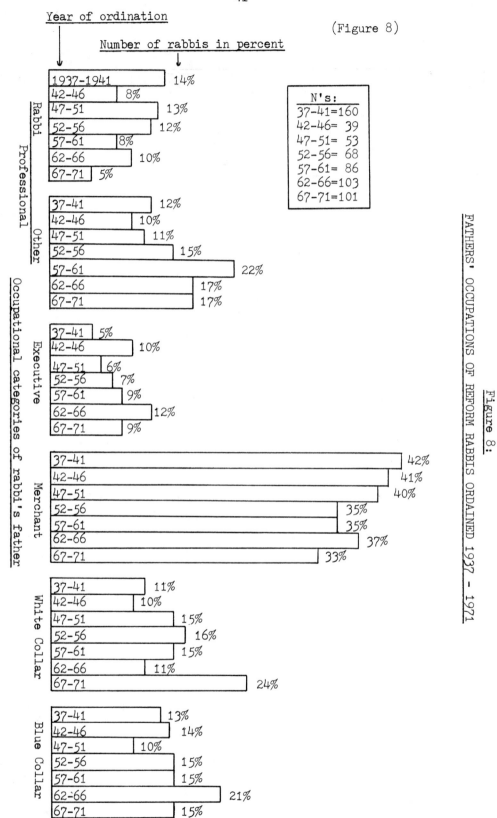

Year of ordination

Number of rabbis in percent

(Figure 8)

N's:
37-41=160
42-46= 39
47-51= 53
52-56= 68
57-61= 86
62-66=103
67-71=101

Figure 8:

FATHERS' OCCUPATIONS OF REFORM RABBIS ORDAINED 1937 - 1971

Occupational categories of rabbi's father

Rabbi Professional
1937-1941 — 14%
42-46 — 8%
47-51 — 13%
52-56 — 12%
57-61 — 8%
62-66 — 10%
67-71 — 5%

Other Professional
37-41 — 12%
42-46 — 10%
47-51 — 11%
52-56 — 15%
57-61 — 22%
62-66 — 17%
67-71 — 17%

Executive
37-41 — 5%
42-46 — 10%
47-51 — 6%
52-56 — 7%
57-61 — 9%
62-66 — 12%
67-71 — 9%

Merchant
37-41 — 42%
42-46 — 41%
47-51 — 40%
52-56 — 35%
57-61 — 35%
62-66 — 37%
67-71 — 33%

White Collar
37-41 — 11%
42-46 — 10%
47-51 — 15%
52-56 — 16%
57-61 — 15%
62-66 — 11%
67-71 — 24%

Blue Collar
37-41 — 13%
42-46 — 14%
47-51 — 10%
52-56 — 15%
57-61 — 15%
62-66 — 21%
67-71 — 15%

3. Summary Highlights (Reform Rabbinate: Social Origins).

1) The majority of Reform rabbis are first generation
   Americans.

2) Only in recent years has the Reform rabbinate stopped
   recruiting first-generation Americans.

3) Some 18% of the Reform rabbinate is foreign-born (as
   against 7% of Reform congregants who are foreign-born).

4) One out of every ten rabbis is the son of a rabbi,
   although not necessarily from Reform ranks.

5) One out of four rabbis comes from a professional home;
   almost half come from homes representing business backgrounds.

6) Seven out of ten rabbis come from solid middle-class
   backgrounds; 14% from working-class homes.

7) On an overall basis, Reform rabbis and Reform congregants
   come from a very similar social stratum.

CHAPTER 5: JEWISH BACKGROUNDS AND RELIGIOUS ORIGINS OF THE REFORM RABBINATE

1. Father's Religious Affiliation.

At the present time, almost exactly thé same number of Reform rabbis
come from Orthodox homes as from Reform homes, 33% and 34%, respectively (Figure 9). Some 18% are the sons of Conservative families,
and another 15% indicate their parents were (or are) unaffiliated.
The finding that more than half of all Reform rabbis come from
Orthodox on Conservative backgrounds should come as no surprise in
light of what has already been seen regarding their generational
status in this country. If the majority of rabbis are first-generation Americans, and if most Jewish immigration to this country since
1892, the birth-year of our oldest rabbinical respondent, has been
from Eastern Europe, where Reform was not very active, then one
can readily understand the situation. This is further supported
by the subsequent data concerning knowledge of the Yiddish language.

2. Reform Rabbis and Congregants Confront the Yiddish Language.

Some 23% of the Reform rabbinate (Figure 10), report their reading
knowledge to be "excellent" or "good," and 20% say the same thing
concerning their ability to speak the language. If we add to this
last figure the additional 14% whose speaking ability is reported
as "fair," we wind up with an impressive number of rabbis whose ties
to Eastern Judaism are far from minimal. The Jewish background of
a very large number, if not the majority, of present-day Reform rabbis
may be different from that of the founders of the American Reform
Movement.

3. Religious Backgrounds by Year of Ordination.

Figure 11 suggests that much is changing, and somewhat rapidly.
There has been a steady drop in the numbers of rabbis coming from
backgrounds other than Reform. Where only 24% of those ordained
prior to 1941 were reared in the Reform tradition, this is true of
more than twice as many (50%) of the most recently ordained rabbis.
The big change in this 30-year process is in the percent now coming
from Orthodoxy. The latter's 54% contribution to the Reform
rabbinate of 30 years ago has dwindled to a tiny 9% in the last

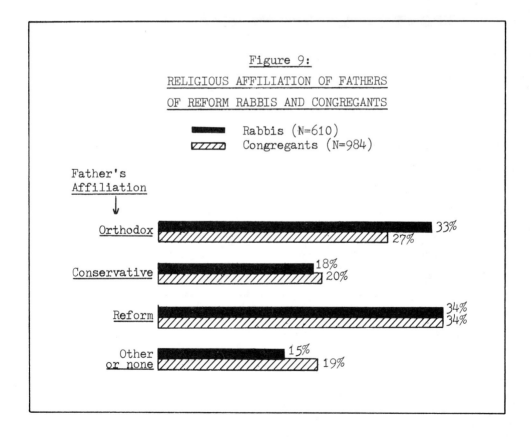

Figure 9:
RELIGIOUS AFFILIATION OF FATHERS
OF REFORM RABBIS AND CONGREGANTS

Rabbis (N=610)
Congregants (N=984)

Father's Affiliation

Orthodox 33% / 27%
Conservative 18% / 20%
Reform 34% / 34%
Other or none 15% / 19%

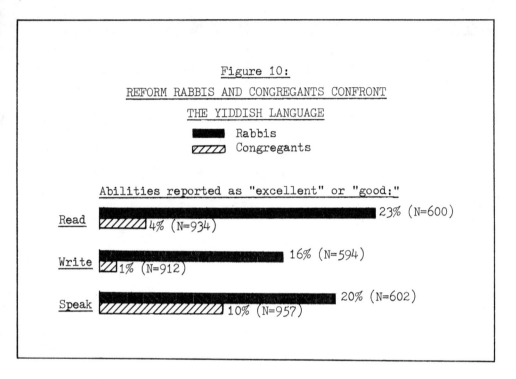

Figure 10:

REFORM RABBIS AND CONGREGANTS CONFRONT

THE YIDDISH LANGUAGE

■ Rabbis
▨ Congregants

Abilities reported as "excellent" or "good:"

Read ▨ 4% (N=934) — 23% (N=600)

Write ▨ 1% (N=912) — 16% (N=594)

Speak ▨ 10% (N=957) — 20% (N=602)

five years. The number of rabbis from Conservative homes, on the
other hand, has fluctuated considerably. Nevertheless, there is a
20-year trend (from 12% to 24%), of an increased contribution from
Conservative sources to the Reform rabbinate.

One is tempted to speculate on this rather dramatic shift which
involves at least two factors. The first is, simply, the growth
of Conservatism and Reform and the relative decline of Orthodoxy in
this country, particularly with respect to religious school
enrollment. This would apply to the period ending in 1960, since
all of our rabbis received their early religious education before
that time. The more recent growth of the Jewish day-school movement,

Figure 11:

FATHER'S RELIGIOUS AFFILIATION WHEN SON WAS ORDAINED

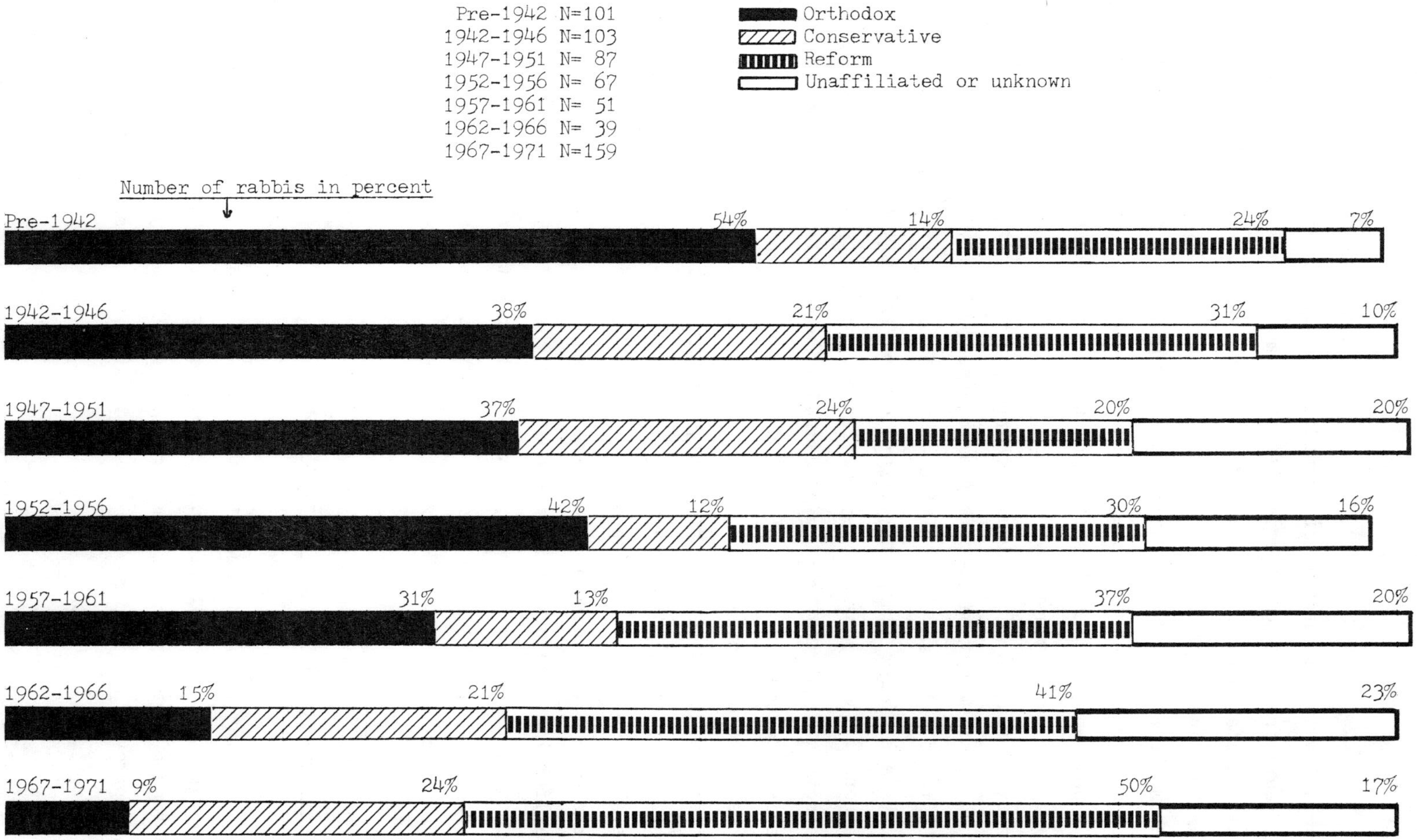

Orthodox
Conservative
Reform
Unaffiliated or unknown

Pre-1942   N=101
1942-1946 N=103
1947-1951 N= 87
1952-1956 N= 67
1957-1961 N= 51
1962-1966 N= 39
1967-1971 N=159

Number of rabbis in percent

Pre-1942   54%   14% 24%   7%

1942-1946   38%   21% 31% 10%

1947-1951   37%   24% 20% 20%

1952-1956   42% 12% 30% 16%

1957-1961   31%   13%   37%   20%

1962-1966   15%   21%   41%   23%

1967-1971   9%   24%   50%   17%

including a large number of Orthodox schools, may change all that
in years to come. The second factor is more complicated and can
only be stated here in a sketchy fashion. Affiliation with Orthodoxy in recent years has been less nominal as that affiliation has
become less normative. For many Jews who are now in their middle
years, a statement that their parents are or were Orthodox means
the home was usually kosher, sons were Bar Mitzvah, and the
synagogue was the neighborhood shul. What else was there? In
short, normative and nominal. Things are somewhat different now.
Much of orthodoxy has become Americanized, and having lost the
stigma of being a religion of unassimilable immigrants, it has
lost less of its adherents (regardless of the legitimacy of the
reasons). At the same time, by virtue of becoming more self-
conscious about the meaning of Orthodoxy vis-a-vis the other
Jewish branches, members of Orthodox congregations may be under
greater constraints to take their membership more seriously. If
this is accurate reasoning so far, then it would follow that the
pool of potential "defectors" would be diminished. Of course there
is also the obvious reason why most of Reform's recruits came
from Orthodoxy during earlier generations. The majority of our
earlier immigrants were mostly Orthodox themselves, or came from
Orthodox backgrounds who may have stopped practicing Orthodoxy
themselves, but who had never really divorced themselves from their
identification with Orthodoxy.

4. Zionism and the Reform Rabbinate.

A second way of looking at the degree of intensity or commitment
to Jewish concerns is afforded by measuring attitudes toward Zionism.
Strength of intensity or commitment varies directly with strength
of approval or disapproval. Thus, if we distinguish among those

with strong views (pro or anti), those with moderate views (pro
or anti), and those with no views at all, we have a useful indicator
of degree of concern with Jewish affairs. Zionism is chosen as an
index for measurement because it is inconceivable that anyone who
is deeply involved in Jewish studies or Jewish affairs will not
have formed some opinion, and usually a strong one, on this issue.

Even if "Zionism" or "Nationalism" or "Jewish homeland" or "Palestine"
or "Eretz Yisroel" were not topics of formal discussion, it is still
quite conceivable that pro or con feelings of parents and home environment were there or were not there. It is also conceivable that overt
attitudes or covert feelings may not have been "expressed" but that
they were there. Hence it is not categorically assumed that Zionism
is the index of all Jewish concerns, but is used here as only one
indicator of Jewish concerns. At least it seems fair to assume that
strongly pro or strongly anti backgrounds are good indicators.

As we see in Table 7, one out of three Reform rabbis comes from a
family which held strong views on the subject of Zionism, another
four out of ten report moderate support or disapproval, one out of
ten is not able to identify what the situation at home was, and one
out of seven tells us that the subject never came up. If we combine the last two categories, and if these data are valid as an
index, we find that one out of four Reform rabbis comes from comparatively uninvolved Jewish backgrounds. The fact that 25% come
from home backgrounds which were indifferent ("mixed" or "rarely
discussed"), to Zionism seems very high indeed. A comparative
view with Reform congregants is also presented in Table 7.

Nor is that the end of the story. Controlling for age, we find
that it is the older rabbis who are more likely to have been brought

Table 7:

PARENTAL BACKGROUNDS OF RABBIS

AND CONGREGANTS: ZIONISM

	Rabbi's family background (N=619)	Congregant's family background (N=984)
Attitudes toward Zionism	%	%
Strongly pro	32	9
Somewhat pro	33	25
Somewhat anti	8	7
Strongly anti	2	5
Mixed	11	9
Rarely Discussed	14	45

up in families that discussed Jewish affairs. The younger the
rabbi, the less this seems to be the case. Thus, 38% of those
rabbis ordained before 1942 report a strong pro-Zionist sentiment
at home, and 5% report a strong anti-Zionist sentiment. Altogether,
more than four in ten come from involved families (Figure 12). Only
one out of six, on the other hand, reports an indifferent atmosphere.
Contrast this with the findings for the most recently ordained
group (1967-1971), where two out of ten are the sons of involved
parents and more than one out of three report little or no interest
at home. It would appear, then, that just as there is an unmistakable
trend in the recruitment of Reform seminarians mostly from Reform

Figure 12:

HOME ATTITUDES TOWARD ZIONISM WHEN RABBIS WERE GROWING UP

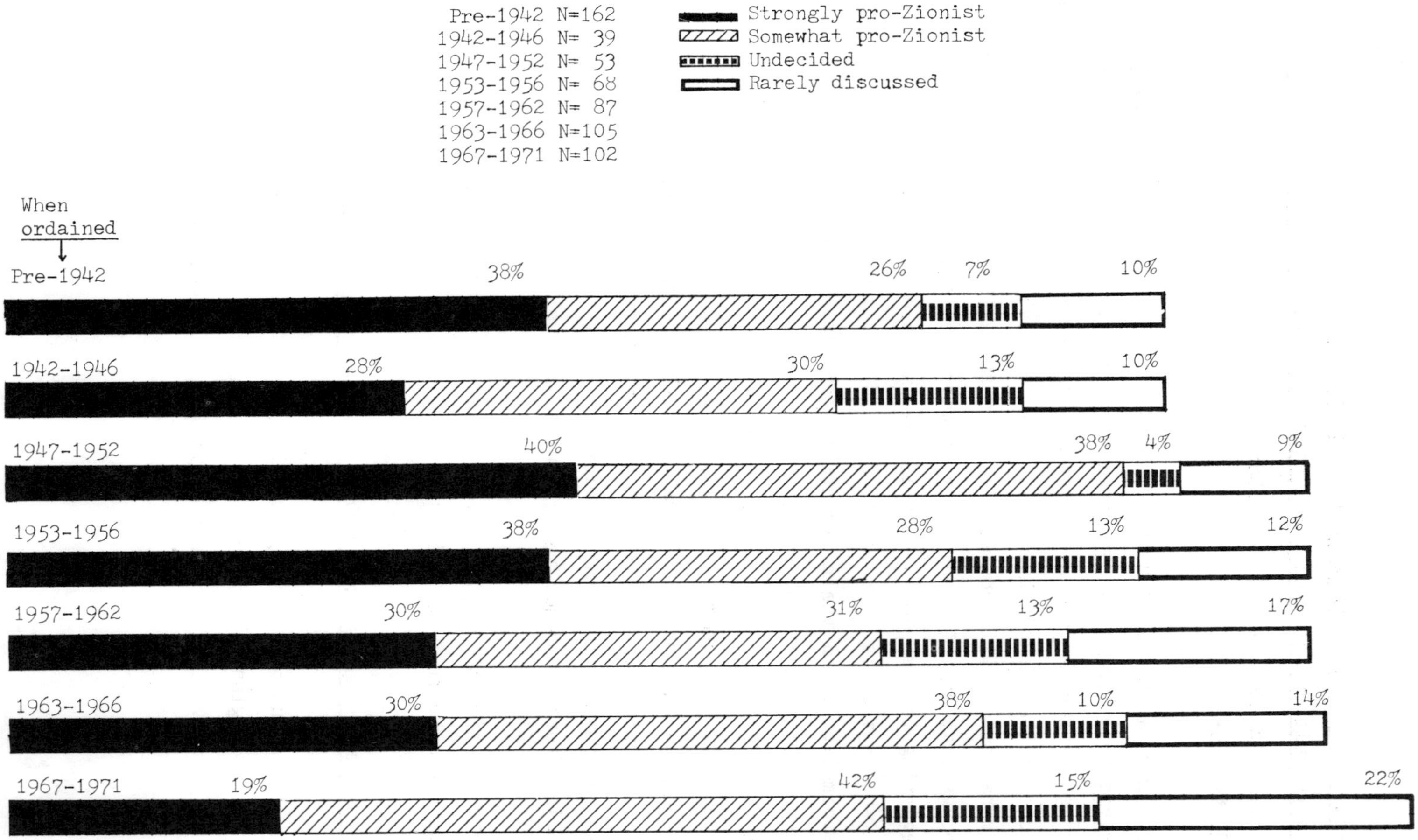

(and unaffiliated) backgrounds, there is also a similar trend in
the recruitment of rabbinical students whose exposure to Jewish
concern at home may be much less than it had been for their other
colleagues.

This should not be misunderstood to imply that Reform rabbis themselves were minimally concerned with Jewishness. But if we were
to assume for the moment that most Reform rabbis had been interested
and committed Jews, themselves, then we have a complex irony on
our hands. It will be recalled from an earlier set of findings that
the generational discontinuity between rabbis and their parents is
beginning to disappear. But if the data are to be believed and if
our assumption is correct, it follows that the Jewish gap between
Reform rabbis and their parents is getting larger. Following this
line of reasoning, Reform rabbis could almost be said to be out of
step as far as the prevailing culture in which they were reared is
concerned. If, on the other hand, we accept the findings but
reject the assumption that rabbis-to-be somehow managed to develop
and maintain a strong interest in Jewishness, then it follows that
the rabbinate itself is increasingly being recruited from the ranks
of indifferent and minimally committed Jews.

We shall see later which one of these models comes closer to describ-
ing the situation as it is unfolding today.

5. Summary Highlights: (Reform Rabbinate: Jewish and Religious Origins).

   1) About one-third of the Reform rabbinate come from Orthodox
       origins; one-third from Reform origins; 18% from Con-
       servative; 15% from unaffiliated homes.

2) Using facility with Yiddish language as an index, the Jewish background of a very large number, if not the majority, of present-day Reform rabbis appears to be different from the backgrounds of the founders of the American Reform movement.

3) Twice as many rabbis now come from Reform backgrounds as was the case one generation (30 years) ago.

4) About 54% of the Reform rabbinate came from Orthodox backgrounds one generation ago. In the last five years, only 9% have come from Orthodox backgrounds.

5) Over the past 20 years, Reform rabbis from Conservative backgrounds have increased from 14% to 24%.

6) As Orthodox living becomes more "assimilable," it is expected that "defectors" to Reform will continue to decrease.

7) One out of four Reform rabbis comes from comparatively uninvolved Jewish backgrounds, on the basis of Zionism involvement as an index. On the basis of same criterion, Reform congregants score much lower than their rabbis.

8) If Zionist involvement is an acceptable index of Jewish
   concern, there appears to be a trend of recruiting rabbinical students whose exposure to Jewish concerns at home
   may be much less then it had been for their older colleagues

CHAPTER 6:   ON BECOMING A REFORM RABBI

Students of occupational choice have made a useful distinction
between the "fantasy" stage, at which time peple play around with
various possibilities, and later stages. Most readers will remember,
in this connection, their own earlier fantasies of becoming motor-
cycle policemen and firemen. Sometimes it happens, however, that
early "decisions" turn out to be the same as the final ones. And
this becomes a useful way of distinguishing between those who
have been preparing themselves for a given career all of their
lives and those whose career commitments, while possibly just as
intense, are of shorter duration. Similarly, information on the
age at which a rabbi first thought of becoming a rabbi may throw a
useful light on the Jewishness of his backgrounds. This is not to
suggest for a moment that all boys whose parents are intensely
committed to Judaism automatically grow up wanting to be rabbis,
but there is surely a greater likelihood of this occurring in such
a setting than in the absence of such early backgrounds.

The data have suggested that rabbis are increasingly being recruited from families in which concern with Jewishness is relatively
low. Does this apply as well to the sons when they were growing
up, - that is, were they, like their parents, not much interested
in these matters? If so, then we should expect to find that younger
rabbis were less likely than their older colleagues to think of becoming rabbis when they were still young. If, on the other hand,
our younger rabbis are different, then we should expect to find
no differences between them and their older colleagues with respect
to the age at which they first thought of becoming rabbis.

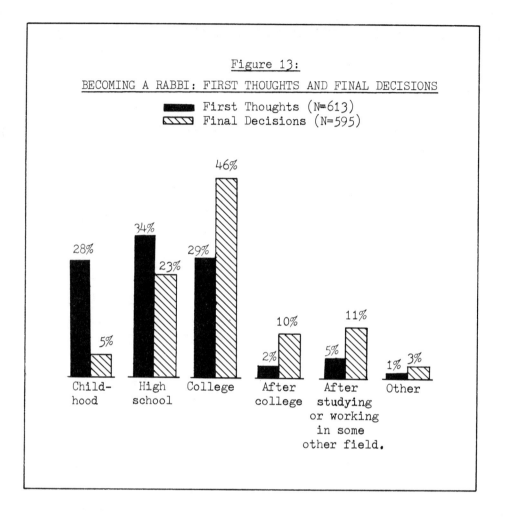

Figure 13:

BECOMING A RABBI: FIRST THOUGHTS AND FINAL DECISIONS

First Thoughts (N=613)
Final Decisions (N=595)

1. First Thoughts and Final Decisions.

First, let us look at the overall picture as depicted in Figure 13. More than one out of four (28%) first thought of entering the rabbinate when they were still children. In terms of motivation, these data are psychologically very significant. This, incidentally, is a high figure when compared with data for lawyers, college professors, and engineers. Another one out of three (34%) first

thought of the rabbinate as a career when he was in high school,
and three out of ten (29%) were motivated to do so while in college.
Only 8% waited until later. In other words, almost <u>two out of three</u>
<u>rabbis were interested enough in Judaism to entertain the idea of a</u>
<u>rabbinical career while they were still either children or in high</u>
<u>school.</u> This is certainly a conservative measure of reasonably high
commitment on the part of a large number of American Reform rabbis.

Now for a look at the figures by various age groups. The first
thing to be noted (Figure 14), is a decline among younger rabbis
in the numbers of very early "deciders," - from 34% for the pre-1942

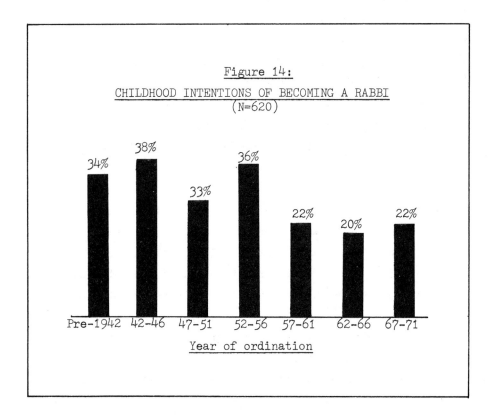

Figure 14:
CHILDHOOD INTENTIONS OF BECOMING A RABBI
(N=620)

Year of ordination

to 22% for those ordained in 1967-1971. This would suggest that
the first interpretation is more correct, that what we have seen
with respect to parental attitudes toward Jewishness (at least as
measured by the intensity of their positions on Zionism), holds for
the children as well. Parental Jewishness, even for those destined
to become rabbis does not appear to play as important a role as it
once did in the early years, at least not as far as career
decisions are concerned.

However, it is only fair to consider the other side of the coin as
well. Even if we do have a decrease from 34% to 22% of those whose
decisions to enter the rabbinate were formulated during childhood
years, we should keep in mind that many more occupational options
were open to those who entered the seminary during the most recent
years than were open to those who entered the seminary in preceeding
years, especially before World War II. Furthermore when we consider the cultural impacts of secularization upon the recently
ordained generation against the situation which confronted their
colleagues of a preceding generation, one might conclude that the
22% figure truly does not represent a decrease, but may very
well be hailed as a firm "holding of the fort," or possibly even
an increase.

Now there comes a big "but." When we look at the figures for
those who thought of rabbinical careers when they were in high
school, things seem slightly complicated. Older rabbis (those
ordained before 1952), usually had first thoughts of the rabbinate
either as children or while in high school. Beginning with 1952,
however, we find a small number (18%) increasing to a respectable
number (41%) in the most recently-ordained group. What does this
mean? Our tentative interpretation is as follows: To the extent
that there is a Jewish youth culture in the United States, it has

been growing in recent years. This development is related to a host of changes in the Jewish teen-age scene, - the growth in the number of Israeli teachers, Hebrew-speaking or at least Jewishly oriented summer camps, work-study programs in Israel, active synagogue youth groups, and other such developments. To the extent that these help generate Jewish values and loyalties, they serve as functional equivalents for the kind of Jewish atmosphere that may be lacking at home. At any rate, if it can be assumed that career plans made during high school and beyond are more likely to be influenced by peer-group climates, one is led to suspect that there is an encouraging trend among Jewish youth today.

So much for the fantasy stage of career decision. We have one more reading on the matter, namely, the time of final decision. As we examine again the data in the aforementioned Figure 13, we see that almost three out of ten made their final decisions before they graduated from high school, but a larger number (46%) did so during college.

Another 10% waited until they were graduated from college before making their commitment, and 11% had actually been studying or working in other fields before switching to the rabbinate. In other words, three out of four rabbis made up their minds before graduation from college, while one out of four made relatively belated decisions.

This same pattern is reflected in Table 8 which shows that 71% of all rabbis began their rabbinical studies as soon as they had graduated from high school or college. Another 20% did so within five years of graduation, leaving only one in ten who had another career before they began studying for the rabbinate.

Table 8:

TIME PATTERNS OF BEGINNING RABBINICAL STUDIES
(N=615)

Immediately following graduation*	71%
Within 5 years of graduation	20%
Between 5 and 10 years of graduation	5%
More than 10 years after graduation	2%

* In some cases from high school; in most
cases from college.

To ascertain <u>motives</u> that are behind one's career choice is something like ascertaining why one chooses a specific marital partner.
A questionnaire which is designed to elicit information from a
large sample cannot do this. Unconscious as well as conscious
<u>individual needs</u> of a person must be probed. Some of the focused
interviews did identify a few clues. But when some of these
responses were later incorporated into the questionnaire, the
findings provided such a scatter that it is impossible to point,
with total accuracy, to any <u>one</u> or even <u>group</u> of explanations
that are satisfactory.

However, some 61% of the rabbis identify with the following explanation as being "most closely" to their own motivation:

As an occupation it offered me the most opportunity to
'do my thing' in terms of my interests, needs and
general fulfillment.

The second and third identifications, 48% and 44% respectively, are made "most closely" with the following two statements.

> I like people and the rabbinate provided maximum opportunities to serve my fellowman.

> My intense belief in God and in Judaism and my desire to continue one of its major traditions, - to be a teacher unto my people.

Lastly, only 5% give the following reason as the one that "most clearly" explains their choice of the rabbinate as a career:

> I suppose I had some insecurities and possibly I felt that the rabbi's robe and position might help to cover these up.

An interesting finding from the interviews is the strong suggestion that the same reasons that motivated most of the rabbis to embark on a rabbinical career are still the same motivations that keep them in the rabbinate today.

A similar conclusion was reached recently by a rabbinical seminar conducted by Professor Eugene Borowitz at HUC-JIR (New York).

> To a man, the rabbis said that they were surprised how much of what they had originally said was bringing them into the rabbinate was, in fact, still motivating them. *

When we look back to some of the previous data concerning how early in life many of these motivations started to take root, it is not surprising to find that the roots have yielded the expected result.

---

* Private communication from Professor Borowitz to the writer.

In the section on the seminarians (Chapter 18, especially Table 47), more will be said concerning the choice of rabbinate as a career.

2. Seminary Attendance.

Hebrew Union College - Jewish Institute of Religion in Cincinnati has turned out the overwhelming majority (71%) of American Reform rabbis. HUC-JIR (New York) has ordained 26% (Table 9). Only a handful (4%) were ordained elsewhere. Moreover, the trend for the last 25 years has been toward an increasing number ordained at Cincinnati. In the period 1947-1951, the figure was 60%. In the more recent period, 1962-1966, it rose to 79%.

3. Educational Attainments.

Virtually all Reform rabbis have had some college training before studying for the rabbinate. As can be seen in Table 10, only 8% went to the seminary directly from high school (virtually all of

Table 9:

SEMINARY ORIGINS OF REFORM RABBIS
(N=616)

Where ordained:

HUC-JIR, Cincinnati ———————— 71%

HUC-JIR, New York ———————— 26%

Other (United States) ———— 1%

Other (Foreign) ———————— 3%

Table 10:

EDUCATIONAL ATTAINMENTS OF REFORM RABBIS
(N=617)

	Highest level attained prior to seminary study	Completion since ordination
	%	%
High school diploma	8	0
Some college	9	0
Bachelor's degree	70	0
Master's degree (HUC-JIR or other Jewish institution)	0	58
Master's degree (secular institution)	10	15
Doctorate (HUC-JIR or other Jewish institution)	0	10
Doctorate (secular institution)	1	12
Non-rabbinical professional degree	3	5

these having been ordained before 1942). The 9% who had only <u>some</u>
college were ordained, in most cases, more than twenty years ago.
On the other hand, where 70% of <u>all</u> rabbis had a B.A. and another
10% an M.A. prior to entering the seminary, the figures for those
holding one of these degrees in the <u>most recently ordained group</u>
is 87% and 7% respectively. Thus, not only is the American Reform
rabbinate a highly educated group, the trend is that it is even
becoming more and more so. This refers to educational achievement <u>before</u> entering rabbinical studies.

Almost six in ten have received a master's degree from Hebrew Union
College - Jewish Institute of Religion* or from another Jewish
institution, while 15% have earned an equivalent degree at secular
institutions of higher learning. And where almost three out of
four have a master's degree, another one in ten has a doctorate
from a Jewish institution, matched by 12% with doctorates from
secular universities. Finally, some 5% hold professional degrees
in non-rabbinical fields. This is certainly a remarkable picture
for a group of religious professionals.

Nor is that all. Almost one in five rabbis is <u>at the present time</u>
working for an advanced degree, half of these at the doctoral level
in a secular institution. Finally, almost three rabbis in ten who
are not now enrolled in a post-ordination degree program plan to
do so. Here again, <u>the most sought-after degree appears to be a
doctorate from a secular institution</u>.

It is worth taking a closer look at trends over time, particularly
with respect to the educational activities and plans of those
rabbis who were ordained within the last 15 years or so. Some 36%
of the 1957-1961 category are now pursuing a higher degree as com-

---

* The Master's degree from HUC-JIR is currently the requirement
for Ordination.

pared with 24% and 33% of those who graduated in 1962-1966 and 1967-1971, respectively. So far nothing too significant. But when we compare the three subgroups (Table 11) with respect to plans for future degree work we come up with the following figures, - 29% (57-61), 49% (62-66), 72% 67-71). Once can interpret this in a number of ways. For example, it can be taken to mean that the somewhat older rabbis are more "realistic," or that they are more burdened with responsibilities, or both of these, But there is another finding buried in the table that is potentially more significant. Again we refer to the last three categories mentioned. There is a definite trend among those who plan to enroll in the future to take doctorates in secular rather than Jewish institutions, - 11%, 26%, 37%. Even if we were to discount the likelihood that all who plan a course of action will carry through, the fact remains that rabbis appear to be oriented in increasing numbers to the secular as opposed to the Jewish academic world.

In a similar vein, we note there is a trend toward professional degrees not associated with the rabbinate. We will be commenting on this trend again at a later point. There appears to be a strong association between low commitment to the rabbinate and the outreach toward graduate studies in non-rabbinical institutions. Thus, while Reform rabbis are highly educated, and while many have advanced degrees from Jewish institutions, there may be a drift away from concern with specifically Jewish learning as measured by the educational activities and plans of younger rabbis. But is this really so? If we look at other evidence, for instance, the amount of time spent on rabbinical scholarship, younger rabbis report more activity along these lines than do older ones. They also appear to value such activities more than do their seniors. How, then, do we account for the findings just reported? One possibility may be, that it is increasingly easier to pursue advanced Jewish studies at secular universities. Not only is this more convenient

Table 11:

EDUCATIONAL ATTAINMENTS OF REFORM RABBIS BY YEAR OF ORDINATION:

I   Degrees earned
II Degrees in progress
III Plans for future studies

I. DEGREES EARNED.	Pre-1942 (N=162) %	42-46 (N=39) %	47-51 (N=52) %	52-56 (N=68) %	57-61 (N=87) %	62-66 (N=105) %	67-71 (N=102) %
Master's from Jewish institution	22	72	60	71	75	70	75
Master's from secular institution	19	23	23	26	9	10	4
Doctorate from Jewish institution	19	15	10	13	9	3	1
Doctorate from secular institution	25	18	19	15	2	5	0
Non-rabbinical professional degree	5	8	6	10	2	3	2

II. DEGREES IN PROGRESS.

Master's from Jewish institution	0	0	0	0	0	0	0
Master's from secular institution	1	0	0	3	3	2	0
Doctorate from Jewish institution	1	0	0	4	6	7	20
Doctorate from secular institution	1	3	17	7	20	12	12
Non-rabbinical professional degree	1	0	2	1	7	3	1

III. FUTURE PLANS.

Master's from Jewish institution	0	0	0	0	0	0	0
Master's from secular institution	0	3	0	1	3	4	8
Doctorate from Jewish institution	0	8	8	3	13	12	14
Doctorate from secular institution	0	5	4	12	11	26	37
Non-rabbinical professional degree	0	0	0	3	2	7	13

and possibly more meaningful for many rabbis, but they may also find the atmosphere at such institutions more to their liking. Our evidence on this last point is not conclusive, but it is perfectly clear that HUC-JIR continues to attract only a minority of its graduates who take advanced degrees.

This study does not probe the specificity of those graduate programs that Reform rabbis are now pursuing. Of course, if further study on the subject would reveal that most are pursuing degrees in non-Jewish studies, per se, then one might conclude that there is truly a drift away from higher Jewish scholarship.

An yet there is another interpretation to the same story, as revealed from the following excerpt from an interview with a pulpit rabbi in his middle 30's.

Interviewer: You're not really very far from (two large) cities) where a graduate program in Jewish studies could be obtained on a part-time basis. Why did you select _____ University?

Rabbi: Well, it would be a chore to get to _____ or _____ . . ., and _____ University (nearby) offers a very good program in Counseling psychology. I've already had my rabbinics. What I need most in my congregation is to help all these people . . . the broken homes, the drugs, and what not. They really need so much . . . (and) it's not just my congregation. You've spoken to other rabbis. Don't they have the same problem? We can't send them all to psychiatrists, and they don't need them either. Thank God they come to me . . .

Interviewer: Since yours is a sizeable city itself, it must have social agencies to deal with some of these problems. Do you make referrals?

Rabbi: These are my members, and they come to me. And I care about them. Why should I send them to (others)? If the Temple lets them down, their religion lets them down. That's the way they see it, and we can't afford that. Counseling is one of

the most bona fide Rabbinic traditions of all time.
You see we in Reform don't render a hard and fast
<u>din</u>, that is to say an autocratic decision, in
terms of Halakhah, but we do provide ethical alter-
natives to their present actions. This type of
counseling in terms of our ethical traditions is one
of our basic obligations as rabbis, all rabbis not
just Reform.

Here are some more comments:

HUC-JIR would really be the best place for me.
But (local university) is ten minutes away. It is
definitely second best, but I must do it part-
time. Unfortunately, Cincinnati would be a luxury
. . . I could not afford taking off a few years for
full-time study. Commuting is, of course, out of
the question (2 hours flying time).

I started at JTS (Jewish Theological Seminary),
but soon realized it really wasn't for me, even
though they're the greatest . . . I wish HUC were
only an hour away, but _____ University will
have to do. It isn't what I really want . . .

First of all, I wanted a Ph. D. Secondly who
can travel to Cincinnati. It's too much for anyone to travel more than an hour, and it's got
to be by car. Flying is too expensive . . .

More will be said about motivation and graduate studies in a
subsequent section devoted to the seminarians (Chapter 18,
especially Table 48).

4. Summary Highlights (Becoming a Rabbi).

1) More than one out of four Reform rabbis thought of entering
    the rabbinate while they were still children; 34% while
    in high school; 29% while in college. This means two out
    of three thought of becoming rabbis before graduation from
    high school.

2) Rabbis ordained before 1942 who were early "deciders"
    amount to 34%; since 1967, this has dropped to 22%.

3) Parental Jewishness, even for those destined to become
    rabbis, does not appear to play as important a role as
    it once did as far as career decisions are concerned.

4) Peer-group climates generated by a growing Jewish youth
    culture appear to be substituting for parental motivations
    for the more recently ordained Reform rabbis.

5) Three out of ten made final decisions to become rabbis
    while in high school; 46% did so during college; 10%
    decided after college graduation; 11% were already in
    other fields when they made their final decisions. Thus
    three out of four made final decisions before college
    graduation.

6) The three motives given by most for entering the rabbinate,
    in rank order, are: (a) " . . . it offered me the most
    opportunity to do my thing ' . . .," (b) " . . . rabbinate
    provided maximum opportunity to serve my fellowman," and
    (c) " . . . intense belief in God and Judaism (and the
    desire) . . . to be a teacher unto my people."

7) Only 5% identify their motivations on the basis of personal insecurities, hoping that "the rabbi's robe and position might help to cover these up."

8) Much of the same motivations that led rabbis to the rabbinate are still the same motivations that sustain them in the rabbinate.

9) Some 71% of today's Reform rabbinate are HUC-JIR Cincinnati graduates; 26% are from HUC-JIR New York; 4% were ordained elsewhere, of which 3% are from foreign seminaries.

10) The Reform rabbi is highly educated before entering HUC-JIR. Among the most recently ordained (1967-71), 87% had a B.A., and 7% had master's degrees before entering the seminary.

11) Almost six in ten have a master's degree from a Jewish institution (including HUC-JIR), and 10% hold a master's from a secular institution; one in ten holds a doctorate from a Jewish institution (including HUC-JIR); 12% hold doctorates from secular institutions; 5% hold professional degrees in other fields.

12) One in five rabbis is now working toward a graduate degree, half at the doctoral level. The most sought-after degree is a doctorate from a secular institution.

13) HUC-JIR attracts only a minority of its graduates for advanced degrees.

CHAPTER 7: ON BEING A REFORM RABBI

1. Career Satisfactions.

Generally speaking, how happy are Reform rabbis with their professional lives? The first and most general answer to that question is
"very much." More than four rabbis in ten say they are "fully satisfied" with their careers and another four are at least "somewhat
satisfied." At the other end of the spectrum, only four in a
hundred see themselves as very dissatisfied and about 9% are somewhat dissatisfied. When more than 80% of the members of a given
profession say they are reasonably pleased with the way things have
worked out for them, it would suggest that all things considered,
the American Reform rabbinate is not a disgruntled group, at least
not in terms of their own careers.

Yet the same data provide us with other, equally sober findings.
Only 43% are "fully satisfied." One might ask how it comes to pass
that a high-prestige profession should provide 57% of its practitioners
with less than complete gratification. Granted, there might be a
few disenchanted personalities, but 57% is not a few. We have to
look at other data in order to figure out what is going on. There
is at least one additional reason for going beyond the finding
already reported. The level of satisfaction is of less interest to
us than its sources. Why are rabbis contented or discontented with
their lot in life? There are the components of power, prestige,
money, ability to do scholarly work and such. Another question has
to do with the factors associated with happiness. Are older rabbis
happier than younger ones, pulpit rabbis more than those who are

Table 12:

SOURCES OF CAREER SATISFACTION TO REFORM RABBIS
(N=620)

Percent reporting
"VERY SATISFYING"

Sources:

	%
Helping people	85
Opportunity to be creative	61
Time for study and reflection	43
Leadership in Jewish community	39
Prestige	37
Social action involvement	33
Presiding over ritual and worship	31
Adequate income	27

not, scholars more than community activists,- or is it all the other way around? These are some of the things we shall pursue at this point.

We will begin with an analysis of a set of questions dealing with sources of satisfaction with one's rabbinical role. The overall results are seen in Table 12. First and foremost, rabbis appear to value and to enjoy their "ability to help people." Some 85% report that this aspect of their work is "very satisfying." Next in order, 61% express greatest source of satisfaction in "the opportunity to exercise (one's) creative abilities." "Time for study and reflection"

is very satisfying for 43%, and "leadership in the Jewish community"
for 39%. The prestige of the rabbinate is gratifying to 37%. Furthermore, 33% enjoy their "involvement in social action," and 31% cite
"ritual and worship services," and, - at the very bottom of the list,
27% are pleased with their incomes. Shortly we shall see how these
sources of satisfaction differ in terms of commitment to calling.

But so much for the overall story. Service and creativity are the
principal ingredients of satisfaction, while extrinsic items such as
prestige and income seem to play a relatively minor role. This finding
is entirely consistent with findings from studies of other professional
groups such as physicians and academicians. By sociological criteria,
therefore, Reform rabbis are a thoroughly professionalized group.
However, one might be tempted to note a somewhat altered self-image
that the Reform rabbi is reflecting in terms of the traditional image
of the rabbi as a man completely devoted to piety, scholarship, and
prayer. The component of service can still be a part of tradition,
but what of the creativity factor? Are the goals for this creativity
explicit in the training of the rabbi?

Let us examine the situation by length of service. One could reason
that older rabbis, by virtue of their positions, might value
different things than those emphasized by their younger colleagues,-
income perhaps, or prestige, or leadership. But that does not happen
to be true. Rabbis, regardless of age or length of service, stress
the same values with respect to job satisfaction (Table 13). Stated
another way, the socialization process whereby young rabbis come to
be full-fledged members of a "moral community" seems to be complete
by the time they graduate from the seminary. For such a situation
to exist implies a normative system to which most rabbis subscribe.
It is the reverse of what would exist if there were no consensus.

Table 13:

SOURCES OF CAREER SATISFACTION TO RABBIS BY LENGTH OF SERVICE

Sources of satisfaction:	Percent reporting "VERY SATISFYING"						
	Pre-1942 (N=163) %	42-46 (N=39) %	47-51 (N=53) %	52-56 (N=61) %	57-61 (N=87) %	62-66 (N=105) %	67-71 (N=102) %
Helping people	87	92	83	81	85	81	85
Opportunity to be creative	58	59	64	51	66	62	69
Time for study and reflection	47	41	45	52	28	38	50
Leadership in Jewish community	44	44	45	34	33	41	32
Presiding over ritual and worship	41	46	38	22	25	22	28
Prestige	37	38	47	32	36	39	35
Social action involvement	36	28	42	31	26	35	29
Income	30	26	34	35	18	23	24

This is a very significant and important finding, and reflects credit on the rabbi's seminary training.

But, while there is consensus as to the sources of satisfaction, let us remember that not everyone is equally satisfied. That is another matter, and we will now examine this in greater detail.

Rabbis were asked two questions: 1) What would they choose as a profession if they could do it over again?, and 1) Did they have any intentions of leaving their present positions? As to the first question, only 53% think they would choose the rabbinate again if they had the chance! With respect to the second question, 34% were very happy and had no intention of leaving. Another 23% were slightly less content, but still intended to stay on. Thus 57% of Reform rabbis are clearly committed to staying put and are happy to do so. On the face of it, we seem to have two findings that appear to be somewhat perplexing. A small majority is content enough to remain in their present posts, and the same proportion think enough of the rabbinate to be willing to do it all over again. It is only fair to comment here that some may wish to leave the rabbinate, or would not again choose the rabbinate, for reasons other than dissatisfaction with the rabbinate per se. One may have personal reasons that have little or nothing to do with the rabbinate.

During the course of one interview, a pulpit rabbi (in his early 40's), expressed his dissatisfaction as follows:

> Rabbi: I can't say anybody - certainly not my parents - pushed me into the rabbinate. We belonged to a large congregation - Reform. I liked the rabbi and he liked me. I guess I was a good student in religious school. You must remember I was in a Talmud Torah for $4\frac{1}{2}$ years before we moved to _____, where my parents enrolled

me in the Temple _____ Religious School. They
didn't actually join the Temple ... I wasn't 10 yet,
so naturally it was the only solution for them and
for me too. I don't regret it one bit. But to come
back to why I became a rabbi, I can't honestly say.
When I see how creative some of my colleagues are -
the things they do. Some of them are also adept in the
business aspects of running a Temple. It's all beyond
me really.

Interviewer: Do you feel the rabbinate was mis-
represented to you by anyone? Did you have different
expectations?

Rabbi: Not really. As a calling, as a profession
it's the greatest. I'm not the greatest for it.
I'm not a businessman. I'm not really a scholar.
Would you believe my weekly sermons almost take a
full week to prepare, otherwise I'm in trouble. On
the plane coming here, another rabbi who came with
me practically prepared his whole sermon for next
week on the plane. I was tired and napped for a few
minutes - maybe a half hour at most. I can't do
that. I'm not creative.

Interviewer: What would be your occupational choice
if you were to start all over again?

Rabbi: Oh, I've thought of that - perhaps a high
school biology teacher - in a small community.

At no time during the course of the above interview was the rabbinate,
per se, criticized. (Possibly a good counselor during college or
even during seminary days might have been able to do much for this
gentleman. Instead we have a dissatisfied rabbi.)

And one wonders about the 11% who say they would prefer something
else. What, for instance? What of the 31% who are in positions
where they are unhappy? Have they tried to relocate? What is the
role of the Placement Office here? Or for that matter, does the CCAR
have any responsibility regarding such a situation? Are there any
national or regional mechanisms available for dealing with this

rather substantial personnel problem? Can anything be done to help these rabbis, regardless of who or what is to blame? After all, congregants are constantly leaning on them for assistance with many and varied problems. Does not the one who is leaned on deserve, even more than others, to do a little leaning himself? Is this what a substantial number of rabbis are referring to when they speak of the rabbinate as a very lonely profession?

It was decided to construct a typology from the responses to the aforementioned two questions. The first type ("satisfied and committed"), consists of those who would still be rabbis and who are very content with their situations. The second type ("unsatisfied but committed"), is made up of those who would rather be something else and who are not happy with their present arrangement. The other two types are made up of discontented who would still choose the rabbinate ("satisfied - uncommitted"), and, on the other hand, those who are willing to "stay put," but would rather not be a rabbi ("unsatisfied - uncommitted"). (Some 12%, incidentally, would have preferred the academic field.) The resultant distribution is most meaningful. The fully committed (those who answered positively on both questions), make up 22% of the total sample. The alienated group makes up 37%. Eleven percent are reluctant. They would rather be something else, but they are ready to stay on. Finally, 31% still want to be rabbis but are unhappy in their current situations.

Now let us see how these four types differ with respect to the question with which we began this discussion,- the amount of overall career satisfaction. The results, which are shown in Table 14, reveal a not too surprising pattern. Where 75% (three out of four), of the highly committed rabbis are fully satisfied, this drops to 17% (less than one in five), in the case of the alienated rabbis. The other two groups are, as we might expect, somewhere in between with

Table 14:

SATISFACTION WITH THE RABBINICAL CAREER

BY TYPE OF COMMITMENT

	Satisfied, committed (N=133) 22%	Unsatisfied, committed (N=66) 11%	Satisfied, uncommitted (N=186) 30%	Unsatisfied, uncommitted (N=223) 37%
	%	%	%	%
Fully satisfied	75	44	52	17
Somewhat satisfied	25	48	43	45
Undecided	0	3	3	8
Somewhat unsatisfied	0	5	3	20
Very unsatisfied	0	2	1	10

44% and 52% respectively. In other words, there appears to be an extremely high and positive relationship between general satisfaction and type of commitment.

But, it will be recalled that there are no differences by age or length of service with respect to the specific sources of satisfaction, and this was interpreted as evidence of a relatively high degree of consensus among rabbis as to what ought to be a source of gratification in one's career. Does the same thing hold true for the four types under discussion, or will there be differences? Table 15, which we have already examined in part, tells the rest of this story. To

begin with, there are virtually no differences with regard to the
matter of helping people. Committed, alienated, or in between,
rabbis mostly report that helping people is a major source of
satisfaction. This also holds true for the importance of time for
study and reflection. While there are modest differences with respect
to creativity and income, they are not very strong. But when we look
at the differences in the number citing social involvement, ritual
and worship involvement, leadership in the Jewish community, and
prestige, the picture changes. Satisfied committed rabbis differ
from the others on all of the latter items.

These findings can be interpreted in one of two ways. Either the
highly committed rabbis happen to get more of what they want, or
they want different things. Either, by virtue of age and position,
they get the prestige and publicity and memberships in important
public bodies (including CCAR committees?), or they are simply more
satisfied with whatever comes their way in these matters, or their
fulfillment in life may be explained, psychologically, in terms of
the commitment component.

It is to be noted that Table 15 enables us to examine the sources from
which rabbis derive their satisfactions in terms of their respective
commitments.

The eight items that constitute the data in Table 15 are derived primarily
from the primary sources that were alluded to in Chapter 2, viz., the
evaluations of the Reform rabbinate which were available to the researcher
at the beginning of this study.

From these findings we are in a position to determine which of our two

Table 15:

SOURCES OF RABBINICAL CAREER SATISFACTION

IN TERMS OF COMMITMENT

Sources of satisfaction	Satisfied, committed (N=133)	Unsatisfied, committed (N=66)	Satisfied, uncommitted (N=186)	Unsatisfied, uncommitted (N=223)
	%	%	%	%
Helping people	90	78	89	84
Opportunity to be creative	70	89	60	58
Prestige	55	34	37	29
Leadership in Jewish community	53	34	34	35
Presiding over ritual and worship	47	29	32	22
Social action involvement	44	28	32	28
Time for study and reflection	43	34	48	43
Income	36	34	21	26

interpretations is more correct. It appears that the more committed rabbis are more likely than their less committed colleagues to derive satisfaction from such things as social involvement and leadership because they value these things more and do these things more. The data provide us with some telling evidence here. It does not appear to be completely accurate, as is claimed by some rabbis, that the alienated rabbis value these activities but find themselves blocked or frustrated from carrying them out. Their own responses reveal that they do not care that much about these things in the first place. Psychologically, one may raise a question about this. Does this phenomenon reflect their pre-rabbinical personalities? If so, could the seminary have done more for them during their student days?

This is not to suggest for a moment that those who are disenchanted in one way or another do not have legitimate problems and legitimate complaints. Far from it. But the data we have looked at thus far do not support the hypothesis that low commitment to a rabbinical career is caused by structural constraints of one sort or another that make it impossible for rabbis to do what they want to do.

(It is to be noted here that the very recent findings concerning the disaffected Catholic clergy tell almost the identical story as ours on this particularly sensitive issue.)

2.   Dissatisfactions.

Now that we know something about what rabbis like about their jobs, let us look at the other side of the coin,- the sources of unhappiness. Such a list (arranged in rank order), is presented in Table 16. A

Table 16: SOURCES OF DISSATISFACTION AS PERCEIVED BY REFORM RABBIS (N=620)	Percent reporting "VERY DISSATISFYING"
	%
1. Lack of systematic arrangement for sabbaticals for study and travel.	29
2. Lack of good operational UAHC and/or CCAR supervised and enforceable arrangements for equitable salary schedules, pay raises, tenure, etc.	26
3. Inability to make much more of religious school program.	25
4. Religiously indifferent congregation.	19
5. Personal loneliness of the rabbi in overall rabbinic situation.	18
6. Lack of any systematic post-graduate programs for the rabbi in terms of location, availability, and needs.	18
7. Apparent insensitivity of Board of Trustees to rabbi's and synagogue's needs.	17
8. Congregation makes more demands of rabbi in "extra-curricular activities," administrative areas, etc., rather than as rabbi qua rabbi.	13
9. Synagogue's policy of indifference in community involvement and social issues.	12
10. Inadequacy of rabbinical training in terms of the scholarly prerequisites for the job.	10
11. Inadequacy of rabbinical training in terms of dealing with many of the practical aspects of a congregation.	10
12. Inadequate income.	9
13. Inability to assess the results of his preaching and teaching.	8
14. Necessity of Friday night service.	5
15. Lack of community involvement on social issues at request of synagogue authorities.	1
16. Lack of prestige.	1

83

number of interesting conclusions may be drawn from these data. It
will be recalled from Table 12 that the <u>least</u> satisfying aspect of
the job was "adequate income," but with only 27% saying that they
were "very satisfied." Now it turns out that the <u>most dissatisfying</u>
<u>job aspect is the lack of a sabbatical system</u>,- and this response is
from 29% only. In other words, the <u>most</u> complained about thing in
a rabbi's job does not upset more than 3 out of 10 rabbis. <u>The</u>
<u>satisfactions clearly outweigh the dissatisfactions by a very</u>
<u>comfortable margin.</u>

Let us continue with the complaints. The most serious has already
been identified. Here are the next four in the order of frequency
of mention,- the lack of a good salary and tenure policy (26%),
dissatisfaction with the religious school program (25%), a religiously
indifferent congregation (19%), and the rabbi's personal loneliness
(18%). As we glance at Table 16, we note that the first theme
(top two items), has to do with the treatment of rabbis, not so much
by his congregations, but by <u>the system.</u> (We shall note later that
"system" is often equated with the CCAR.) Note, for instance, that
complaints against the congregation (salary, prestige, constraint,
etc.), are mentioned by very few. <u>The second theme has to do with</u>
<u>the rabbi's sense of frustration with himself at the ineffectual nature</u>
<u>of his own performance.</u>

The reader is referred back to p. 28, where comments on this subject
from rabbis were presented as part of the data on <u>income.</u> The

aforementioned comments, along with the following one, were selected
at random, from over 100 similarly categorized written expressions,
each from a different rabbi-respondent.

> If I had to do it over again, I would still choose the
> rabbinate. I am not critical of it per se, as a calling.
> I object to 1) the employee stakes, 2) the 'business'
> relations between rabbi and congregation (Board), 3) the
> authority of laymen in areas belonging to the rabbi,
> 4) the frittering away of the rabbi's time and energies
> on non-rabbinic tasks. Frankly, I feel strongly we need
> a union for self-protection and bargaining purposes.

The second interesting set of findings in regard to dissatisfaction
tells us that while there are differences between the various
commitment types, viz., that those who are highly committed are less
critical than those who are alienated, the differences between the
two groups are not very great. In other words, not even the alienated
ones are doing very much complaining. The loudest chorus from this
latter group comes in regard to the matter of sabbaticals and here
it is a mere 35%. Table 17 portrays the data in detail to support
this important fact.

Table 17 presents a few generalizations about rabbinical dissatisfactions with their careers in terms of commitment. (Table 16
presented general overall dissatisfactions regardless of commitment.)
Close scrutiny of these two tables is very important. Both are arranged in terms of rank-order of the response patterns. (Of course,
the rank-order arrangement for Table 17 can only be done for any one
of the four commitment categories. In this case, it was done for the
first category,- the "committed and satisfied"). Table 17 tells us
that dissatisfaction with one's rabbinical career tends to increase

Table 17: SOURCES OF RABBINICAL DISSATISFACTION IN TERMS OF COMMITMENT (PERCENT REPORTING "VERY DISSATISFYING")	Committed, satisfied.	Committed, unsatisfied.	Uncommitted, satisfied.	Uncommitted, unsatisfied.
	(N=136)	(N=66)	(N=190)	(N=227)
1. Lack of systematic arrangement for sabbaticals for study and travel.	24%	32%	24%	35%
2. Inability to make much more of religious school program.	19%	23%	19%	33%
3. Lack of good operational UAHC-CCAR supervised and enforceable arrangements for equitable salary schedules, pay raises, tenure, etc.	15%	33%	21%	34%
4. Religiously indifferent congregation.	13%	15%	15%	27%
5. Lack of any systematic post-graduate programs for the rabbi in terms of location, availability, and needs.	12%	23%	18%	22%
6. Apparent insensitivity of Board of Trustees to rabbi's and synagogue's needs.	12%	12%	15%	23%
7. Personal loneliness of the rabbi in overall rabbinic situation.	11%	10%	12%	28%
8. Inability to assess the results of his preaching and teaching.	5%	8%	5%	12%
9. Synagogue's policy of indifference in community involvement and social issues.	5%	8%	13%	16%
10. Inadequacy of rabbinical training in terms of the scholarly prerequisites for the job.	4%	12%	8%	12%
11. Congregation makes more demands of rabbi in "extra-curricular activities," administrative areas, etc., rather than as rabbi qua rabbi.	4%	11%	11%	20%
12. Inadequate income.	4%	3%	7%	6%
13. Inadequacy of rabbinical training in terms of dealing with many of the practical aspects of a congregation.	3%	12%	10%	14%
14. Necessity of Friday night service.	3%	5%	2%	9%
15. Lack of community involvement on social issues at request of synagogue authorities.	1%	3%	1%	1%
16. Lack of prestige.	0	0	1%	1%

in terms of decrease in commitment. Thus we may view the situation
in terms of two negative relationships.

1) As commitment increases, dissatisfaction decreases.
2) As commitment decreases, dissatisfaction increases.

Psychological evaluation comes into play here. The psychiatric and
psychological consultants to this study, after thorough review of the
findings, based on the quantitative and the qualitative data, point
out that in the case of the least committed rabbis, there may be
projection of fault-finding with others (persons, organizations, the
system), in order to assuage their own lack of fulfillment. This
lack of fulfillment may be due to one or more inadequacies that might
pertain in the life of any person, and thus does not necessarily
suggest personality pathology. There may be a malfunctioning marital
or family situation. There may be felt deficiencies (felt by the
individual himself) in income, scholarship, or in interpersonal
relationships. These are just some of the areas that may induce
personal inadequacy. There are others. Thus the adjustment mechanism
of projection comes into play. It is the individual's way of keeping
his head above water even if he isn't a good swimmer. But to blame
others will never make him a good swimmer. Perhaps all he needs is
some assistance and encouragement. Perhaps he should never be in
the water in the first place.

In terms of the projection hypothesis, we particularly note in Table
17, Numbers 3, 4, 5, 6, and 11. Here we see where others are viewed
as letting the rabbi down,- the UAHC and the CCAR in terms of arrangements for his economic needs; the congregation in terms of his
expectations from them as Jews; the lack of post-graduate availabilities
in terms of his educational needs; the Board of Trustees in terms of

his own role sensitivities. Numbers 7 and 8 may be viewed as further
manifestations of one's lack of fulfillment. It is not suggested
here that what we have is a bunch of sick rabbis who need intensive,
long-term psychiatric treatment. But we have some honestly unhappy
rabbis. We should not equate dissatisfaction with incompetency or
with inadequate performance. Industrial psychologists have provided
us with evidence that we have no high and positive correlation here.
On the contrary, it is from among those who experience dissatisfaction
that innovative change often comes forth. Of course, it is how the
process of change is called for, how it is introduced, how it is
given meaning that often make for difficulties. As for the responses
to Numbers 11 and 13, our consultants have rendered a split-decision.
One interpretation is that these rabbis may not be doing too well in
their present congregations and are projecting their problems on the
College for providing inadequate training, and on their congregations
for being too demanding. Another interpretation that might pertain
here is that these are rabbis who are content with their abilities,
but are still dissatisfied with their respective performances and
are expressing a sincere desire to do even better, because in their
opinion there is so much more that needs to be done and can be done.

Of course, in the extremes, we are dealing here with the white-hot
core of the constant forces of change versus status quo. The chief
problems are often not really the issues themselves, but the opposing
value-systems of human beings whose personal feelings and emotions
are on the line. And this may have little or nothing to do with being
a rabbi. It is a part of all of us. But one aspect begs to be
answered. What is the motivation for one who is uncommitted and
unsatisfied? There are explanations, but are they answers?

An area of dissatisfaction that merely surfaced in the written
comments that accompanied the questionnaire, but made itself felt a
little more strongly in interviews, came from a rather small number
of rabbis, mostly from those who have been pulpit rabbis some twenty
years or more. The dissatisfaction expressed itself as a general
disappointment with some of the younger rabbis. One such rabbi
devoted considerable attention to the matter during the course of an
interview. He is a rabbi of a substantial urban congregation who
views younger rabbis as honest and committed Jews, but is in a
quandry as to why some of them become rabbis. A former assistant
rabbi who had worked for him had previously described him as a most
wonderful boss, and a very hard-working rabbi - a credit to any
congregation. "I didn't always see eye-to-eye with him on some things,
but he's a great man."

While ambling through an unstructured interview with this not-so-
older gentlman, he seemed distressed with the new generation of rabbis.
And his comments are reasonably typical of others who express themselves on the same subject.

> They come out (of the HUC-JIR) with a certain disdain
> for the rabbinate. They think that we're just wasting
> our time with many of the things that we're doing.
> They . . . feel that they are the spokesmen of world
> Jewry, and not concerned with the little day-to-day
> functions of the rabbi. Whether it's the preaching -
> they get very sloppy about it, because there may be
> only 200 people there. They think there ought to be
> 1000 or 2000 people there listening to the great wisdom
> that flows from them . . . I happen to be a very
> cautious preacher. I prepare meticulously week after
> week . . . if there are 50 people or 1000 people . . .
> I take as much pain emotionally for a Shabbos morning
> service as I do for Yom Kippur . . .
> . . . .

Also one of the reasons that they have this disdain for
the rabbinate, I think, is because the men who are
running (HUC-JIR) have no understanding of the rabbinate.
They don't know what it's all about . . . If they were
to turn out great scholars, I would say fine, but they
don't even do that . . . They (the younger rabbis)
will undertake a spectacular program, but they will not
stick with it. (They haven't the) persistence to stay
with it . . . I have to do this job over and over again.
To me every funeral is another funeral,- it's not the
same funeral, every wedding is another wedding,- it's
not the same wedding . . . I think these young men see
it as another utility that they hand out. The (HUC-
JIR) does not teach them how to deal with the laymen.
They have nothing but disparagement for the laymen.
They feel that on every issue, they know the answers.
These young men assume that when you speak of God you
are dealing with a rigid concept, so they have
difficulties in their belief in God. If they were to
know more, they would know that our rabbis - our
predecessors - had grave complications about God,
themselves, precisely because they believed.

While only a small number of senior pulpit rabbis were displeased
with their assistant rabbis almost en toto, there were many more
who pointed to specific rabbinical shortcomings concerning their
younger assistants. Typical of this latter category are the
following comments:

The newer men seem to be satisfied with passing the buck
to Religious School Directors, to committees . . .

They think that getting in with the kids means being a
kid. They forget they are rabbis. And they overlook
that some of the brighter boys and girls lose respect
for them.

(My assistant), I think, sometimes forgets he is in a
synagogue. He's the really chummy sort. Unless everyone calls him by his first name, he feels offended.
This means the little children in the religious school
. . . this isn't so bad . . . (compared with) the
older congregants who don't like to be called by their
first names by such a young man, even if he is a rabbi
. . . he's a boy to them. They've complained to me
and when I told him so, he shrugged it off.

It should be noted that less than two dozen senior rabbis articulated
these particular dissatisfactions. It is because they speak from the
vantage point of years of experience as pulpit rabbis, that their
views become important.

We have, then, a situation that can be summed up with a reasonable
degree of clarity. Reform rabbis, as far as their overall careers
are concerned, are a satisfied group. More important, the rabbinate
appears to be a profession with many more attractive than objectionable
features, so much so that even those who want to leave it can think
of few things to complain about. At least this is what they tell us
when they are pinned down to the specific components of role satisfaction that are contained in the aforementioned Table 16.

But there is at least one other way to view all these data concerning
satisfactions and dissatisfactions. Up to this point we have been
classifying rabbis with respect to career orientation. Are they
satisfied or not? Do they want to remain rabbis or not? Now for a
different kind of question. How satisfied are they with Reform
Judaism itself? What about all this talk about crisis? How bad are
things? How close are we to the brink? A good many rabbis brought
up the matter of crisis in preliminary interviews, and so a number
of items touching on this issue were built into the questionnaire.
Put together, the responses make up what we shall call "The Crisis
Index."

Here are the preliminary results:

1) Of all rabbis surveyed, 21% are strongly convinced that the Reform Movement is undergoing a serious crisis.

2) Another 21% share this view somewhat less strongly.

3) Some 27% lean to the opposite view.

4) Some 31% say we are not in any crisis.

Summed up, the story is that 42% of the American Reform rabbinate say there is a crisis in Reform Judaism and 58% do not identify much, if any, crisis in the Reform movement.

And here we have an interesting phenomenon. Those who are "strongly convinced" that there is a "crisis" differ more from those who are less convinced with respect to sources of dissatisfaction. The same applies to those who are committed from those who are alienated! Take the example of not being able to make more of the religious school program. Of those who are highly convinced that we are in a crisis, 45% are distressed with the religious school program, while only 15% of those who question crisis indicate such dissatisfaction. Another large difference occurs in regard to the "apparent insensitivity of the Board" to the rabbi's and congregation's needs,- 33% to 6% respectively (Table 18).

What does all this mean? One possible interpretation, in terms of behavioral assessment, is that, since men do not live in personal vacuums, those who perceive the situation "outside" as being in bad shape are more likely to be critical of the rabbinical career regardless of how well things are going for them personally. Here we may be dealing with the projection hypothesis again. Stated another way,

Table 18:

"THE CRISIS INDEX" AND SOURCES OF RABBINICAL DISSATISFACTION

	"THE CRISIS INDEX"			
	High (N=128)	Fairly high (N=129)	Fairly low (N=169)	Low (N=189)
1. Inability to make much more of religious school program.	45%	28%	17%	15%
2. Lack of systematic arrangement for sabbaticals for study and travel.	41%	37%	19%	24%
3. Religiously indifferent congregation.	40%	19%	15%	9%
4. Lack of good operational UAHC-CCAR supervised and enforceable arrangements for equitable salary schedules, pay raises, tenure, etc.	35%	32%	22%	19%
5. Apparent insensitivity of Board of Trustees to rabbi's and synagogue's needs.	33%	18%	16%	6%
6. Personal loneliness of the rabbi in overall rabbinic situation.	31%	20%	17%	7%
7. Lack of any systematic post-graduate programs for the rabbi in terms of location, availability, and needs.	27%	18%	17%	13%
8. Synagogue's policy of indifference in community involvement and social issues.	25%	13%	10%	3%
9. Congregation makes more demands on rabbi in "extra-curricular activities," administrative areas, etc., rather than as rabbi qua rabbi.	24%	14%	8%	7%
10. Inability to assess the results of his preaching and teaching.	18%	6%	4%	5%
11. Inadequacy of rabbinical training in terms of dealing with many of the practical aspects of a congregation.	15%	10%	11%	5%
12. Inadequate income.	14%	10%	10%	4%
13. Inadequacy of rabbinical training in terms of the scholarly prerequisites for the job.	13%	13%	8%	4%
14. Necessity of Friday night service.	13%	4%	2%	2%
15. Lack of community involvement on social issues at request of synagogue authorities.	2%	2%	1%	1%
16. Lack of prestige.	1%	1%	2%	0

complaints about their own careers seem to be closely related to a
general anxiety that some rabbis have about the future of Reform
Judaism.

The opposite assumption, however, also may exist in many cases.
There may be those individuals who are presently experiencing
personal dissatisfactions and personal discomforts with life. Thus
the rabbinate, as an overall world, is not viewed too kindly, and
may even be blamed for it all. We shall be exploring this further
in Chapter 10 when we examine some rabbinical views on the subject
of crisis in Reform Judaism.

Let us look at a few diverse rabbinical observations at this point.
They are reasonably representative of several dozen such expressions.
They are all different. The only unifying theme is personal
dissatisfaction.

> All of the problem areas spotlighted in this study are
> vital and important. Yet there is one which differs
> from the others in a most critical respect: I speak
> of the rabbi's economic viability. The rabbi's satis-
> faction or dissatisfaction with his seminary, his
> congregation, his Reform Movement -- these he suffers
> through himself, in essence . . .
> . . . .
> . . . No rabbi expects to get rich in this work; but
> neither should he and his family have to live on the
> edge of genteel 'poverty' having to give his family
> subliminal support . . .
> . . . .
> . . . Make this a profession in which a rabbi's remun-
> eration is truly commensurate with his needs, and you
> will have done much to make it a profession in which
> the men are better adjusted; they and their families
> happier!!!

> . . . I feel that the major reasons for so many
> Reform rabbis being dissatisfied are: 1) their
> feelings of <u>personal</u> inadequacy which they have <u>prior</u>
> to entering rabbinical school and which are carried
> over into their rabbinical roles and 2) an over-
> glorification of the role and the effectiveness of
> the rabbi (essentially a naive view).
>
> Although I have for some time thoroughly enjoyed
> my rabbinate, I recognize that is largely due to my
> <u>outside</u> activities which, supplementing congrega-
> tional work, makes my rabbinical life gratifying.

It would appear that with some of our rabbis that this <u>personal</u>
component for fulfilling oneself <u>outside</u> of his rabbinical context
may have started while the rabbi was still a student in the seminary.
A very recently ordained member of the rabbinate has this to say
on the subject:

> . . . other considerations, outside of college,
> usually determine the student's motivation and in-
> terest in the College. This is a rather sad commen-
> tary on an already problem-ridden institution. It
> is a common understanding at HUC, that in order to
> survive the five or six years, spend as little time
> there as possible, have a life apart. The seminary
> should be such an institution where students go for
> many things and participate in the life of that
> institution.

3. <u>Summary Highlights (Being a Reform Rabbi)</u>.

A. <u>Satisfactions</u>:

1) More than 80% of Reform rabbis say that they are satisfied
    with the way things have worked out for them in terms of
    their <u>professional</u> <u>careers</u>.

2) Some 43% are "fully satisfied," only 4 in 100 are "very dissatisfied;" 9% are "somewhat dissatisfied."

3) The top two <u>sources</u> of satisfaction are: "helping people" (85%), and "opportunity to be creative" (61%).

4) The least two <u>sources</u> of satisfaction are: "presiding over ritual and worship" (31%), and "adequate income" (27%).

5) <u>Regardless of length of service</u>, rabbis stress the same values with respect to job satisfaction.

6) Some 57% of the rabbinate are clearly satisfied with and committed to remaining in the rabbinate.

7) Some 54% think they would choose the rabbinate again if they had it to do all over again.

8) There is an extremely high and positive correlation between general satisfaction with the rabbinate with type of commitment; 75% of the <u>highly committed</u> rabbis are <u>fully satisfied</u> to be in the rabbinate; only 17% of the <u>alienated</u> are so satisfied.

9) Highly committed rabbis derive more satisfaction from <u>social involvement</u> and <u>leadership</u> than do alienated rabbis.

10) Although alienated rabbis often claim they are blocked and frustrated in their performance in the areas of social involvement and leadership, actually there is hardly any evidence that they care to assume these roles with any degree of commitment.

B. Dissatisfactions:

1) The single most dissatisfying job aspect is the lack of a
    sabbatical system, but only 29% make this complaint.

2) The lack of a good salary and tenure policy is the second
    most noted dissatisfaction. This is voiced by 26%; 25%
    are dissatisfied with their religious school program;
    19% complain of a religiously indifferent congregation;
    18% note the rabbi's personal loneliness next.

3) Differences between committed and non-committed rabbis are
    not very great when it comes to types of dissatisfactions.

4) Dissatisfaction with one's rabbinical career tends to
    increase in terms of decrease in commitment.

5) Basic dissatisfactions are primarily aimed at the "system"
    (the CCAR, the HUC-JIR, the Union, the Congregation,-
    separately and in combination).

6) Psychological interpretation explains some of the dis-
    satisfaction as a case of projection,- blaming others
    (mostly the "system") for one's own inadequacies.

7) Some of the more experienced rabbis are displeased with
    what they identify as a lack of commitment on the part of
    their junior colleagues.

8) Some 42% of Reform rabbis say there is a crisis in Reform
    Judaism; 58% do not identify much if any such crisis.

9) Those rabbis who strongly identify a crisis are also most
    often those who express much dissatisfaction with their
    respective careers. There are exceptions.

10) Those rabbis who strongly identify a crisis are also most
    often those who come from the less committed ranks. There
    are exceptions here, too.

11) There seems to be a need for national or regional mechanisms
    for identifying the dissatisfactions and for dealing with
    the situation, starting with admissions to the seminary,
    seminary personnel capabilities, and later with the
    employed rabbi and his individual situation.

CHAPTER 8: RELIGIOUS BELIEFS OF REFORM RABBIS

1. Belief in God: Traditionalists, Moderates and Radicals.

There may once have been a time when a study of a rabbinical group
would not have included a chapter thus entitled, since it was taken
for granted that everyone shared the same belief system. If that
was ever true, it certainly is not so today. The data, from the
questionnaires and from focused interviews, tell us that many rabbis
are seriously questioning their own beliefs, or diverge in their
beliefs from their colleagues. The trend, if age is any indication,
is strongly in the direction of stepped-up debate in this area
in the immediate years ahead. In short, the counter-cultural
dimensions of the contemporary American social system does not exclude
American Reform Judaism.

Here is how some of the self-labeling goes:

> "Agnostic"
> "Atheist"
> "Bahai in spirit, Judaic in practice"
> "Conservative"
> "I can't really label myself"
> "Jew"
> "Monotheist"
> "Polydoxist"
> "Reconstructionist at heart"
> "Religious Existentialist"
> "Theist"
> "Theological Humanist"
> "Traditionalist"

Thus we shall devote this chapter exclusively to the Reform rabbi's
religious beliefs. As Figure 15 points out, only one in ten rabbis

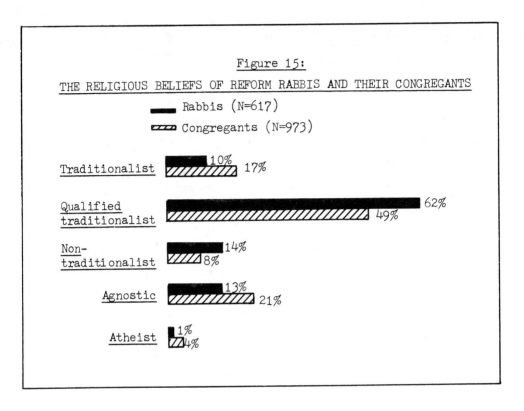

Figure 15:

THE RELIGIOUS BELIEFS OF REFORM RABBIS AND THEIR CONGREGANTS

Rabbis (N=617)
Congregants (N=973)

Traditionalist   10%   17%

Qualified traditionalist   62%   49%

Non-traditionalist   14%   8%

Agnostic   13%   21%

Atheist   1%   4%

states that he believes in God "in the more or less traditional
Jewish sense". Some 62% qualify their belief in God by adding,
"in terms of my own views of what God is and what he stands for."
Finally, more than one in four (28%), see themselves, either as
non-traditionalists (14%), agnostics (13%), or atheists (1%).

There appears to be an unmistakable trend. Take traditionalism,
for example. While 10% of the total Reform rabbinate see themselves
believing in God in the "Traditional" sense, the proportion is as

high as 13% and holding steady for rabbis ordained before 1957.
Since that time, however, the number has declined to such an extent
that only 3% of the youngest group (ordained 1967-1971), so define
themselves (Table 19).

Or take the "qualified traditionalists," those who believe in God
subject to some private interpretation. Their numbers have dwindled
from a high of 70% to a bare majority of 55%. Conversely, where
the less traditional-minded make up only 17% of the oldest group
of rabbis, the number grows to 42% in the case of those most recently
ordained. This is indeed a significant finding, particularly in
view of the likelihood that it is a conservative one. Based upon a
large number of interviews with individual rabbis, especially with
those ordained in the last ten years or so, it would appear that the
response pattern which came forth from the questionnaire could be

Table 19:

RELIGIOUS BELIEFS OF REFORM RABBIS BY LENGTH OF SERVICE

Ordained →	Pre-1942 (N=162)	1942-46 (N=39)	1947-51 (N=52)	1952-56 (N=68)	1957-61 (N=87)	1962-66 (N=105)	1967-71 (N=101)
	%	%	%	%	%	%	%
Traditionalist	13	13	13	13	11	7	3
Qualified Traditionalist	70	72	67	63	53	58	55
Non-traditionalist	6	3	13	10	16	23	21
Agnostic	11	9	7	11	20	11	20
Atheist	0	3	0	3	0	1	1

modified on this point. When one examines the qualifications which many rabbis have in mind concerning the nature of God (as revealed in the interviews), it is very possible that many more rabbis hold non-traditionalist views than is even revealed by the bare statistics as reaped from the questionnaire instrument. Thus it would appear that one may have a situation where an increasing number of Reform rabbis reject or question the central religious tenets of Reform Judaism. What this portends for the future might well be a very serious question presently confronting the whole Reform movement.

The remainder of this section is a measure of religious belief which includes not only the question already mentioned but a number of other items which deal with various aspects of religiosity. All are found to be highly correlated with one another so that the resultant measure is highly reliable. Moreover, the basic distribution denoting overall religiosity does not change very much. On the basis of their own evaluations, the data tell us that 10% are identifiable as traditionalists, 62% are identifiable as moderates, and 28% are identifiable as radicals. Nor does the picture change with respect to age. Some 15% of those 55 or older are traditionalists as opposed to 7% of those under 40. On the other hand, the 14% figure for radicals over 55 increases to 42% in the case of those under 40.

2. Traditionalists, Moderates and Radicals: Backgrounds, Attitudes and Practices.

Who are the traditionalists and how do they differ from their more liberal and radical colleagues? We shall see that some of the answers are not only interesting, but provide profound insight of possible future trends of Reform Judaism. Every finding reported here represents a sizable statistical difference between one group and the next. The findings in Table 20 (possibly one of the most important compilations of data in this whole study), will be presented by giving three percentages in sequence. The first figure will represent rabbis who hold "traditionalist" positions, the second figure identifies the "moderates," and the third figure represents the "radicals." Thus, the data provide us with a plethora of insights regarding origins, backgrounds, attitudes, and behaviors of Reform rabbis who by their own responses identify themselves in these respective categories.

On the basis of what Table 20 tells us, Traditionalist rabbis appear to be vanishing indeed if their orientation depends in large measure on the possession of characteristics such as Items 1-3. If the social origins of rabbis are related to religious values, then changes in the first are likely to produce corresponding changes in the second. Items 4-9 suggest that the happiest rabbis appear to be those who are on the verge of disappearing. This does not suggest that their less traditionalist successors will be less happy, but it is noteworthy that the more traditional, the more content is the man with less, and one wonders whether their origins and orientation might not have made them better suited for the rabbinical life.

Do items 10-16 suggest that the happiest rabbis are also the more conservative in their approach to the rabbi's many roles? If this is so, then we have further documentation to substantiate such an hypothesis. Despite all the preceding attitudes and behaviors, however, traditionalists are _less_ likely to engage in Items 28 and 29. Perhaps one should not say "despite all," since rejection of the chuppa and the breaking of the glass are entirely consistent with the modes of classical Reform. Classical Reform is being seriously questioned from within by a generation of rabbis who are themselves largely the products of Classical Reform. Young, with possibly little first-hand knowledge of other Jewish modalities, they are nevertheless concerned, possibly romantically, with

Table 20:

BACKGROUNDS, ATTITUDES AND PRACTICES OF REFORM RABBIS:

TRADITIONALISTS, MODERATES, AND RADICALS

T - Traditionalists
M - Moderates
R - Radicals

	T (N=62)	M (N=383)	R (N=173)
1. Come from rabbinical family backgrounds.	16%	11%	5%
2. Have (or had) Orthodox fathers.	42%	35%	22%
3. Able to write classical Hebrew.	31%	21%	16%
4. Satisfied with their careers.	57%	41%	36%
5. More satisfied now than they were when first ordained.	36%	32%	31%
6. Content with their present posts and have no plans for leaving.	44%	34%	25%
7. Would want to become rabbis if they had it to do all over again.	67%	54%	43%
8. Receive lower salaries (under $10,000).	15%	6%	5%
9. Have pulpits in smaller congregations (under 100 families).	23%	11%	8%
10. Emphasize the conduct of services and their preaching as essential ingredients of their identities as rabbis.	66%	45%	22%
11. Do considerable preaching.	61%	54%	36%
12. Work very _little_ with youth groups.	12%	15%	26%
13. Are involved in social action.	11%	16%	26%
14. Feel that rabbis should not risk antagonizing their congregations by engaging in social activism.	27%	19%	13%
15. It is important to conduct weddings, preside at funerals, etc.	55%	49%	34%
16. Use the Union Prayer Book "_as is_."	65%	34%	23%
17. Much stress on the importance of attendance at Sabbath services.	58%	38%	15%
18. _Oppose_ the abandonment of emphasis on the sacred.	39%	31%	18%
19. Much stress on the importance of a well-prepared sermon.	67%	62%	46%

104

T - Traditionalists
M - Moderates
R - Radicals

	T	M	R
20. Experiment with formats of religious services.	13%	32%	46%
21. Believe that Reform should pay less attention to decor and more to emotion.	14%	28%	36%
22. Oppose the Israeli Supreme Court ruling in the Shalit case.	21%	12%	6%
23. Believe that "faith is an encounter of the whole personality with God."	49%	42%	14%
24. Believe that "God is a merciful healer."	31%	18%	5%
25. Believe that "it is impossible to have peace of mind without God."	23%	12%	4%
26. Believe that "prayers ... furnish a close bond with Jews and Judaism."	88%	60%	26%
27. Almost never pray privately.	29%	11%	1%
28. Favor the use of the chuppa.	15%	24%	29%
29. Favor the breaking of the glass at weddings.	10%	17%	20%
30. Sense a "Jewish distance" between themselves and their congregations.	14%	25%	28%
31. Feel that their congregants are unconcerned with Judaism.	3%	9%	17%
32. Feel that the "Jewish distance" is the single most frustrating experience for them.	9%	19%	20%
33. Uncertain about the future of Reform Judaism.	10%	16%	23%
34. Derive much satisfaction from involvement in school and social action programs.	21%	31%	41%
35. "Judaism must speak out on the great social issues of the day or find its very existence threatened."	43%	60%	68%
36. Involved in community affairs.	44%	49%	58%
37. "Jewish leadership has not done an adequate job in facing up to civil rights issues."	10%	21%	26%

ecstatic movements within Judaism (such as Hasidism), bordering
possibly, on the anti-sacramentalism of progressive Protestantism.
These are the Reform rabbis of the future. It goes without saying
that some will change their minds as they grow older, others will
possibly leave the rabbinate. But it is difficult to believe that
a group whose de facto orientation is so radically different from
that of their older colleagues will disappear, or will become much
more conservative over time. The attrition rate may be higher than
it was in the past. At any rate, the data would suggest that
Reform is in for more change before it achieves more equilibrium
within the Movement. (Of course, one can only agree to this in
its entirety if congregations move along in similar directions.)

The traditionalist rabbis appear to be most composed. In response
to a series of questions dealing with the possibility of a crisis
in Reform Judaism today, almost four out of ten traditionalists
denied that such a crisis exists, or, if it does exist, would
grant that it is very important. The comparable figures for moderates and radicals are 31% and 27%. In short, the more involved
one is in pressing for change, the greater the sensitivity to
potential or real crisis. (Or is this the other way around. Is
it that stable and secure rabbis are not afraid to face a crisis?)
For the present, the traditionalists do not see themselves as
"embattled." They may feel some discomfort with their more
radical colleagues as a good many do indicate in the course of
confidential interviews, but they do not see themselves as fighting
a rear-guard action. According to some traditionalists, they
are simply more secure with basic overall Judaism than are some
of their colleagues.

Here is one older respondent's reaction:

> I found myself choosing a statement that seemed to me
> too smug because I couldn't accept the alternative
> statement of anger or despair. Incidentally, there
> are young rabbis who are glad they are rabbis, as well
> as cheerful mossbacks like me!

We have already seen several indications of the traditionalists'
views,- their level of general satisfaction, their commitment to
the rabbinate, their willingness to stay put. Let us look more
closely at the differences between traditionalists, moderates,
and radicals as they view their congregations (Items 30-37).
Not only are the younger rabbis pressing for changes with respect
to liturgy, ritual, and belief, they seem to be even more concerned with the rabbi's role in the outside world. Despite the
fact that it is the traditionalists who appear to have slightly
more working contacts with Protestant and Catholic clergymen, it
is the radical group that press for involvement in social action.

To summarize, the older Reform rabbi, who believes in God, is
happy in his work, is content with tending to the needs of his
congregation, - this man is not only in the minority today, but
his numbers seem to be becoming fewer and fewer.

An older Reform rabbi (over 20 years a pulpit rabbi), typifies this
position. When asked if he believed in God in the traditional
sense, his reply was spontaneous:

> I have always believed in God, and to me there is
> neither traditional nor non-traditional. His existence
> is clear to me. If I did not believe in God, I could
> not read the service ... How can a rabbi, or any Jew
> for that matter say the words, 'Hear, O Israel: The

Lord our God, the Lord is One,' and not mean it? For
a rabbi, especially, it would not only be fraudulent
and degrading, but a flagrant insult to his congregation and to his calling.

Another Reform rabbi, recently retired, explained it this way in

one of his sermons:

> On this night - Kol Nidre Eve - which is so mightily
> charged with what we call Religion, I want to ask and
> attempt to answer the question: Does Man Need
> Religion?
>
> I approach this theme with a major assumption which,
> for me, is also a profound conviction: There is a God!
> I shall not try to prove this. I shall not even argue
> about it. For me - this is axiomatic and I affirm
> it categorically: There is a God!
>
> I hold also, that in its simplest definition Religion
> means belief in God; and conversely, I hold that with-
> out such belief there is no religion! An atheist,
> however zealous he may be, is not religious. Godless-
> ness cannot be a synonym for religion if we use words
> honestly and responsibly.

We will be taking an intensive look at congregants' views on these

same matters in subsequent pages. But this much can be said now.

There may not be a "Jewish distance" between rabbis and their con-

gregants, but there may be a growing distance.

Or it might be viewed through the eyes of one of our older rabbis,

who made this observation:

> Since I was a young man . . . (as a student rabbi),
> there were those who spoke of a "Jewish distance"
> between themselves and their congregations. I still

hear it today ... (usually) from the younger (rabbis).
Believe me, there is no greater 'Jewish distance'
between these men and their congregations, than the
'Jewish distance' ... (that exists) between some of
(them) and their God.

3. Summary Highlights (Reform Rabbis: Religious Beliefs).

1) One in ten rabbis states that he believes in God "in the
more or less traditional Jewish sense".

2) Some 62% believe but qualify "the more or less traditional
Jewish sense" with "in terms of my own views of what God
is and what He stands for."

3) Some 14% Reform rabbis identify themselves as non-traditionalists; 13% are agnostics; 1% are atheists.

4) In terms of belief in God and other aspects of religiosity,
Reform rabbis can be categorized as traditionalists (10%),
Moderates (62%), and radicals (28%).

5) Of rabbis 55 and over, 15% are traditionalists, and 14%
are radicals; of rabbis under 40, 7% are traditionalists,
and 42% are radicals.

6) Traditionalist rabbis seem to be disappearing by some
criteria (e.g., rabbinical family backgrounds, Orthodox
fathers), but radicals two-to-one over the traditionalists
favor the re-introduction of some traditional rituals
(e.g., chuppa and breaking of the glass). More than two-
to-one over traditionalists, the radicals also believe
in the need for more emotion in Reform ritual and services.

7) Traditionalists, three-to-one over radicals, emphasize "the conduct of services and their preaching as essential ingredients of their identities as rabbis."

8) Radicals, over two-to-one compared with traditionalists, are involved in social action; Traditionalists, over two-to-one over radicals say that "rabbis should not risk antagonizing their congregations by engaging in social action."

9) Traditionalists use the <u>Union</u> <u>Prayer</u> <u>Book</u>, <u>as</u> <u>is</u>, three-to-one over radicals.

10) Traditionalists, over three-to-one compared with radicals, believe that "faith is an encounter of the whole personality with God."

11) Four of ten traditionalists deny the existence of a crisis in Reform. Crisis is claimed by 31% of the moderates and 27% of the radicals.

12) On the basis of 37 factors concerning backgrounds, attitudes, and practices (Table 20), it appears that Classical Reform is being seriously questioned from within by a generation of rabbis who are largely products of Classical Reform.

CHAPTER 9: THE PULPIT RABBI AND HIS ESTABLISHMENT

Of the 620 rabbis who completed questionnaires, 506 or 82%
occupy or share a synagogue pulpit. The information analyzed
in this chapter comes from these pulpit rabbis only.

1. Synagogue Affairs and Synagogue Politics.

First, a look at how their respective synagogues are run (on
the basis of the rabbis' assessments). We shall start by
suggesting that there is a distinction between synagogue affairs
and synagogue politics, that is, between serving the needs of
the congregation, and maintaining a power status. As to major
activity (Figure 16), in synagogue politics, some 76% of our rabbis
mention the Board of Trustees with the Sisterhood getting 13% of
their votes, and the rest scattered. As to which group makes the
greatest contribution to the congregation, the answers are significantly different. While the largest number of rabbis (45%) still
mention the Board of Trustees, there is a drop of 31%, and it would
appear that most have switched to the 34% who mention the Sisterhood in this connection. Are the rabbis saying that men are too
often just politicians? It is worth noting that, with respect
to both criteria, the Men's Club and other auxiliaries, according
to most rabbis, are only minimally involved. It is also worth
noting how many rabbis cite individual members rather than
groups as strong contributing agents to synagogue growth.

On the whole, rabbis see their congregations as tractable.
Thus, in rating their respective Boards and general memberships
as to willingness to experiment and to accept change in synagogue

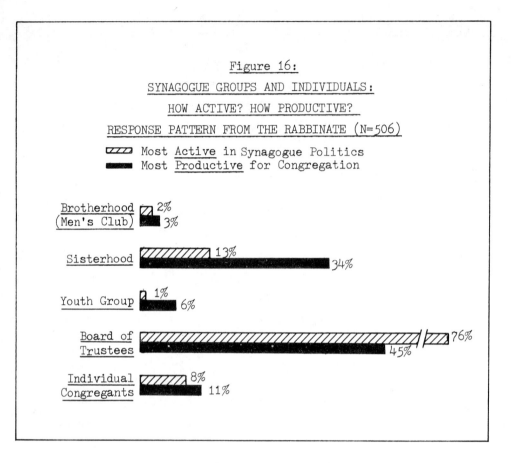

Figure 16:
SYNAGOGUE GROUPS AND INDIVIDUALS:
HOW ACTIVE? HOW PRODUCTIVE?
RESPONSE PATTERN FROM THE RABBINATE (N=506)

policy (Figure 17), some 74% say that the Board would be willing,
and 76% say the same thing for the general membership. Indeed,
only 24% and 20%, respectively, are viewed as being unwilling.
On the basis of this, one would conclude that most Reform rabbis
are relatively free of shackling restraints, that their congregants
give them a certain amount of latitude in initiating change, or
would do so if they chose to exercise the option. This means,
of course, that most rabbis could assume more leadership if they
chose to do so.

From the interviews, however, most rabbis felt that the <u>initiative</u>
almost always had to come from them (the rabbis). One rabbi,
in his mid-fifties, now heading up one of the larger Reform
congregations in the country, felt this way about it:

> In the past my greatest mistake was to let things
> go along for long periods of time, and we were all -
> The Board and I, and the other auxiliaries too, all
> too complacently satisfied. But then when all of
> a sudden something had to be done about something,

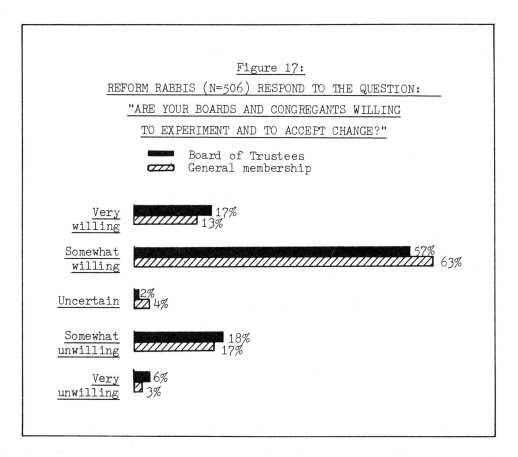

Figure 17:

REFORM RABBIS (N=506) RESPOND TO THE QUESTION:

"ARE YOUR BOARDS AND CONGREGANTS WILLING

TO EXPERIMENT AND TO ACCEPT CHANGE?"

███ Board of Trustees
▒▒▒ General membership

Very willing — 17% / 13%

Somewhat willing — 57% / 63%

Uncertain — 2% / 4%

Somewhat unwilling — 18% / 17%

Very unwilling — 6% / 3%

and after I had done a lot of thinking on it
... I would present it to the Board, only to
be met by a wall of inertia. Now this is the
rabbi's fault ... He can't expect to be asleep
at the switch for months or years ... (and)
allow the leadership to be equally lethargic,
and then all of a sudden hit them with something new, and expect them to react favorably
without wincing. The rabbi should always be
innovating if only to keep the leadership
tuned-up, so to speak, so that when they are
needed to really give leadership to something
big, they can be relied upon. This is the way
I do it now, and it's a lot easier, too, for all
of us.

One of the findings of interest in Figure 17 is the fact that our
rabbis view their general memberships approximately in the same
light as they view their Boards of Trustees when it comes to
experimentation and the acceptance of change. If this assessment by the rabbinate is accurate, then it would follow that
Boards are truly representative of their respective congregational memberships, at least with regard to change and
experimentation.

While on the whole, Boards and congregants alike are seen as
reasonably permissive, and while there are no important differences between satisfied and dissatisfied rabbis in their perception of the membership's attitude, there is a large difference
where the Board's attitude (Table 21) is concerned. Of those
who view their Boards as "very willing", 53% of the rabbis
say they are very satisfied and another 40% are somewhat
satisfied. Of those with "somewhat willing" Boards, the figures
are 45% and 40%. Of those with "somewhat unwilling" Boards, the
number of satisfied rabbis drops to 29% and 47% respectively.
Of those who see their Board as "very unwilling", only 22%
and 35% respectively, report a measure of satisfaction.

Table 21:

RABBI'S PERCEPTION AND SATISFACTION REGARDING BOARD'S
WILLINGNESS TO EXPERIMENT AND TO ACCEPT CHANGE

Rabbi's degree of satisfaction

Rabbi's Perception of Board's Attitude	Very satisfied	Somewhat satisfied	Undecided	Somewhat unsatisfied	Very unsatisfied
Very willing (Rabbi N=84)	53%	40%	0	7%	0
Somewhat willing (Rabbi N=283)	45%	40%	5%	8%	2%
Somewhat unwilling (Rabbi N=92)	29%	47%	4%	12%	8%
Very unwilling (Rabbi N=28)	22%	35%	4%	17%	22%

Now it goes without saying that the relationship could be the
other way around. It could be that satisfied rabbis are more
likely to perceive their Board members as permissive and
friendly. Happy people are generally more prone to see others
as cooperative. But in this case we have an independent check, -
the absence of differences where the congregants are concerned.
If dissatisfaction is causing the perception that the Board is
uncooperative, then it might follow that the general membership
is also perceived by the rabbi as unwilling to cooperate.

One needs to note an important psychological component of a
group's willingness, and sometimes even their ability to
experiment and to accept change. This is the personality of
the leader. One can not disregard the role of the rabbi's
basic personality. His own leadership qualities are capable
of having a profound effect on the Board and on the congregation. The interpersonal relationships between the rabbi and
his various synagogue constituencies may explain in many cases
why experimentation and change are or are not possible in his
congregation.

Here are two comments from congregants:

> When I was asked to go on the Board for the past
> eight years, I just couldn't because I knew I just
> couldn't work with him (former Rabbi). It's
> different now. I'm not even on the Board ...
> that isn't important - I'm active on two committees.
> I think I'm speaking for one or two others. Let's
> face it - Rabbi ____ (present rabbi) is a friendly
> man. He's interested - in you - in what you're doing -
> the kids like him.

Interviewer: As a Board member, do you feel
any differently toward your rabbi than before?

Congregant: You know it's a strange thing.
I really didn't like my rabbi at all. I didn't
know him all that well and the kids used to
come home with those crazy stories about how
he would dismiss the class ... he seemed un-
organized. I don't want to say disorgranized.
But he's a real leader - a real competent guy
who could hold his own anywhere. He doesn't
say too much, but when some of us get tangled
up - he steps in and comes up with good work-
able solutions. I don't think many (congregants) know this part of him.

The fact that we find it for one group (the Board) and not for
another (the congregants), suggests that Board behavior counts
for more in causing rabbinical job satisfaction than does the
conduct of the general membership. Not that rabbis are necessarily always pleased, or ought to be, with what the
general membership is up to (or not up to, as the case may
be), but the rabbi's job satisfaction does not appear to be as
directly influenced by the general membership's behavior or
attitudes as it is by the Board's feelings and doings. And,
of course, this is not too difficult to understand.

2. Prerequisites to Membership.

Returning to synagogue affairs, our rabbis report three very
different situations with respect to prerequisites to membership
in their respective congregations (Figure 18). Some 18% of the
congregations require it for a marriage ceremony, while 18% will
make some exceptions. Another 60% require membership for religious

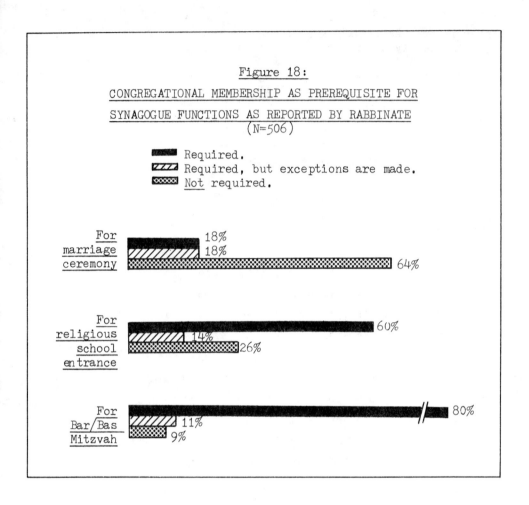

Figure 18:

CONGREGATIONAL MEMBERSHIP AS PREREQUISITE FOR
SYNAGOGUE FUNCTIONS AS REPORTED BY RABBINATE
(N=506)

■■ Required.
▨ Required, but exceptions are made.
▧ Not required.

For marriage ceremony
18%
18%
64%

For religious school entrance
60%
14%
26%

For Bar/Bas Mitzvah
80%
11%
9%

school enrollment, while another 14% will make some exceptions.
By far the largest number of congregations, 80%, require it for
the Bar/Bas Mitzvah, and an additional 11% require it but will make
some exceptions.

3.   What Role for the Hebrew Language?

Hebrew is used in all but two congregations as reported by the
506 pulpit rabbis who responded, but the kind of Hebrew varies
and what may be disturbing (at least to some congregants), is that
it even varies <u>within</u> **same** congregations (Figure 19).   Whereas
48% use Ashkenazit for worship, only 23% of these same congregations use it in the religious school, the remaining 25%
using Sephardit.   The reasons are two-fold: (1) Many religious
school teachers are far more likely to be familiar with Sephardit,
and (2) in older congregations, where Ashkenazit has been used
for decades, a sudden change would almost be traumatic for some

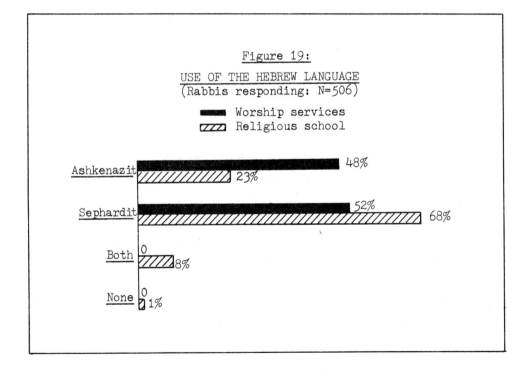

Figure 19:

USE OF THE HEBREW LANGUAGE
(Rabbis responding: N=506)
■■■ Worship services
▨▨ Religious school

Ashkenazit   48%
             23%

Sephardit   52%
             68%

Both 0
      8%

None 0 1%

119

rabbis and congregants alike.   Younger rabbis are far more
likely to report the use of Sephardit in the worship services
than do their older colleagues, - some 69% of the most recently ordained as opposed to 31% of the rabbis who were ordained
prior to 1942. If things go on this way, Ashkenazit appears
to be a doomed havara except among some Orthodox groups.

4. The Worship Service and Music.

Virtually all Reform congregations (99%) these days, have Friday
night services (Figure 20), and of these, 61% also have services
on Saturday morning. Only two congregations report having
Sunday morning services instead. As for the use of musical
instruments other than the organ, the vast majority (89%) of
the rabbis report that they are used occasionally or never.
Only 5% report regular use of musical instruments in addition
to the organ.

5. The Union Prayer Book.

The Union Prayer Book (Volume I) continues to be used by most
rabbis, but only 38% use it without some modifications. The
statistical breakdown is presented in Figure 21. If, for
Sabbaths and Festivals, only 38% and 45% of our rabbis, respectively, report using The Union Prayer Book "as is," it can
easily be deduced that the Reform prayerbook is not meeting
the complete needs of Reform rabbis and their congregations.
And the responses regarding the use of Volume II are reasonably similar to the response patterns concerning Volume I.

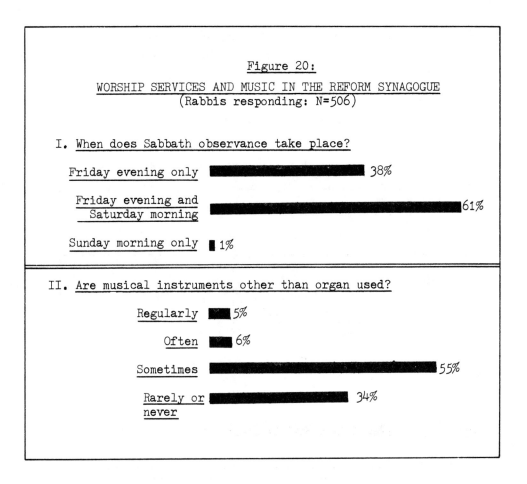

Figure 20:

WORSHIP SERVICES AND MUSIC IN THE REFORM SYNAGOGUE
(Rabbis responding: N=506)

I. When does Sabbath observance take place?

Friday evening only — 38%

Friday evening and Saturday morning — 61%

Sunday morning only — 1%

II. Are musical instruments other than organ used?

Regularly — 5%

Often — 6%

Sometimes — 55%

Rarely or never — 34%

Of course, on the face of the total statistics, by including the "as is" users with the "with modifications" users, we can easily be misled into accepting the fact since 90% do use the prayerbook, the prayerbook is here to stay. Not so. From written comments, and even more so from data that were elicited from the interviews, the findings suggest that substantial numbers of rabbis are very disenchanted with substantial portions of the present prayerbook, and have been for a number of years. One of the most vigorous complaints from pulpit rabbis throughout the country, aimed at

the Central Conference of American Rabbis, can be summed up
thus, - "Will they ever finish the revision of the prayerbook?"
The many original written prayer services that have been prepared by rabbis throughout the country also testify to the
fact that the present prayerbook is not "wearing well".*

Furthermore, it should be noted that those who respond as users
"with modifications," represent a very broad range. Some insert
minor modifications. Others use a completely original Sabbath

Figure 21:
USE OF THE "UNION PRAYER BOOK, VOL. I"
(Rabbis responding: N=506)

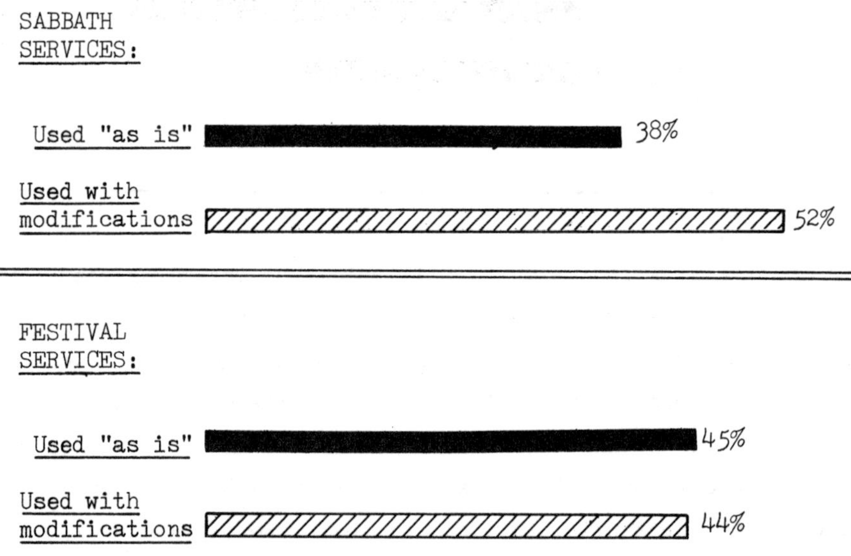

SABBATH
SERVICES:

Used "as is"   38%

Used with
modifications   52%

FESTIVAL
SERVICES:

Used "as is"   45%

Used with
modifications   44%

* See Chapter 18, Section 4, pp. 330-332, for further analysis of
   the Union Prayer Book, primarily as seminarians evaluate
   it. Some comparative rabbinate-seminarian findings are
   presented (Figure 56).

service from one to as many as three Sabbaths during the course of every month, so that the prayerbook may only be used "as is" once or twice a month in some cases. As was just mentioned, a great many creative services have been introduced during the past few years, and in many different parts of the country. Some of these are of "multi-media" format, i.e., a single service may include specially composed music (sometimes of a "rock" nature), arranged for chorus and/or instrumental performance, as well as color film excerpts depicting flashes of poverty, pollution, student campus action, - all backed up by lighting effects to induce mood. Somewhere, brief traditional prayers are also included. Some of these creative services have been poorly re-ceived by rabbis and congregants as well. Others have been extremely moving and beautiful and well received.

It should be noted here that close to two hundred rabbis have seen fit to comment, in writing and in interviews, that there are those in the Conference who are making more of the need for a prayerbook revision than the situation requires. The tone of these, and they represent almost all age-groups, is that the prayerbook is a scapegoat more than a malady. One rabbi admits he is using the Conservative prayer book (edited by Rabbi Morris Silverman), along with the Union Prayer Book in his congregation, but this is only because he now has a more traditional congregation than in his former position. Previously the Union Prayer Book was fully satisfactory for him and for his congregation.

He concludes:

> It's not very different from a college course. It's
> <u>not the textbook</u>, it's the <u>professor</u> who makes the
> course a good one or a bad one, <u>not the book</u>.

Some further comments from Reform rabbis are as follows:

> On the general question of prayerbook revision,
> it is my sober judgment that most of the cries
> or calls for change, 'creative services,' etc.
> come from colleagues who are, in the last analy-
> sis, non-believers in the efficacy of prayer
> <u>qua</u> prayer. The 'Sefer Chassidim' says it
> better: 'When the heart does not know what
> the lips utter - there is no prayer.' The
> truly earnest worshipper finds no prayerbook
> page dull or 'irrelevant,' for he clothes the
> words on those pages with his own spiritual
> need, hunger, hurt or yearning. As the human
> experience varies from week to week, the wor-
> shipper's attachment of meaning to the prayers
> varies - from week to week. No amount of 're-
> vising' can ever be adequate for the one who
> merely reads pages or passages.

> The <u>Union Prayer Book</u>, it seems to me, was
> written by men who were terribly anxious not
> to give offense to non-Jews. For example,
> the handling of the Kol Nidre.

> The reason why the Reform (and other) Jews
> 'can't relate to prayer' is not, I think, due
> to the format or the use of the vernacular
> (which it is asserted allows comprehension to
> overcome affectivity) but simply because he
> doesn't believe what he is saying. No amount
> of 'structural' change in the synagogue will
> be able to overcome this particular barrier

to the effective performance of its mission. No
fooling with the vocabulary, no tampering with
the format, no increase in aesthetic properties
is going to overcome this little defect, and we
are probably just going to have to wait this one
out.*

Whether or not the final results of the present efforts of the

Central Conference of American Rabbis to revise the Union Prayer

Book will meet the needs of the Reform Movement is hard to pre-

dict at this point. One Regional group of the Central Conference

of American Rabbis already boasts of a sufficient number of

original services (albeit without CCAR Imprimatur), to be able

"to go it alone" if a new and satisfactory revision is not

forthcoming in the immediate future. Said one rabbi from this

group, "We'll probably be discarding most of what we have

already done ... and be into our second or third revisions

before the Conference comes out with anything ...."

6. Intermarriage and Mixed Marriage**.

The issue of intermarriage and mixed marriage is a thorny one

for many Jews, as the 1971 annual meeting of the Central

Conference of American Rabbis attests. Magazine and newspaper

articles on this subject abound. And more often then not, all

---

* Bernard Z. Sobel, "The Future of the Reform Synagogue," (Part
   2 of a Symposium), Dimensions Summer 1969, p. 14.

**Intermarriage is used here to denote marriage between a Jew
   and a non-Jew who has converted prior to the marriage
   ritual. Thus intermarriage is, in effect, a Jewish
   marriage. Mixed marriage is used here to denote marriage
   between a Jew and a non-Jew who has not converted to
   Judaism prior to the marriage ritual.

sorts of so-called findings are quoted. It would be wise to note
that almost no accurate scientific studies have been made to date
on this subject for our society as a whole. The reasons are obvious.
We do not have uniform national statistics on everything we want
to know on intermarriage and mixed marriage. Hence most hard research finds it necessary to focus on limited population samples.
To generalize from any specific finding is scientifically hazardous,
and sometimes even reckless.

To be sure these "findings" are often couched as "estimates,"
"tentative conclusions." or in other properly cautious formats.
Unfortunately the reader sees only the figures and these are
taken as the findings. And they make good newspaper copy. Yet
another way is simply to skip the hard data, and present, in their
place, a type of summary conclusion. Such an example appeared
recently in one of the nation's leading newspapers.

A Reform rabbi was represented to have reached the following
conclusions:*

> He (the rabbi) ... estimated that roughly a third
> (of Reform rabbis) officiate at such (mixed)
> marriages regularly, a third do it in so-called
> emergency situations - such as when the bride is
> pregnant or there isn't time for conversion, and
> a third won't do it under any circumstances.

---

* The New York Sunday Times, September 5, 1971, p. 42; Some rather
  good statements on current rabbinical thinking on the
  subject is portrayed in David Max Eichorn et al, "Symposium
  on Mixed Marriage," Reconstructionist, January 15, 1971,
  pp. 14-22; and Herbert Weiner, "Conversion: Is Reform
  Judaism So Right?" Dimensions, Winter, 1971, pp. 4-9.

It should be noted that in our study this question was addressed to pulpit rabbis only. Of the 506 pulpit rabbis who responded to most questions that were addressed to them, only 478 responded to questions relating to intermarriage or mixed marriage. Nevertheless, a small handful did insert comments to the effect that the question was not being answered (usually), for one of three reasons:

1. It is not yet a reconciled situation in their own mind.

2. It is not properly a CCAR or "public" matter, but a private matter between rabbi and congregant.

3. The subject is much too involved with so many different variables that apply in each case, that the "statistical answers can't be given" with accuracy.

Here are excerpts from some comments:

This is my first year here. It's a small group, and thank God I haven't been called upon to perform an intermarriage (without conversion) ... I'm preparing two women for conversion now. I really don't know what my position is ... I'm hoping you will shed some light ...

... Reform Judaism will disintegrate if this (mixed marriage) keeps up. Once I accepted the idea. I know differently now ... I can't really answer the question because of my changed position.

> I have always maintained, and I have written
> on it . . . (that) the rabbi, that is, all
> clergymen, more even than a lawyer or a doctor,
> have a privileged relationship with each member
> of his congregation, or for that matter with
> any human being who seeks him out for anything
> . . . (and) this is a confidence that cannot
> and must not be betrayed. The personal re-
> quirements of a marriage ritual, or funeral
> arrangements, are a personal matter and it is
> really nobody else's affair.

With regard to the preceding statement, one wonders if the rabbi
might be confusing two things. Confidentiality is one thing.
Ethical considerations are something else again. Does he consider his officiating at mixed marriages as less than ethical
behavior, and thus prefers not to talk about it? Or does he
view it as unethical to talk about it even with complete
confidentiality as far as his congregants are concerned?

Figure 22 presents the findings from this study. We see that
better than four out of ten of our Reform rabbis, based on our
sample, officiate at mixed marriages for one reason or
another.

A rabbi, ordained less than five years, explains himself this
way:

> If I don't, they'll simply go to a Justice of
> the Peace or shack up. At least this way I make
> contact with them, and for most it's probably
> the first time that Judaism has responded by say-
> ing, "We give a damn . . ."

The above statement was given considerable consideration by the
psychiatric and psychological consultants to this study inasmuch as it reflects similar comments from many rabbi-respondents.

Figure 22:

DISTRIBUTION OF PULPIT RABBIS (N=478)

WHO OFFICIATE AT MIXED MARRIAGES*

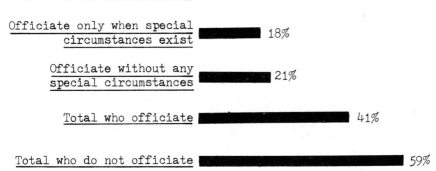

Officiate for members only ▌ 2%

Officiate only when special circumstances exist ▬▬▬ 18%

Officiate without any special circumstances ▬▬▬ 21%

Total who officiate ▬▬▬▬▬▬ 41%

Total who do not officiate ▬▬▬▬▬▬▬▬ 59%

---

*Intermarriage is used here to denote marriage between a Jew and a non-Jew who has converted prior to the marriage ritual. Thus intermarriage is, in effect, a Jewish marriage.

Mixed marriage is used here to denote marriage between a Jew and a non-Jew who has not converted to Judaism prior to the marriage ritual.

As _professionals_ in their fields (not necessarily _personally_),
they agree with the position. In terms of the persons who are
petitioning to be married (both Jew and non-Jew), they see the
rabbi's action as _recognition and acceptance versus rejection_.
This is submitted as a _psychological_ interpretation with no
implications, of course, that this interpretation should or
should not transcend any religious principles or doctrine.

Another rabbi, after eight years out of the seminary and who
is just beginning in his own rather small pulpit, put it this
way:

> From personal knowledge, I know that Rabbi _____
> (ordained over 30 years), although he strongly
> rejects my position (to freely officiate at
> an intermarriage)*, really does the same thing
> only thinks he doesn't. He spends two or three
> hours chatting with the couple, suggests some
> books to read, but doesn't test them on anything ..
> and if it's a woman, he gives her a piece of
> paper with the blessing of the candles - in
> transliteration - asks her to light the candles
> when she can, - and that's it ... It's a marriage!

One rabbi said he only officiates at mixed-marriages if the non-
Jewish party is willing to be his "student," and to be "educated."
"I educate, I don't convert, as such. Whether the person converts
or not is secondary."

Then there is the other side of the coin. Let us hear from Reform
rabbis who will _not_ officiate at mixed marriages. A rabbi who had
completed a few years as an assistant to an older man, but now,

---

* By our definition, the rabbi was referring here to mixed
    marriages (one spouse not converted).

has his own pulpit, tells us this:

> I performed intermarriages (mixed marriages by
> our definition), under Rabbi _____ ... (but)
> I will no longer do it. I shall now require
> conversion, including mikveh and even circum-
> cision, if it is medically o.k. ...
>
> Interviewer: Why this change?
>
> Rabbi: I guess because I've grown up as a
> rabbi. With all due respect to Rabbi ___,
> I think he and others like him have missed
> the boat. Reform Judaism isn't an isolated
> non-Judaism. We are part of a mainstream
> of one God and one Judaism. Strange as it
> may seem, it was from some of (Rabbi)
> _____'s own sermons that this (grow-
> ing up) came to me.

Many rabbis deliver many sermons on this subject. One such sermon,
by a rabbi, some 20 years in the pulpit, who is asked often to
officiate at mixed marriages recently explained it this way to
his congregation:

> ... a rabbi's chief obligation, as a rabbi, through
> his highly specialized calling and training, is to
> preserve Judaism, Jewish peoplehood and Jewish
> family values, through Jewish education, through
> the Jewish home, through the Jewish community,
> and throughout Jewish life. While we rabbis,
> of course, realize that there are a lot of
> Jews who are not living proper and fulfilling
> Jewish lives, ... this, in no way, diminishes our
> prime function and responsibility as rabbis, to
> commit and inspire our people to live in accord
> and with the basic traditions and principles of
> our faith.
> ....
> What many laymen fail to understand about a
> Jewish wedding ceremony is that it is not the
> rabbi who makes the ceremony Jewish by his pre-
> sence. What makes it Jewish is that two Jews

are promising faithfully and honestly to create
a <u>Jewish</u> home for themselves, and with God's
blessings, for their children, 'according to the
law of <u>Moses</u> and the faith of <u>Judaism</u>.' That is
to say, <u>they</u> are pledging to live their lives
according to the Mosaic code of morality and
according to the rites, ceremonies and beliefs
of the Jewish <u>religion</u>, either in its liberal
Jewish interpretation if I'm the rabbi, or in
its traditional Jewish interpretation if it's
one of my Conservative or Orthodox colleagues.
The <u>rabbi's</u> role at the Jewish wedding is
merely to represent the 3000 year old Jewish
rabbinic and priestly tradition before that
which the couple vow to uphold. <u>My</u> role in
the ceremony is to represent <u>Judaism</u>. The
couple's role and responsibility is to pro-
mise to live Jewishly, as Jews, in their future
Jewish married life together - Not just the
husband and not just the wife but <u>both</u> ...
....
The only realistic advice for all rabbis to
give such couples who just can't agree before
marriage on the wisdom of a single, <u>unifying</u>
religious influence is that under <u>no</u> circumstances should we agree to a pathetic-farce-
like token mix-marriage ceremony, which is
Jewish in <u>nobody's</u> eyes - neither in the eyes of
such rabbis who officiate, nor in the eyes of
the Jewish religion, nor in the eyes of those
assembled, Jewish or Christian, and, most
important, certainly not in the eyes or in
the hearts or in the minds of the couple
themselves...
....
As to the propriety of a rabbi co-officiating
with a priest or a minister ... Either the
ceremony is legitimately <u>all</u> Jewish, <u>all</u>
Catholic, or <u>all</u> Protestant or else it is <u>not</u>
in conformity with the legitimate and fulfilling historic dictates of any one of these
great religions.

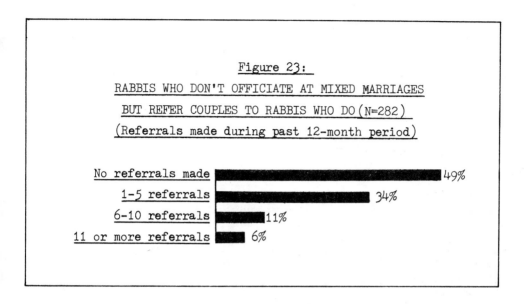

Figure 23:

RABBIS WHO DON'T OFFICIATE AT MIXED MARRIAGES

BUT REFER COUPLES TO RABBIS WHO DO (N=282)

(Referrals made during past 12-month period)

No referrals made — 49%
1-5 referrals — 34%
6-10 referrals — 11%
11 or more referrals — 6%

Now let us look at the 59% of our respondents who flatly refuse to officiate at any mixed marriage for whatever reason. Well, it isn't such a flat refusal after all, - at least not by all of them. Of those who do not themselves officiate, we have only to look at Figure 23 to see that over half of this group refer couples to colleagues who will do what they won't do themselves.

When a rabbi in his late 30's, who does not perform mixed marriages was asked by the writer if he experienced any conflict by referring such couples to other rabbis, his answer was succinct:

> Not at all. It's just a referral like to a psy-
> chiatrist or to a social agency. I don't see it as
> a Jewish matter only. It's a human problem. I'm
> simply helping a fellow human being to solve his
> own problem in his own way...I perform a public
> service,... and Rabbi _____(a Conservative
> colleague in the same city), does the same thing
> for his people... and he feels the same way as
> I do about it...Believe me, it's a lousy situa-
> tion all around.

A rabbi of a congregation under 200, who is very happy with his
overall situation, said he was most troubled by this one particular problem. He would not, under any circumstances, perform a
mixed marriage, but did make referrals.

> Interviewer: When the non-Jewish party won't agree
> to conversion, do you refer them to another rabbi
> who will marry them?
>
> Rabbi: I do. I feel guilty about it. And yet by
> the same token, I feel that in some respects I
> have to facilitate it, so as not to push them
> away completely. So I've got tremendously
> ambivalent feelings about that. There are a
> few rabbis in the area who do (perform mixed
> marriages)... I feel guilty because in essence
> I'm sanctioning it.

When seminarians who were interviewed were asked if they would
officiate at mixed marriages, their responses very largely
reflected the same scatter of responses that come forth from the
rabbinate, except that they oppose mixed marriages four to one
on their questionnaire returns. While 7% approve, 28% disapprove.
None approve it "for synagogue members only." Some 16% "approve,
but only in the most unusual circumstances." (Significantly,
many of these saw fit to underline the words "most unusual.")
Many seminarians did not answer this question on their questionnaires.
In interviews, many indicated they had not yet reached a firm
position in their minds. They were still searching.

Here are some seminarians' comments:

> I cannot answer this; I have not made a decision,
> although I disapprove.

> I don't really know.

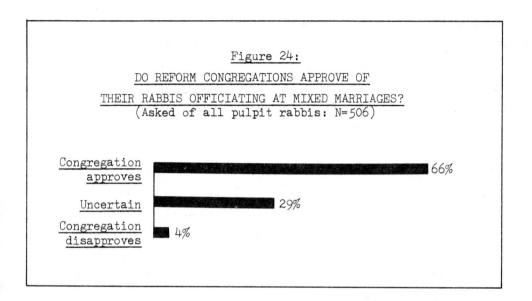

Figure 24:

DO REFORM CONGREGATIONS APPROVE OF
THEIR RABBIS OFFICIATING AT MIXED MARRIAGES?
(Asked of all pulpit rabbis: N=506)

Congregation approves — 66%
Uncertain — 29%
Congregation disapproves — 4%

I say no now, but haven't others said no until
they were faced with it. I just don't really
know.

Until Rabbi _____ came here to speak, there
was no question in my mind that I would . . .
(officiate at mixed marriages). But he really
rocked some of us a little . . . I'm in a
quandary . . .

Well, if "it's a lousy situation all around" and not a single rabbi
who was interviewed and who officiates at mixed marriages indicates
that he is happy about it, - then what is it like for the rank and
file Reform Jew. Actually we look into this, in depth, in Part III
(The Reform Congregation), later on. But what do the rabbis think
or know about the feeling that their congregants hold on this
matter? Rabbis were asked this question, Their responses
appear in Figure 24.

135

And so we have it. Reform Judaism is a party to a lot of mixed
marriages. Later on we shall see some of the ramifications of
this in terms of what goes on in these families in such areas
as synagogue attendance, religious school attendance, and
Jewishness in the home (Chapter 11, especially Section 2).
But let us go on a bit farther with the rabbis.

There are virtually no age differences in regard to the rabbi's
willingness to perform mixed marriages. This is an important
finding, particularly in view of the other differences we have
noted among the various generations of rabbis.

Although the record shows that less than half of our rabbis perform
mixed marriages, the view from some quarters is that mixed marriage
is an acceptable position to the Reform Movement, contrary to the
fact that the CCAR long ago had taken a position designed to
discourage such practice.

A prominent Israeli writer views Reform on the subject of mixed
marriages as follows:

> For various reasons the Jewish Reform Movement is
> gradually turning away from its original assimila-
> tionist course and is by slow and still careful
> steps returning to the fold ...
> ....
> ... the Reform Movement should be willing to abandon
> its general laxity that verges on total license and
> permissiveness to the extent that there practically
> are no longer any barriers to mixed marriage, assimi-
> lation and complete apostasy.*

---

* Dr. Yisrael Sheib Eldad, The Times of Israel, Tel Aviv, 17
    July 1970, pp. 6-7.

The actual behavior of rabbis in regard to mixed marriage is mirrored
in their attitudes as to what the CCAR's position ought to be on
the issue, notwithstanding the CCAR position that presently exists.
About half (52%), feel that the CCAR should require prior conversion, another 36% say it should be left up to the rabbi, 8% would
rather avoid an official stand by The Conference and a mere 2%
state that the Central Conference of American Rabbis should accept
mixed marriages without conversion.

Lest the subject of intermarriage and mixed marriage be ended without
any evidence that Reform rabbis are confronting the situation, it
should be noted that special courses have been set up by many rabbis
to deal with the situation throughout the country. The joint efforts
of Rabbi Marc Brownstein (Temple Sinai, Newington), and Associate
Rabbi Charles Sherman (Temple Beth Israel, West Hartford), have received considerable attention in the Greater Hartford area:*

> Two area Reform rabbis stated this week that for
> a variety of reasons - including the increased
> rate of mixed marriages, greater exposure among
> students to Judaism and Jews, and an increased
> interest in Judaism among dissatisfied Christians
> (and because) the number of converts seems to be
> on the rise (as special course has been created.)
> ....
> The course consists of 12 two-hour sessions.
> Utilizing lecture, audio-visual material, and
> informal discussion, the Rabbis present an
> introduction to each of the following areas:
> Jewish history, Holydays, and Festivals, Jewish
> life cycle ceremonies, synagogue and home cere-
> monial objects, the prayer book, Bible, post-
> Biblical Jewish literature, Israel, and the
> American Jewish community.
> ....

*Connecticut Jewish Ledger, August 26, 1971, p. 16.

Students are advised to make no firm decision with
regard to conversion until they have completed
their course of study.
....
In cases where individuals are married or con-
templating marriage to a Jew, the Jewish partner is
expected to attend all classes with the prospective
convert.
....
Students in the class are required to read a total
of eleven books.
....
The course is taught from a basically liberal
Jewish perspective, although comparisons are
frequently drawn between traditional and liberal
practices...

7. "Jewish Distance" Between Rabbi and Congregants.

What do rabbis think of their congregations? If, as we have seen
earlier, they see them as fairly tractable, does it mean that the
rabbis see eye to eye with them, or is the perceived tractability
of the congregation merely a reflection of the perceived indifference?
(Table 22) Some 71% express a feeling of "Jewish distance" between
themselves and members of their congregations. Some 50% identify
a definite lack of concern for Judaism on the part of their congregants. Almost half, indeed, refer to "Jewish distance" as the
single most frustrating obstacle that they are experiencing in
their careers as rabbis. Rabbis seem to have little trouble with
their congregations in the routine affairs which are involved in
running a synagogue. Only 12%, for example, complain of unreasonable
demands made on them by their congregations. But when it comes
to things Jewish, it's a different matter. Perhaps this can best
be summed up by the fact that more than 60% of the fully satisfied
rabbis complain of a "Jewish distance" between themselves and their

138

Table 22:

THE RABBI (N=506) VIEWS A "JEWISH DISTANCE"

BETWEEN HIMSELF AND HIS CONGREGATION

	%
There is a "Jewish distance" between me and my congregation.	71
Most members of my congregation seem unconcerned with the Judaism that I try to bring to them.	50
The "Jewish distance" is probably the single most frustrating obstacle to me in my rabbinical experience.	46
Members of my congregation have little understanding of my objectives and goals as their rabbi.	42
I often have the feeling that my congregation doesn't care for Judaism.	32
I often have the feeling that my congregation doesn't believe in Judaism.	26
My congregation has been unreasonable in its expectations of me.	12

congregations. As one rabbi put it. "... and it grows, as I keep studying." Of the dissatisfied rabbis, a total of 78% pointed to this "Jewish distance" factor as a basic thorn in their lives.

Now, while the percentage difference points to a relationship between general satisfaction and perception on this issue, the more important point is that a clear majority even of those rabbis

who are fully satisfied feel that the situation is still not what
it ought to be.

Here are some rabbinical comments on the subject:

> Most (congregants) understand what I'm trying to
> get at, but do not get themselves to move in these
> directions. They care for Judaism, believe in it
> vaguely, but do not act. More effective dynamics
> must be found.

> There are, thank God, a few (congregants)who care and
> whose interest makes the effort worthwhile.

Psychiatric assessment of the data in Table 22 suggests that
substantial numbers of Reform rabbis must be experiencing serious
discomforts with their congregations as a whole. The data suggest
sufficient cause for serious alienation, serious frustration, and
disillusionment on the part of many of our rabbi-respondents. A
rabbi needs an extra-strong personality, and a tremendously strong
and durable ego to live with this and yet continue on a day to
day basis in his overall mission to give of himself to his people,
both personally and rabbinically, to give to his family, and to
fulfill his own needs to a reasonable degree.

8. Confrontation with "Chuppa and Glass."

It was not expected that the use of the chuppa and the breaking
of the glass at weddings would constitute a separate section in this
study. But we shall soon see why. Reference has already been made

to these practices earlier (Table 20, pp. 103-104), and more will
be said later, but let us look at the way Reform rabbis feel about
these once-discarded (by Reform) practices.

The question was put to our rabbis this way:

> Two traditional wedding rituals - the chuppa and the
> breaking of the glass by the bridegroom - are not
> required Reform practices. What are your feelings
> in regard to these?

Let us now see what Table 23 tells us.

The boldest statistic is that only 2% and 6%, respectively, say that
the chuppa and glass "should not be permitted." A far cry from
earlier classical Reform days. That one out of four is saying
the chuppa should be required seems also to be a vast shift
toward tradition. But the most meaningful and majority response
pattern from our rabbis is that it should be left to the discretion
of the bride and groom. Some 59% say this regarding the chuppa,
and 60% say so regarding the breaking of the glass.

Here are some random comments from rabbis who were interviewed:

> As you know, the membership is changing over the
> years. Many joined us after the war (WWII), who
> came from so-called Orthodox homes. It's the
> yarmulka bit all over again. And now it's break-
> ing a glass and the chuppa. ... and is there any
> harm bringing happiness to a grandparent or even
> a great grandparent? That, too, is a mitzvah.
> After all, the kids do it for them mostly ...

Table 23:

REFORM RABBIS CONFRONT THE CHUPPA AND THE GLASS
(N=600)

	Chuppa	Breaking the glass
	%	%
It should always be done.	25	17
It should be at the discretion of the bride and groom.	59	60
It depends on the policy of the synagogue.	3	2
It should be up to the rabbi to decide.	8	10
It should not be permitted.	2	6
Other.	4	4

When I have a chance, I prefer to draw from the
symbolism and the ritual of our own rich tradition.
This is why I am very happy when young people ask
for these (chuppa and glass) ... Lord knows they
ask for everything else. They create their own
rituals - with poetry - with tracts from Indian
philosophy or from Malcolm X. This can all be
fine too, but to me, personally, there is greater
beauty and feeling in our own traditions. I
honestly think that if I were to give blessing
to what Malcolm X and Indian philosophy brings,
and at the same time say no to traditional
Jewishness, - this would be chutzpah on my part.

When one of our most beloved members took his daughter to the Hotel _____, so that they could be married there (by a Conservative rabbi), under a canopy and could break the glass, then it became necessary for me to re-think some of my own views. The irony is that some of my strongest trustees are strongly against it as a result of my own teaching over the years.

... and we mustn't forget that a wedding brings many who have never stepped foot into a Reform Temple. They have no orientation about us at all ... we sit smugly in our own world, either unaware or not seeming to care about the sensitivities of our fellow-Jews from the Orthodox and the Conservative folds. The chuppa and breaking of the glass are part of their required ritual! Relatives and friends come from (far-away cities) to many of our weddings ... if one of our people wants to marry someone from Temple _____ (Conservative), we have to have the wedding there because my Board just wouldn't allow a chuppa ... that's all it would take.

Another respondent, almost 20 years a pulpit rabbi, for many years the rabbi of a congregation of almost 1000 families, who feels the matter should be left up to the bride and groom, nevertheless, sees it a little differently:

Interviewer: Is the breaking of the glass a part of your wedding ritual?

Rabbi: Yes it is - most reluctantly! I find it, if you pardon the pun, a shattering experience ... I have warm feelings for all traditional things. The one thing that bothers me very much is the breaking of the glass.

Interviewer: How about the canopy?

Rabbi: ... I have no feelings about it. It's
perfectly permissible. The other (breaking of
the glass), is sheer superstition with all kinds
of psychoanalytic obscene undertones. It has
absolutely no redeeming idealistic value at all.

And so it goes. Thus a separate section on the "chuppa and the
glass." Later we shall hear from the congregants on the same
subject.

9. Rabbis Confront the Central Conference of American Rabbis,
   and the Union of American Hebrew Congregations.

Is the CCAR the rabbi's friend or is it a "bureaucratic monstrosity"
as one rabbi labelled it? Opinions, as one might expect, are mixed,
and the detractors seem to be almost equal in number with the
defenders. Thus, 48% of the respondents agree with the statement
that the CCAR "promulgates the values of success and competitiveness
among its members to the point that it pits one man against another
..." Only 30% disagree with the statement. What is more, the
preponderence of evidence, both from written statements and from
interview material, reveals that the younger rabbis tend least to
defend or support the CCAR. Where 39% of the rabbis ordained before
1942 disagree with the above quotation, the number declines to
16% for those most recently ordained. (This situation appears to be
similar to what is now being experienced in the American Medical
Association and in several national academic associations.)

Here are random comments (<u>not limited to pulpit rabbis</u>), regarding
the CCAR:

It seems to me that the CCAR has become an oligarchy
with little opportunity for the rank and file membership to serve on committees. I am opposed to
the present committee structure of the CCAR. It
would seem to me that a rabbi might well be unhappy because of the way in which his professional
organization operates.

It is surprising that a questionnaire designed to
study the American Reform rabbinate has not also
gone into considerable detail concerning the nature,
structure and function of the CCAR and the UAHC.
Both of these organizations play a major role ex-
tending over the lifetime of the rabbi. Thus,
this questionnaire and the study that flows from
it cannot be complete.

Would have preferred more questions on individual
rabbi's involvement with CCAR and Reform colleagues.
I was surprised to find no questions dealing with
the current and/or past placement procedures and
with the governmental structures of the CCAR.

I really would like to respond to the idea of the
CCAR but there is no room for it. I think it is
a self-serving club, based on nepotism and a
'club' atmosphere. The administration has been
honest but short-sighted in the extreme. The
waste of money on committees which do little
but supply a paid trip to N.Y.C. for members or
prestige for the chairman is shocking. May I
suggest a questionnaire on the CCAR and its
placement committee -- and see how the men
respond, I consider my own successful rabbinic
career a combination of luck and fortitude -
and give no credit to the CCAR.

Some feel such a hatred and disgust for the politics
of both the College and the CCAR, that I know they
threw out these forms. Others, in the same frame
of mind, took the time to complete theirs. Good
luck. I'm looking forward to laughing at your results.

The CCAR should help us to become a band of brothers, and help us to resist the corrosive values of American society with its emphasis on prestige and success.

I would suggest CCAR regional meetings to discuss this instrument, not merely to criticize it, as I am sure it will be criticized out of a need not to deal with the many issues it raises. I do not know who constructed this instrument, but I commend him (them) for their hard work and deep concern for the perplexities which face honest and dedicated rabbis, of whom there are too few. I urge further exploration of the various themes begun in this instrument.

So much for an overall criticism of the CCAR. As for more specific ones we have the finding reported in an earlier section. Some 46% feel that the CCAR does not do enough in setting up enforceable standards for salary schedules, increments, and tenure. And an even larger number (70%), are very vigorous in their demands that something ought to be done about it without delay.

The most difficult task that confronted this study was to identify uniformities to represent accurately the many adverse feelings toward the CCAR. (Physicians and attorneys have informed the writer that similar conditions also prevail within their respective parent organizations.)

One partial interview with a pulpit rabbi in his mid-30's went like this:

Interviewer: Some of your random comments thusfar give me a feeling that you have some discomfort regarding the CCAR. Is this true?

Rabbi: If you mean do I hate the CCAR, of course not. They are all my colleagues. But as a professional organization it is bad, very bad indeed.

Interviewer: How so?

Rabbi: Well there's little concern for the individual rabbi! You know we're not a bunch of truckdrivers, but the Teamster's Union shows more concern for their members than the CCAR does for us.

Interviewer: You use the word concern. I'm sure you mean something there.

Rabbi: Of course, do you think the average rabbi knows what's going on on the national level? We don't know if they are even aware of the seriousness of the situation.

Interviewer: What is it that the Teamster's Union does that perhaps the CCAR might do?

Rabbi: It isn't just what they do. It's how they treat people. For instance the Board has absolutely no contact with 99% of its members...

Interviewer: What specific contact would you make with the members, if you were on the Board?

Rabbi: Well, I know what I wouldn't do. I wouldn't disregard the wishes of the rank and file. We are having a crisis in Reform Judaism!

Interviewer: What, in your opinion, can the Board do about this crisis in Reform Judaism?

Rabbi: First of all we've got to take stock of ourselves. I mean not just the rabbinate, but the College and the Union too ... especially the College. Maybe we ought to have regional 'think-tank' sessions ... (then) maybe someone would come up with some ideas.

Interviewer: You have apparently given this much thought, would you care to share your ideas with me. Where is the CCAR failing? What specifically would you recommend.

Rabbi: Well, the first and most important thing
is to recognize that an awful lot of guys (Reform
rabbis) are unhappy. Let's just not try to sweep
that one under the rug. It's a fact. They're
unhappy with their jobs, they're unhappy with
their Boards, who look at the rabbi as a hired
hand. First of all they're goyim (reference
was supposedly to the Boards). Except, I don't
think goyim would push around their ministers
like we get pushed around. And there's no one
to turn to. The CCAR and the Union could do
a lot if they wanted to.

(After approximately another 15 minutes in the same
vein-)

Interviewer: Mostly, I get the feeling that you
would like to see the CCAR become something of
a strong labor union that would help rabbis to
stand up against injustice in the rabbinate.

Rabbi: I mean that exactly.

Interviewer: Who is inflicitng these injustices?

Rabbi: It's the nature of our Movement. You
have to understand the history of our Movement.
Many of our people are still running away from
Judaism.

The above is not a completely typical interview, but it contains
the tone of things when an attempt is made to elicit some focused
data relative to the subject. In unstructured interviews, on the
other hand, individual rabbis are able to talk for the hour (maximum
length devoted to an individual interview), naming many things
that, in their opinion need correction, and for which the CCAR is
held accountable. But while one rabbi will emphasize one thing,
another will emphasize something completely different, and might
actually make very light of what the first rabbi had to say.
Hence the difficulty to identify uniformities.

One uniformity, not an exceptionally strong one, but at least
receiving more consensus than others is the desire for "effective"
CCAR Regions.

Here are a few rabbinical comments on the subject of Regional
involvement:

> Regional offices should share programs with each
> other, and then each Regional head ought to be
> able to give us (those rabbis in his Region)
> strong leadership ... (on the basis of) what's
> going on on the national level. The Conference
> can't really do this for us from New York. But
> I hold them responsible for not implementing
> such arrangements. ... I'm not asking for un-
> attainable ideal ... utopia ... I'm talking just
> plain tachlis.

> Some Regions have already solved certain problems
> that other Regions are still grappling with.
> We're too large a body (the Conference) to deal
> with the every-day needs of rabbis and synagogues
> and school needs, and camps and recalcitrant
> trustees, and even with colleagues sometimes.
> Our problems are daily ... Maybe we need Regions
> and even sub-Regions. Maybe the whole business
> of Regions should be reconsidered and reorganized,
> I mean maybe combining the Union and the Conference
> into single strong Regions, with strong leaders,
> lay as well as rabbinical, and good full-time
> staffs. And these, especially the Regional rabbis
> should be experienced and competent, a little
> older than some of them are: It is very im-
> portant that Regional leaders should have proven
> experience as congregational rabbis. They should
> be screened very carefully. I'd like to see the
> Regions elect someone from their own group, or at
> least have a strong say who this man should be.

Strong, well organized regions can enhance the
national program and administration of the CCAR ...
....
Stronger regions also mean better programming
within the regional organizations, all of whom
are doing something at the present time. We
already have a perfect example of this in what
appears to be the increased quality in the
programming of the annual conventions or re-
treats of the various regions since the CCAR
took over the subvention of the visiting
scholar, but insisted on setting the standards
for such scholars. However, programming within the region need not and should not be academic only: Regional problems would be better
discussed and analyzed if the region is well
organized and in close, official liaison with
the national leadership.
....
Strong, well organized regions, working closely
in liaison with the national CCAR, could probably
be far more effective in the sensitive and ex-
plosive field of mediation and ethics, at least
in the more remote regions...
....
A strong, unified CCAR is extremely important
because of its national impact, both with respect to national and community issues, and with
respect to the strengths that it can exert for
the benefit of its own members. No one would
want to go so far in developing 'strong regions'
so as to weaken the national CCAR.
....
The use of regional meetings, kallot, symposia,
practica, and study groups would tend to free
the CCAR convention to spend its time in taking
up the broad issues to which a convention of
our size and prestige should speak.

Let us look at some further reactions, selected at random:

They (CCAR Board) should send their minutes to
us (the membership). It would be helpful if
minutes of important committees would come to
us. Then we'd know what's going on, and not
wait for the convention to find out. We're
not a part of our own organization, until we
find out that something has already happened.
This study is a good example. No one knew
anything about it, until it was announced. If
all minutes came to us, some of us could make
suggestions, be a part of things while things
are being considered.

We need a Schulchan Aruch for Reform Judaism . . .
we have most of what we need now, but it's all
over the place. We need it all together. It
should be subject to revision, but it should
always be there. The Conference is too large
(to work this out) . . . We need to work this
out on a Regional basis first.

The CCAR should take a stand against the Masonic
ritual.

We (the CCAR) have certain stands, but many
flaunt them. Our offical position on intermarriage is a good example (The rabbi meant
mixed marriage by our definition.) At least
the congregation (of a rabbi who officates at
mixed marriages), should be informed (that he is
doing this). Why do we have a UAHC and a
CCAR? This should be their responsibilities.
If they don't have the machinery for this
. . . they should institute it. These organizations should be the leaders of our Movement, not just the repositories and receptacles
of everything and anything that goes on that
passes for Reform Judaism.

The CCAR doesn't look after its men. For
example, who will do anything with the results
of (this) study?

There's nothing wrong with it (CCAR) if you don't
take it seriously.

The time has come for CCAR to provide placement
for rabbis in non-congregational positions.
My assistant is a fine young rabbi, but he's
not for a congregation - any congregation. Someone, either the College or the Conference should
(provide them with information and guidance)
before they enter the College, and certainly
before they are ordained. What are we doing?
Nothing!

Age differences on CCAR committees are not the
solution. A young man, and I can think of a very
prominent younger rabbi here, might be more conservative than an older one, like Rabbi _____
for example (a man in his early 60's).

Possibly the most chilling statement comes forth from a group of

fifteen rabbis who had recently completed a seminar under Professor

Eugene Borowitz (HUC-JIR):

Instead of binding the rabbis together as a
community of brothers so that our beliefs and
commitments would be reinforced by a common
understanding and concern, our College-Institute,
the UAHC and most particularly the CCAR per-
petuate all the worst of the American values
of competitiveness and success. So they tend to
pit one man against the other in a struggle for
prizes of power and preeminence rather than to
provide the one place in our society where we
might reenforce our Jewish sense of what constitutes true personal accomplishment and worthy
social association.*

If all the interviews regarding CCAR complaints are to be summed

up, an unwieldly procedure at best, the results come out some-

thing like this:

---

* Personal communication to the writer from Professor Eugene Borowitz.

1. There is a desire to have more effective regional mechanisms for meeting the individual needs of some individual rabbis.

2. These needs can be broken down as follows:

   a. Functional support of the rabbi in his confrontations with his Boards on synagogue policies regarding the whole gamut of rabbi-synagogue interaction.

   b. Inexpensive means for social and professional interaction with fellow-rabbis and their families.

   c. Provide recognition (and possibly some rewards, honors, etc.) for achievement, and to make this known throughout the Movement, especially to the CCAR Board.

   d. Constantly to provide guidelines (meaningful to the individual rabbi's needs), for knowing what's going on, who's doing what, what should he be doing and not doing, - more regarding policy and administrative procedures of how to serve a synagogue, as well as in rabbinical-theological area.

3. The individual rabbis seem to want a more provocative and outspoken leadership. They seem to want the world to know about the MOVEMENT of which they are a part, and they want to be proud to be a part of this MOVEMENT. (In this respect they mention the need for the Union and the College to "shape up" just as often as they mention the CCAR's need to do so.)

4. Many individual rabbis seem to be less than proud of some of their colleagues. They hold the CCAR Placement Bureau responsible for not always recognizing merit, and therefore making possible many desirable positions for some less than adequate rabbis.

In line with all this, one wonders if some new and different mechanisms, national and/or regional, need to be considered.

That the problem is similar with other ministerial groups, and that
they,too, are confronting the situation with some new thinking is
evidenced by what is happening in the United Presbyterian Church.
In a recent memorandum on the subject, prepared by their Director,
Northeast Career Center, we note the following:*

> It is the purpose of this paper to present occupa-
> tional counseling or career guidance services as an
> effective 'core' effort in professional development
> programs for church leadership . . . Several basic
> principles must be considered in the establishment
> and operation of this service, however, if it
> is to be more than a personal rescue service for
> the few who are serious misfits in the ministry.
> Among such principles are the following:
>
> 1. It must be broad enough to provide assist-
>   ance to the 'strong' as well as to the 'weak,'
>   to the 'healthy' as well as to the 'sick';
>
> 2. It must be structured and operated in a way
>   that contributes to the ability of each
>   professional to be self-actualizing rather
>   then dependent, in his professional planning;
>
> 3. It must provide for competent and serious
>   attention to the theological concerns of
>   church professionals;
>
> 4. It must be objective enough, and competent,
>   to help some who wish to leave the pro-
>   fessional service of the church for another
>   endeavor, as well as those who continue in
>   church work;
>
> 5. It must be available throughout a man's life
>   and useful with all age groups.

---

* Thomas E. Brown, "Occupational Counseling as a Way to Assist Church
  Professionals in Development of Leadership Capability,"
  (Mimeo), 1970.

One overall observation of the rabbi's view of the CCAR is that he
speaks of the organization as some separate and lofty entity, far
removed from the daily needs of the average pulpit rabbi. When
pressed, during the course of interviewing, many rabbis do not feel
that they are truly part of a parent organization.

> Here I am all alone with a pack of troubles. I
> don't blame Stern (Rabbi Malcolm Stern, CCAR's
> Director of Placement). His letters have bucked
> me up, and I'm sure he did the best he could
> . . . But these congregations have no concep-
> tion that they're hiring a rabbi, not a main-
> tenance man. Maybe the CCAR ought to have
> some field representatives who would be on
> call if a rabbi got in over his head with his
> "machers " (trustees) . . .

When the interviewer asked about assistance from the Regional Office,
the reply was, "Forget it. I've worked with two regional directors
in two different cities . . . and the less said the better."

And along this same line, comes this reaction from another rabbi:

> No Rabbi lasts more than three years here (a
> 200-family congregation). If I visit an unaffili-
> ated Jew in the hospital, my Board says I'm
> wasting time. They will not provide for pen-
> sion, medical insurance, any travel expenses
> or anything else. When I conducted a youth
> group to Israel for ten weeks, they deducted
> ten weeks salary. If I conduct a wedding or a
> funeral for a non-member, I must charge $100
> and give it to the Temple. I taught a course
> in Hebrew at the high school (in a nearby commun-
> ity), and the Board wanted my salary. (The
> Rabbi explained there was no synagogue in that
> community, and in this way he reached many
> of the unaffiliated Jewish children there.)
> My board now tells me that I am to perform mixed
> marriages for Temple members. Of course I can't
> stay here any longer. I've already given them
> my notice . . .

Interviewer: In situations like this, is there
anything the CCAR or your Regional office can
do to help?

Rabbi: The CCAR, forget it . . . (Rabbi _____)
from our Regional office was over here about a
year ago, but nothing was accomplished, and the
situation has deteriorated too, it's ludicrous!

With regard to the above, the Rabbi's Regional director was interviewed later. When the gentleman informed the writer that one of
his functions was "to help create new congregations, and to strengthen
existing congregations," the interviewer asked the following question:

What has this office done in the past six months
to strengthen a congregation?

Regional director: That's an interesting question. Normally I'm called in to congregations
when there's a problem within the congregation
. . .

Interviewer: Rabbi, could you tell me what you
did these last six months to strengthen a congregation?

Regional director: That may be difficult. Let
me give it some thought. Of course you have to
understand that within the course of a given
day I will work with a dozen congregations.

The Regional director than proceeded to tell the interviewer what
his previous day was like, starting with a breakfast meeting with
the president of a congregation because of some difficulty with
regard to allocation of office space for the senior rabbi and the
new assistant rabbi. Then came a number of additional tasks that
confronted the director during the course of that one day. It was
a trying day, and the problems were real ones to those who called

upon him for help. But mostly, the interviewer found himself thinking
about the aforementioned rabbi whose situation was becoming "ludicrous?"
From whence cometh his help? (Even if it possibly means helping him
out of the rabbinate.)

Regarding the CCAR Regions, many mixed feelings prevail:

> The CCAR regions are excuses for organizations,
> not real organizations. It's a front. All is
> decided top-side (by the CCAR Board) . . . We
> have meetings. Some are a complete waste of time,
> and I don't even care to go anymore. The Union's
> regions, that's something else again. If a Temple's
> Board wants anything . . . not only the Regional
> office, but the Union itself gets going on it
> immediately. They've got paid staff, of course
> . . .

There is obviously a very strong mandate for change, even if from
what and to what are not always clear. Almost two out of three
rabbis want to see the CCAR play a vigorous role in setting up
enforceable standards for the treatment of its members (especially
with regard to working arrangements). With regard to other views
concerning the CCAR establishment, it is to be noted that only 14% agree
with the proposal that the CCAR's headquarters should be built
somewhere else, together with a seminary, near a city, but far
enough away for peace and quiet to reign. And, in response to
another question dealing with moving, 62% favor remaining in New
York, while another 23% are indifferent to the whole question. This
last item may or may not serve as an indicator of the negative attitude that many rabbis have toward the CCAR, for we will see later
how many more are interested in site changes where the HUC-JIR is
concerned.

Our rabbinical respondents were presented with three proposed
courses of action that the UAHC might undertake in behalf of the
rabbinate. Needless to say, the overwhelming majority approved
of all three plans with 79% voting for a plan that calls for a
vigorous and systematic public relations campaign aimed at the
congregations, particularly the Boards, with the primary intention
of improving working conditions. And 75% approved of a proposal
that calls for the "implementation of a better 'protective'
position" for the rabbi in dealing with his congregation.

With the exception of the few questions that involved the UAHC this
study did not pursue any in-depth probing of the role of the UAHC.
It was not the mission of this study to do so. Nevertheless, many
voluntary expressions, in written form and exhibited during the
course of many interviews, brought forth some penetrating observations concerning the UAHC vis-a-vis the rabbinate. Reasonably
typical of some such comments is the following:

> A fifth section might have been included in this
> study, namely, the attitude of rabbis to the
> UAHC and the role the Union plays in Reform Judaism.
> Over the years I have found many rabbis and con-
> gregational leaders dissatisfied with the various
> functions of the Union and greatly concerned
> because of the unilateral control it desires
> to exercise over its Reform affiliates through
> its domination of pulpit placement as a threat
> to congregations that fail or refuse to conform to
> its financial demands.

Table 24 gives us a clue to some feelings about what rabbis would
like to have from the Union and/or the Conference regarding salary
arrangements with their congregations. Some 50% are asking for
some clear-cut norms or guidelines concerning salary schedules.
However, they do not wish to have any CCAR/UAHC intrusion on any

Table 24:

WHAT DO PULPIT RABBIS (N=506) WANT OF
THE CENTRAL CONFERENCE OF AMERICAN RABBIS /
UNION OF AMERICAN HEBREW CONGREGATIONS
REGARDING SALARY ARRANGEMENTS WITH SYNAGOGUES?

CCAR/UAHC should work out a binding salary scale for pulpit rabbis.	14%
CCAR/UAHC should set up and maintain up-dated norms. Final arrangements should be left to rabbi and Board.	50%
UAHC should negotiate with congregations, and rabbi's salary should come directly from UAHC.	6%
Satisfied with present situation.	30%

final arrangements that concern their negotiations with their congregations. This, they feel, should be left to the rabbi. Only
14% express a desire for a CCAR/UAHC enforced salary scale that would
be binding on congregation and rabbi alike. Almost one-third (30%)
are sufficiently satisfied with their present situation, and presumably do not want any CCAR/UAHC intervention regarding any
salary arrangements with their respective congregations. Of course,
it should be noted that how a rabbi feels about the situation in
his present relationship with his congregation concerning money matters

(salary, raises, pension benefits, insurance coverage, sabbaticals,
travel expenses and other such related factors), may be very
different from how he might yet respond in any subsequent position
with another congregation. It might be proper, however, to raise
a few questions. Less than one-third of the rabbinate indicates <u>no</u>
need for "outside" help in handling these matters with their respective congregations. Could we assume that only in about one-third of
our congregations can rabbis expect a reasonably easy time in dealing
with these matters? After all, Boards do change. Or would it
be out of line to assume that only one-third of our rabbis have
sufficient business acuity in terms of overall "rabbinical economics?"
If so, they would probably not rate much differently from academicians.

Lastly the data in Table 24 suggest a strong need that these and
related issues be aired in a constructive manner so that the Conference might be strengthened. <u>The airing process itself might well
serve as a welding instrument between the individual rabbi and the
Conference.</u> It is a manifestation of concern, and what the individual
rabbis in their sometimes lonely outposts seem to be asking is for
someone (their parent organization, their Regional organization), to
be <u>concerned.</u>

10. Reform Rabbis Confront the Hebrew Union College - Jewish Institute of Religion.

Probably no college or university has ever had a completely satisfied
group of alumni, and so it is with the alumni of Hebrew Union College -
Jewish Institute of Religion. Actually, 64% of our rabbinate <u>rejected</u>
the proposition that "HUC-JIR served to inculcate its students . . .
with lasting ideals (making for) a band of brotherhood." Additional
findings (Figure 25) sum up some of the salient features. These
compare the rabbinate with the seminarians. On three of the five

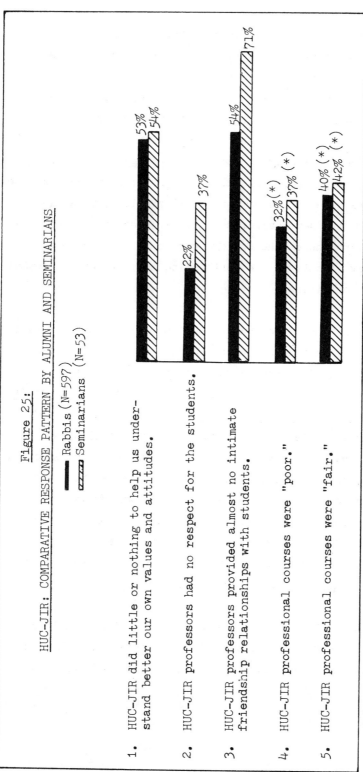

Figure 25:

HUC-JIR: COMPARATIVE RESPONSE PATTERN BY ALUMNI AND SEMINARIANS

▉ Rabbis (N=597)
▨ Seminarians (N=53)

1. HUC-JIR did little or nothing to help us understand better our own values and attitudes.

2. HUC-JIR professors had no respect for the students.

3. HUC-JIR professors provided almost no intimate
   friendship relationships with students.

4. HUC-JIR professional courses were "poor."

5. HUC-JIR professional courses were "fair."

(*) These responses should not be construed to mean that those who did not indicate "poor" or "fair"
    have necessarily rated these or all non-professional courses as "excellent."

evaluative factors, there is an extraordinary similarity of feelings
expressed by both students and alumni. The data add up to something of an indictment of the seminary system not only as it now
exists, but as it has existed in the past. Many rabbis do not, on
the whole, come away from HUC-JIR with pleasant memories. As will
be indicated in Chapter 18, rabbis' wives who were "student wives"
express themselves similarly. Some of our younger rebbetzins,
especially, are very acrimonious about their "student days" at the
seminary. To be sure, there were personal problems, financial problems, and such, but many harbor some bitter memories of chronically
unhappy situations where "the College was no help!" We shall
have more to say on this in the forthcoming sections on the seminarians and the rebbetzins.

It should be noted that disenchantment with HUC-JIR is not limited
to those rabbis who are least satisfied with their careers as
rabbis. While there is indeed a correlation in the expected
direction, what is far more important is that even the most satisfied rabbis are equally critical of HUC-JIR. Many rabbis feel
strongly enough to write long comments concerning their feelings
about their seminary days. We shall excerpt some of these shortly.
Also throughout the interviewing stage of this research, few rabbis
by-passed any reference to the HUC-JIR. There was praise, but
there was also considerable dissatisfaction. However, the criticism
never approached the point where one was ashamed of the institution
he had attended. The criticism took the form of the need to make a
good institution much better, - and why not the best!

A summary score of the five components which are itemized in Figure
25 was formulated for the purposes of ascertaining the relationship between career satisfaction on the one hand, and criticism

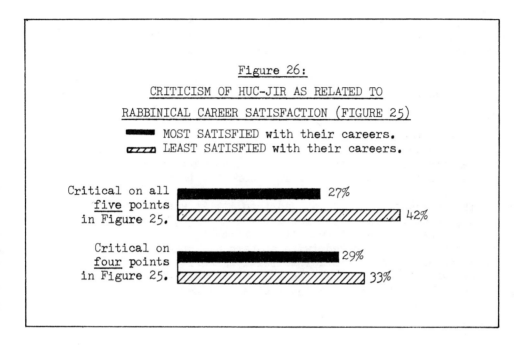

Figure 26:

CRITICISM OF HUC-JIR AS RELATED TO

RABBINICAL CAREER SATISFACTION (FIGURE 25)

▬▬ MOST SATISFIED with their careers.

▨▨ LEAST SATISFIED with their careers.

Critical on all five points in Figure 25. 27% / 42%

Critical on four points in Figure 25. 29% / 33%

of HUC-JIR, on the other. A total of 56% of even the "most satisfied" rabbis and 75% of the "least satisfied" rabbis are critical on at least four of the five components   (Figure 26).

To get the _feel_ behind the statistical data, it is helpful to read from their own hands and to hear from their own mouths (excerpts not limited to pulpit rabbis):

A faculty that recognized its students as intelligent adults who are deeply committed to learning a tradition of which they know tragically little would be an improvement over the current situation in which students are damned and ridiculed daily as irretrievable ignoramuses because they weren't born with the Talmud in their mouth. This psychological castration is great training for lying flat on your back, in a congregation, or cavorting like a trained seal, because you know deep down inside that you have nothing to offer.

HUC-JIR has peddled pipe dreams and turned out
hostile alumni for too many years. Hopefully, a
fuller picture of the real world outside the
schools will bring about changes in curriculum
and attitudes beneficial to the entire Reform
movement.

I can't really blame the (HUC-JIR). Like
(undergraduate school) . . . there were professors who were tops, and some not so hot.
But, as I look back, . . . They were all pretty
good. I had a few bad experiences . . . but
if you really put all you had into it, it was
a good education. With the exception of the
language (Hebrew), it wasn't a difficult
course, . . . I worked twice as hard at (undergraduate school) in order to really make it.
At (HUC-JIR), it was a breeze . . . (comparatively). But I don't think that should be a
criticism against the school. It was a
different program.

The College is to blame for not preparing the
rabbinate for synagogues or for scholarship.

Medical school prepares a man to practice medi-
cine. Law school prepares a man to practice law.
HUC does not prepare a man to practice Judaism
. . . I regret I didn't go to law school.

I learned more about Jews and Judaism from my
boss (the senior rabbi) in the two years I've
been here than during all my years at (HUC-JIR).
I regret to say my professors were not all good
Jews. They should spend a few years here
. . . (with his senior rabbi).

When I was in the Seminary I found that the
vast majority of the faculty were extremely
antagonistic toward the congregational rabbi.

The congregational rabbi was frequently downgraded
for being ignorant, for selling out to the congregation as well as to the non-Jewish community.

HUC-JIR should concern itself more with the psychological problems of its students and their motivations for becoming rabbis.

A very recently ordained rabbi, now an assistant rabbi, revealed
that he had wanted to be a rabbi since he was eight, and the only
times he wavered was while at HUC-JIR.

Interviewer: As you were going through the seminary
did you ever feel shaky about having chosen the right
future - the right career?

Rabbi: Being at the college and being exposed to
some of the "top men" in the field, I was wonder-
ing whether this was really what I wanted. Not
because I wasn't committed to what I was studying
and to what our people stand for, but because
. . . I saw a lot of people who were humanists in
the rabbinate, and it was kind of depressing very
often. A lot of the top men in the field who
are political - speak out of both sides of their
mouth - will do one thing and say another. It
was very depressing and sometimes very discourag-
ing. And you often ask yourself the question,
'In twenty years from now, am I going to be the
same kind of person?'

Interviewer: Are you talking of faculty rabbinate?

Rabbi: No, I'm talking about people who would
come in - HUC Board of Overseers, CCAR Board of
Overseers, rabbis who would come in every year
to speak . . . (With regard to the teaching
rabbinate there was this one Professor _____)
. . . I hated the man, I despised the man.

Interviewer: How about the course, per se, not the
man? Did it stretch your mind?

Rabbi: It distorted my mind . . . I don't like
what he stands for . . . I don't mind a man questioning assumptions that other people make - that's
part of academic work, but the man is an arrogant,
antagonistic, bitter human being.

Now let's return to the statistical data. Some comparative re-

sponses from rabbis and from seminarians are very informative.

What are some of the areas where change is indicated? And let

us note the different responses that come from the alumni as

against what the students have to say.

First let us look at what rabbis and seminary students have to say

about the curriculum. Questionnaires to both rabbis and students

carried an identical question designed to elicit from them their

assessment of each course on the basis of a five-point scaled

response pattern, ranging from "very important" to "very unimpor-

tant." Seventeen courses, based on the latest catalogs from the

three HUC-JIR centers in this country, and listed alphabetically

from Bible to Theology, were provided for the respondent's

evaluation.

The specific question and instructions read as follows:

Assume you come from a classical Reform home,
have just received your B.A. in English from
your State University, and are now beginning
your studies for the rabbinate. From the
list following, which courses would you consider necessary and which unnecessary? (For
purposes of answering this question, assume
that all courses were equally well taught.)

Table 25:
HUC-JIR CURRICULUM:
A RANK ORDER ASSESSMENT BY ALUMNI AND BY SEMINARIANS

	Rated "VERY IMPORTANT" by	
	Alumni (N=597)	Seminarians (N=53)
	%	%
Rated TOP FIVE:		
1. Bible	94	85
2. Jewish Religious Thought	83	65
3. History	83	87
4. Hebrew Language	82	78
5. Theology	70	72
Rated MIDDLE FIVE:		
6. Human Relations	64	57
7. Homiletics	62	46
8. Midrash	59	68
9. Liturgy	57	54
10. Philosophy	56	60
Rated BOTTOM SEVEN:		
11. Education	54	48
12. Commentaries	50	56
13. Speech	44	39
14. Comparative Religions	43	57
15. Talmud	39	46
16. Codes	34	35
17. Jewish Music	15	18

Table 25 provides a rank-order evaluation in terms of rabbinical
responses. Student responses are then matched with the rabbis'
responses. Since the findings are self-explanatory, no further
comments are necessary on Table 25. As to Midrash specifically,
there is the additional finding that 22% of the rabbis and 42%
of the students strongly approve of the proposal that Midrash
(and Commentaries) be taught simultaneously with the Bible, rather
than as separate courses. And as to homiletics, it appears
that 35% of the rabbis and only 11% of the students feel that
it would be a good learning device for students to be required
to evaluate printed sermons and to deliver them before the class.
(Yet this was precisely what a group of five seasoned rabbis
had recommended to the writer during an informal discussion at
a Regional conference. Hence the question in the first place.)

Both the rabbis and students were asked to express themselves
on a few other items, some related, some unrelated, regarding HUC-
JIR. These are questions that had been raised by individual rabbis
and seminarians during the earliest interviewing stage of the
research.

One such question concerned the name of the seminary. Some had
expressed chagrin. One rabbi labelled it as "cumbersome, unclear
and misleading . . ." The findings are rather revealing. While
only 35% of the rabbis are favorably disposed to the name "Hebrew
Union College - Jewish Institute of Religion," this is true of 70%
of the students. Similarly, where 22% of the rabbis are willing
to consider a name such as The University of Reform Judaism, only
2% of the students are similarly inclined. In this regard, then,

the students are definitely more conservative than their elders.
They are clearly on the side of keeping the name of the seminary as it
has been. Could it be that rabbis who have been "in the field"
have had some unfavorable experience with the seminary name, -
experiences that students are yet to encounter?

By and large there is very little that alumni or present students
would wish to delete from the curriculum as it now stands. Jewish
music appears to be the only clear-cut case of a "dispensable"
course. In the evaluation of all the other courses that constitute
the curriculum on the three United States campuses of HUC-JIR,
there appears to be a strong consensus to retain the present format.
Let it be noted, however, that this does not mean that all courses
are held in the same esteem.

After close scrutiny of Table 25, and in addition to what has been
observed already, it is worth noting a few small but important
differences between alumni and students as they rate the following
three specific courses (in terms of "importance"):

	Alumni rating.	Student rating.
Jewish Religious Thought..........	83%	65%
Comparative Religions.............	43%	57%
Homiletics.......................	62%	46%

On the whole, then, while we may be witnessing a shift in interest
from specifically Jewish religious thought to religious thought and
action in general, and while students appear to have less interest
in the art of preaching, there is substantial agreement as to what

the HUC-JIR is being asked to include. The top five for both groups is the same in four cases out of five, the exception being the replacement of Jewish Religious Thought by Midrash.

But there are other and more important matters than the name. Take the question of bringing the seminary more into contact with what is going on in other academic centers. Only 8% of the respondents are definitely opposed to developing cooperative programs with other academic institutions. On the other hand, 52% are unqualifiedly for the proposal, and another 4% approve with certain stipulations. This proposal, be it noted, does not include the reorganization of JUC-JIR, or building new institutions. It simply seeks to enlarge the present scope of HUC-JIR activities, and virtually everyone is in favor of that.

But are the present institutions ideally located? Perhaps not. In answer to the proposal that seminaries should be located in major academic centers, 69% of the rabbis, and 85% of the students express approval. In other words, while they are not explicitly urging the actual move, they would certainly do things differently if they were starting from the beginning.

What would they do if they could start over again? Well, we have seen that they would not initiate very many curricular innovations. And we also find that they do not want to move into a suburban Gan Eden (Figure 27).

Because so many references, comments, and recommendations (re: HUC-JIR), had been noted in the primary sources and during the pre-questionnaire stage, it was decided to put them all together into a hypothetical model. Thus a proposed model of a multi-university, incorporating

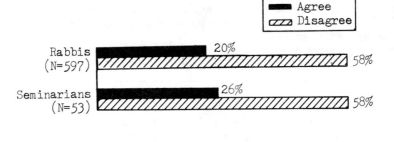

Figure 27:

RELOCATING HUC-JIR, UAHC, AND CCAR:

COMPARATIVE ATTITUDES OF RABBIS AND SEMINARIANS

"A completely new plant combining a Reform seminary, the UAHC, and the CCAR headquarters ought to be planned for the not-too-distant future to be located near a large urban area, but in a country setting removed from the distractions that normally intrude on contemplation and study."

■ Agree
▨ Disagree

Rabbis (N=597) 20% 58%

Seminarians (N=53) 26% 58%

almost all the separate recommendations that had been submitted earlier, was formulated and presented to both rabbis and seminarians. At best, the whole process was a complicated exercise, and made very formidable demands on the respondents. It was a most atypical demand for survey research. It is the type of probing most often relegated to personal interviewing. It is gratefully noted that the responses which came forth from rabbis and seminarians makes possible the development of some excellent data. (The reader is now asked to review the multi-university model, Appendix, so that the findings in the next few pages will be more easily understood in the context of the overall question.)

And now we are ready for the responses to many questions that were raised concerning the model (Table 26). First of all, they like it.

Table 26:

HEBREW UNION COLLEGE - JEWISH INSTITUTE OF RELIGION:
RABBINICAL AND STUDENT RESPONSES TO A PROPOSED MODEL
(PERCENT REPORTING AGREEMENT)

	Rabbis (N=597)	Students (N=53)
1. The flexibility factor regarding the ability to take electives in other schools, and providing for enriched interdisciplinary programs between the schools is a good idea.	88%	90%
2. A School of Basic Studies is a good idea.	74%	66%
3. Ordination should depend much on the student's background, thus the program should be flexible and allow for completion anywhere between four and six to seven years as needed.	70%	73%
4. A doctorate should be conferred with ordination.	69%	71%
5. The School of Judaica and Cognate Studies and The School of Rabbinical Studies should be combined, possibly providing the D.H.L. for ordination, and the Ph.D. for research and scholarly pursuit for those who do not wish to be rabbis.	60%	69%
6. The different campuses should be under separate boards of governors.	16%	39%
7. A School of Music and Music Education is preferable to a School of Sacred Music.	33%	39%
8. The D.H.L. and the Ph.D. should require the same number of years for completion.	34%	28%
9. Ordination should take no more than four years after bachelor's degree.	23%	15%
10. Ordination should take no more than five years after bachelor's degree.	57%	58%
11. Ordination should take no more than six years after bachelor's degree.	44%	60%
12. The B.H.L. should be discontinued.	49%	60%

Over two-thirds (69%) of the rabbis and almost three-fourths (74%)
of the students agree it is a good proposal. And 69% of the rabbis
as well as 86% of the students deny that the proposal is a "dream."
(An example of good response reliability.) Since several very drastic
recommendations for change are included in the hypothetical model,
it goes without saying that if a substantial majority agree that
the overall model "is a good proposal", there must be many rabbis
(actually the majority), and seminarians, who are not satisfied
with the present structure and function of today's HUC-JIR.
(It is for the purpose of eliciting the rabbinate's general assessment of their seminary in terms of their self-evaluation needs,
rather than to intrude on the seminary with recommendations for
change, that these findings are herein reported.)

More specifically, let us examine those aspects of the proposal
with which most rabbis and students are in agreement, by having
indicated they either "strongly agree" or "agree." The percentages
in all cases combine both responses.

The high percentage of agreement that both alumni and students give
to the first five proposals is quite convincing. On other proposals,
students differ in various degrees with their elders. With regard
to the length of time that should be required for ordination, some
respondents favored more than one plan.

The crucial part of the hypothetical model concerns itself with
various plans for achieving ordination from the proposed School
of Rabbinical Studies. Table 27 repeats the four plans that were
proposed in the questionnaire and provides the responses that came
forth from alumni and students.

Table 27:

A SCHOOL OF RABBINICAL STUDIES FOR HUC-JIR:

ALUMNI AND STUDENTS CHOOSE FROM FOUR HYPOTHETICAL MODELS

Alumni (N=597)
Students (N=53)

IN AGREEMENT:

	Alumni %	Students %
Plan 1: Bachelor's + 2 years M.H.L. (Incl. 1 year in Israel) M.H.L. + 2 years D.H.L. D.H.L. + 1 yr. (ORDINATION) 5 yrs. Ph.D.	37	40
Plan 2: Bachelor's + 1 yr. in Israel B.H.L. B.H.L. + 1 year M.H.L. M.H.L. + 3 yrs. (ORDINATION) 5 yrs. D.H.L. D.H.L. + 1 year Ph.D.	36	39
Plan 3: Bachelor's + 1 yr. in Israel B.H.L. B.H.L. + 1 year M.H.L. M.H.L. + 3 yrs. (ORDINATION) 5 yrs. Ph.D.	21	32
Plan 4: Bachelor's + 1 yr. in Israel M.H.L. M.H.L. + 2 years D.H.L. D.H.L. + 3 yrs. (ORDINATION) 6 yrs. Ph.D.	20	32
No answer	21	24

Now let us again get the _feel_ of things by going behind the statistical findings, and read what some rabbis and seminarians have to say about the model as a whole or parts of it.

The following are a random selection of rabbinical comments on the model:

> The school curriculum should allow time away from the classroom for working with prison chaplains, hospital chaplains, army chaplains, and pulpit rabbis similar to the method used by Antioch College.

> Excellent - finest thing to come over the pike in years.

> Don't like separate campuses - think all schools in U.S. should be combined into one of the existing schools or a new one in a new locale should be built.

> The plan is too 'pat' - but brilliant since something _is_ needed.

> Instead of 'conglomerating' under one roof, plug in with universities in area and create an interacting network with them. Each university benefits from the others and vice versa. Use existing facilities in this manner not only of HUC-JIR but other universities.

> I strongly favor this idea. But the School of Arts and Humanities should be strong in Jewish content; i.e., courses in Hebrew, Religion, Jewish History, etc. should be required.

I strongly believe that the Rabbi should be educated in a Yeshiva or Rabbinical Seminary.
He will thus be fully indoctrinated in Jewish
thought, Jewish life, history, philosophy,
Hebrew, Bible, Talmud (abridged) and cognate
subjects ... The four HUC-JIR schools should
all be equal in faculty and in complete
courses leading towards ordination. Continuing to hallow Cincinnati as the Queen City
is ridiculous, - Jewish life has passed it by.

I would urge a strong centralized system, ad-
ministratively and physically. Duplication of
staff, faculty, plants, etc. is wasteful. Recognition should be made of existing inadequate
preparation in Judaic disciplines. Reform
rabbis should be no less versed in the tradition
than Orthodox rabbis.

I agree in principle that it would be ideal
if the school were to serve 'the total Jewish
community...'

In Rabbinic studies the highest degree towards
which we should devote our psychological attention is ordination ... I say this despite the
fact that I have an earned D.H.L. for which I
worked damned hard for three years and enjoyed
immensely ...
....
I believe that the Cincinnati and New York schools
should merge and ... (establish) in the East. I
recognize the historical significance of Cincinnati,
of course, but many factors suggest this to me
and to many other people also.

... it is an understandable but curious fact
that nobody, in any discussion, seems to think of
'Rabbi' as something superior to a doctorate
(I have a PH.D. - no sour grapes).

My chief complaint with HUC-JIR was that it all
but prevented serious scholarship while it emphasized busy-work - even when the students
were capable of much, much more. Doing graduate
work elsewhere after HUC is like moving from
High School to College. Any new plan would
have to incorporate serious scholarship for
at least the last three years - especially
one leading to a PH.D. The Cincinnati school
should be closed down - it is an unnecessary
drain on funds and a much too parochial atmosphere.

An excellent achievement for so difficult and
diffuse a task ...
....
... Most alumni and students are unhappy about
HUC-JIR, it appears, because of the dehumanized
administration ... The academic set-up or failure
of scholastic achievement are secondary causes
of irritation, dismay or despair.

HUC-JIR has demonstrated its incapacity to train
adequate Rabbis, cantors and teachers in the
sense that its graduates have in any significant
way fostered the growth, quality and advancement
of Jewish life or stemmed its decline.

... One grave mistake, however, is keeping Cincinnati
as the center of Reform studies. The center
should be in a large city with several large
universities and with a large Jewish population.

Though a complete reorganization of the program
of rabbinical studies is desirable, I believe that
these proposed changes ... will do little to reduce
the anxiety or the ambivalence of many rabbis.
For the real problem, in my opinion, does not
lie in the process of acquisition of knowledge
and the professional skills and techniques, but

in the depth and intensity of the spiritual
and ethical convictions of the individual ... A
humanism, which could exist without God, or
without the Jewish people cannot - in my opinion -
provide a sufficient motivation for the rabbinical call. Unless one is willing to sacrifice
for the sake of his convictions and ideals, he
will be ambivalent in time of crisis or difficulty.
....
How can this faith be taught? By the life and
example of a new type of teacher - less interested
in credits and more in spiritual and ethical
values.

I like the idea of broadening the base of the
College - this will better serve the needs of
American Jewry, if the College could ever be
reorganized.

The congregants are demanding more emotional
depth in their services ... in their rabbis ...
they are reaching out for more symbolism, more
affective elements in the worship service ...
they want more authority ... (and) the Reform
rabbi (represents) this authority infrequently.

Interviewer: Are you suggesting his training is not
good enough?

Rabbi: Right, I think it's inadequate. There
have to be practicums as far as counseling is concerned ... as far as emotional (needs) are concerned ... (We need) courses dealing with the
affective nature as well as just the scholarly.
A great deal of what is taught at HUC-JIR is as
superficial as a Sunday school education that
we offer in the congregation.

... The seminary is a unique experience. It's
terribly competitive. It is an incestuous pre-
datory family ... The seminary is very unreal,
nor is American Judaism really related to the
seminary ... and it has to get off the hill in
Cincinnati ... and get to where the people are
(in it's thinking.)

The following comments, also randomly selected, are from <u>seminarians</u>:

> The entire last part - a revised total academic model - seems predicated on the idea of a unified movement. Given the bickering and political in-fighting that I have seen thus far, I find this assumption somewhat questionable - to say the least!

> I am strongly in favor of a diversity of programs to fill various interests and career goals. In our present system, the multiplicity of individual desires are never satisfied. The person who wants to be a pulpit rabbi is inadequately trained be-cause of the attempt to satisfy the needs of graduate students of other interests. Similarly, the graduate student is hindered because of the need to train rabbis.

> HUC is not a Yeshiva - it is a professional school aimed at a career. The increased enrollment threatens that career with lack of jobs.

> The year in Israel should definitely come after being at the college for a period of one to two years after the student has a knowledge of Hebrew and a vested interest in the college. Going to Israel for the first year is a mistake.

> It would demean the PH.D. to give it to all. Plans #1 & #3 would be OK if they only gave the DHL for 5 years.

> You have written a 28 page questionnaire that does not once mention how the student is sup-posed to finance 4, 5, or even, heaven forbid, a 6 year education!!!

I could possibly envision a separate program for
pastoral rabbis and a separate one for scholar-
rabbis. Perhaps a difference of degree (simple
ordination vs. earned academic degree) would be
in order. Courses such as Bible, Midrash and
Talmud would not necessarily be taught in Hebrew
after preliminary work was completed, but in
English, stressing idea content rather than form
criticism, etc. in the pastoral program. This
would in no way limit a person in the scholar-
rabbi program from entering the congregational
rabbinate but it might make available, as Rabbis,
people specializing in fields such as psychology,
sociology, etc. without it being necessary for
them to be concerned with a host of textual
labors. The scholar-rabbi would receive an
earned academic degree and would have a larger
period of study before receiving that degree.
Ordination in this program would come with
successful completion of the course study so one
would have to be pretty sure before he began -
Perhaps aptitude and psychological testing would
be appropriate in formulating such decisions.

11. Summary Highlights (Pulpit Rabbi and His Establishment).

   1) The Board of Trustees and the Sisterhood are viewed by Reform
      rabbis as the two synagogue groups that do most for the
      congregation. The Men's Club rates very low in terms
      of the same criteria.

   2) Reform rabbis see their congregations as reasonably
      tractable. Rabbis give similar ratings to their Boards
      and to their congregants on the issues of willingness
      to experiment and accept change. Less than 20% say their
      Boards and congregants are "very willing," but the large
      majority say they are "somewhat willing." Only 6% rate their
      Boards as "very unwilling," and 3% say the same of their
      congregants.

3) Many experienced Reform rabbis feel change is usually the
   result of their own initiative, not the result of the Board's
   initiative.

4) The rabbis' satisfaction with his Board is closely related
   with the latter's willingness to experiment and to accept
   change; conversely, rabbis report dissatisfaction with
   their Boards where the latter are non-receptive to experimentation and change.

5) Board behavior has a greater impact, than does general membership behavior on rabbinical job satisfaction.

6) With regard to synagogue policy concerning the requirements
   of affiliation, rabbis report that people must first affiliate
   with the synagogue if they are to be married there (36%);
   before their children will be accepted in the religious
   school (74%); and especially before children will be Bar/Bas
   Mitzvah (91%). In some cases, exceptions may be made.

7) Ashkenazit still lingers on in Reform, but appears to be on
   its way out as an havara. Less than half of all Reform synagogues still employ it in their services, and only 23% of
   our synagogues teach it in their religious schools. Some
   Reform synagogues,while using Ashkenazit in services, teach
   in Sephardit in the religious school.

8) Sabbath services are held only on Friday evenings in 38% of
   Reform synagogues. In 61% of the synagogues there are both

Friday and Saturday services. Only 1% have Sabbath services on Sunday. One-third of our synagogues rarely or never employ any musical instruments other than the organ at services.

9) Generally speaking, the present prayerbook is not "wearing well". There is great demand by the majority of the rabbis for a revision as soon as possible. Many Reform rabbis have written their own services. Many "creative" services are constantly being substituted for the Union Prayer Book. The Temple Youth contribute considerably to the latter type.

10) Some 41% of Reform rabbis officiate at mixed marriages (no prior conversion); some do so for members of their congregations only, or only "when special circumstances exist." Over half of those who do not officiate refer the parties to rabbis who will officiate.

11) A large majority of Reform rabbis (71%) feel there is a "Jewish distance" between themselves and their congregants. Almost half the rabbis see it as "the single most frustrating obstacle" in their rabbinical careers.

12) Some 60% of Reform rabbis say that the use of the chuppa and the breaking of the glass should be at the discretion of bride and groom. Only 2% say the chuppa should not be permitted; 6% say the same for the glass ritual.

13) Approximately half the rabbinate expresses discomfort with the CCAR. Discontent cannot be categorized because of the

many different reasons given by different rabbis. Almost
half say that the CCAR "pits one man against the other."
Younger rabbis, as a whole, are more disparaging than their
older colleagues.

14) By their criticisms of the CCAR, the Regions (and the Union
and College as well), a majority of Reform rabbis seem to
be asking for two things: (1) Effective apparatus (national
and regional) for helping them in their "business" arrangements
with their congregations (including placement, salaries,
increments, insurance and pension benefits, sabbaticals and
tenure), and (2) Effective apparatus for the promotion of
a community of kindred souls with kindred personal and professional (scholarship and administrative) needs. Most are
saying a Regional apparatus could possibly do these things
better than the parent organization.

15) The majority of Reform rabbis (64%) do not feel that HUC-JIR
had inculcated its students "with lasting ideals (making for)
a band of brotherhood." On several salient characteristics,
rabbis and seminarians assess the HUC-JIR similarly. Over
half of both groups say that the institution "did little
or nothing to help us understand better our own values and
attitudes."

16) Criticism of HUC-JIR appears to be equally divided between
those rabbis who express satisfaction with their careers and
those who express dissatisfaction.

17) Courses rated the top five at HUC-JIR by both rabbis and
seminarians are: Bible, Jewish Religious Thought, History,

Hebrew language, Theology. The bottom five, in terms of
importance, are identified as Speech, Comparative Religions,
Talmud, Codes, Jewish Music.

18) Twice as many seminarians as rabbis (70% to 35%) are favorably
disposed to the name Hebrew Union College - Jewish Institute
of Religion.

19) Three-fourths of the rabbinate (some with stipulations) want
the HUC-JIR to enlarge its present scope of operations by
developing programs with other academic institutions.

20) Some 69% of the rabbis and 85% of the seminiarians would
prefer the seminaries to be located in major academic centers.

21) Many rabbis and seminarians are making many different recommendations for HUC-JIR to consider. Most of these recommendations (many are new and drastic) are incorporated in a
hypothetical multi-university model (Appendix A); 69% of
the rabbis and 74% of the seminarians say it is "a good
proposal."

CHAPTER 10: WHAT LIES AHEAD?

1. CRISIS!

During the course of pre-questionnaire interviewing of rabbis from all sections of the country, many expressed concern that Reform Judaism was in the midst of a crisis,- a situation that will become worse, many felt, before it becomes better. Most often the respondent spoke of the crisis as an overall Jewish problem rather than just a problem that Reform is facing. Concurring with the interview information were the many written comments that had accompanied the questionnaires or were sent along as private communications. A rather typical expression from one rabbi was subsequently included in the questionnaire to the rabbinate. Both the statement and responses from the rabbinate (and from the congregants), constitute Table 28.

Some 50% of Reform rabbis accept the proposition that a crisis (as identified in Table 28), applies to <u>themselves</u>, whereas a somewhat larger number say it applies to their respective <u>congregations</u> (64%). We shall see later that when the congregants are asked the same question, a reasonably similar number (52%) also agree there is a crisis. However, a much larger number of congregants over rabbis give a "don't know" answer.

There is, then, a somewhat pervasive feeling of crisis. But if a reasonably large number of rabbis are persuaded that things may be worse than they actually appear to be on the surface, the same level of agreement does not exist when it comes to <u>identifying</u> the crisis. Take the matter of proselytizing, for example. Only 8% feel "strongly" and another 25% agree "somewhat" that more time and energy should be given in making an effort to win Jewish recruits to Reform. The numbers in favor of proselytising among non-Jews are roughly the same. Some 12% are "strongly" in favor, and 19% are "somewhat" in favor of doing this.

Table 28:

ROLE CONFUSION AND CRISIS IDENTITY

"Despite the external appearance of success and apparent synagogue vitality, Jewish life, secular and religious, is undergoing a crisis of existence and commitment which may test Jewry's will to live . . . Part of the crisis lies in a growing anxiety within the rabbinate and congregations as to their true roles. Once well-grounded conceptions about their tasks and their identities are becoming confused."

DO YOU FEEL THIS APPLIES TO YOURSELF? WHAT ABOUT YOUR CONGREGATION?

	AGREE	DISAGREE
Response from rabbis (N=620):		
This situation applies to me.	50%	47%
This situation applies to my congregation.	64%	31%
Response from congregants (N=984):		
This situation applies to me.	52%	16%

Quite recently a Reform rabbi, pursuing a doctorate at a secular
university on the subject of rabbinical-congregational role relationships, submitted a proposal for his doctoral dissertation with the
following introductory remarks:

> The rabbinate has changed in recent years from a stable
> calling to a crisis ridden profession. This is somewhat
> surprising in view of the thousands of years of tradi-
> tion of the role of the rabbi. However, reports of con-
> flict in synagogues between rabbis and congregations are
> becoming routine; conflagrations are flaring up daily
> in all areas of the United States.

To identify uniformities in order to describe the concern of the
many rabbis who were interviewed is not an easy task. What is crisis
to one rabbi in his given situation may be almost a totally unknown
factor to another rabbi. We are in a similar situation here as we
were with rabbis who were asked to identify their grievances with the
CCAR. It will be recalled that grievances were many and varied. So
varied, in fact, that uniformities were hard to come by. And now we
have a malais with regard to crisis. Many will tell us that there
is a crisis. But, again, what they tell us is so varied, as to defy
any honest formulation of uniformities. Yet a thread of discontent
with Judaism in general, and with the Reform Movement in particular,
continued to weave itself throughout the investigation. Needless to
say the Union of American Hebrew Congregations, the Central Conference of American Rabbis, and the Hebrew Union College - Jewish Institute of Religion all come in for their share of criticism.

2. The National Scene: Is Merger Desired?

By raising a question about the possibilities of merging Reform with
one or both of the other branches of Judaism, some clues began to

Table 29:

HOW REFORM RABBIS FEEL ABOUT MERGING

WITH CONSERVATIVE AND ORTHODOX MOVEMENTS (N=620)

1. In favor of merging all three branches.	6%
2. In favor of merging Reform with Conservatism.	22%
3. In favor of separate status for Reform, but incorporating more of traditional Judaism in its beliefs and practices.	43%
4. In favor of separate status for Reform, but moving further away from traditionalism toward humanism.	29%

appear concerning the nature of the Reform rabbinate's discontent and possibly an identification of "the crisis."

We find these data in Table 29. Almost 3 out of 4 rabbis want to continue to remain a separate branch of Judaism, but they are then split 60-40 on the direction to take. Is this possibly some clue to the crisis in Reform today? One of the interesting things about this situation is that there are no meaningful differences by age. The split seems to occur across the board among rabbis of all ages. It is significantly not a generational difference.

If most Reform rabbis do not prefer a merger, there is nevertheless a good deal of interest in a merger with their Conservative colleagues provided that the latter would liberalize their own position. Realizing that Reform rabbis would also have to become more traditional as part of such an arrangement, we find 40% saying that they would "definitely" enter such a combined movement and another 21% say they "probably" would. This is a definite and important finding. Reform rabbis, while they would prefer to go it alone, are showing an increasingly receptive attitude toward a merger with Conservatism, with the understanding that this means becoming more traditional in the process. What we do not know from this finding, however, is what would happen in the case of those who would be staunchly opposed. Would this be the start of a new schism? It is impossible to tell. But we do have one additional bit of information. Rabbis, it seems, think that they are far more likely than their congregations to go along with such a move. Only 14% think their congregations would approve, while 38% think they would disapprove. Another 37% think that with proper planning and preparation they could win their congregations over to the pro-merger position. Does this mean that the rabbis themselves see a ready market for a schismatic movement? In view of what we shall see about Reform congregations (in a subsequent section), one is forced to agree that their assessment is quite possibly correct.

Both in written comments and in interviews, many rabbis reveal even stronger thoughts for a Conservative-Reform merger. They share these thoughts, from time to time, with Reform colleagues, with colleagues in the Conservative rabbinate, with some of their congregants, and with others. Most feel that the mechanics of such a merger is probably the most formidable block. Others (very few), identify strong theological differences that need to be respected by all concerned.

Comments from seminarians and rabbis are reasonably similar, pro and
con. Following are two comments, one pro, the other con, chosen
randomly:

> (From a Reform Rabbi)
> At the present time there are not too many theological
> or philosophical differences separating American Reform
> and Conservative congregations. The way of life of
> most of the members of such congregations is most in-
> distinguishable . . .
> . . . .
> . . . The main problems standing in the way of a merger
> are the vested interests of seminaries and synagogues
> as well as practical questions regarding liturgy and
> ways of worship. Hats on or hats off--to wear or not
> to wear a tallith--instrumental music or not--these are
> the stumbling blocks. I consider it a serious mistake
> made by the early Reformers that they dispensed with
> head covering during worship because this created an
> artificial and unnecessary division between Jews.

> (From a Reform seminarian)
> The idea of combining Reform and Conservative and/or
> Orthodox seminaries into one is absurd. Reform is so
> different than the other two denominations that to
> make any combination would be tantamount to stunting
> Reform's ongoing development.

3. The Local Scene: Community Team Rabbinate?

So much for merger at a national level. How do they feel about some
kind of cooperative working arrangement with Orthodox and/or Conservative rabbis at the local level?

Another postulation that was submitted to the Rabbinate was as follows:

> It would be desirable in terms of 'Jewish community,' if
> rabbis were employed by local or regional Jewish community

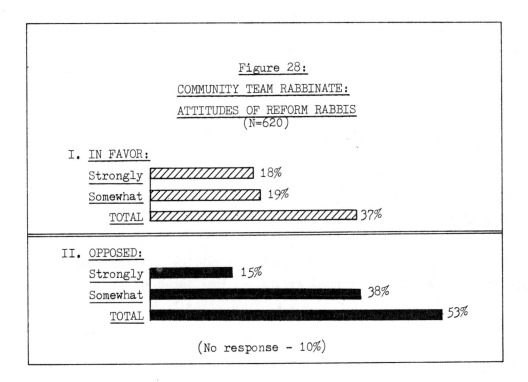

Figure 28:

COMMUNITY TEAM RABBINATE:

ATTITUDES OF REFORM RABBIS
(N=620)

I. IN FAVOR:
Strongly 18%
Somewhat 19%
TOTAL 37%

II. OPPOSED:
Strongly 15%
Somewhat 38%
TOTAL 53%

(No response - 10%)

councils (perhaps by an existing Jewish community agency
or by the creation of a new one), and then be assigned to
tasks so as to serve the total Jewish community, including
the conducting of worship services, rituals, education,
counseling, etc.

Assume that this would include the Orthodox and Conservative rabbis also, and that a very sophisticated machinery
would be worked out so that rabbi and 'client(s)' would be
compatible as a result of the 'division of labor' and the
'assignments' of rabbis.

How do rabbis feel about the aforementioned idea? The results show
non-acceptance, with only 18% "strongly in favor" of the proposition,
as indicated in Figure 28. The overall figures are 37% in favor, and
53% opposed. But now a curious finding. Those rabbis who, as we

saw a moment ago, are more in favor of liberalizing Reform and moving
toward humanism are <u>also</u> more in favor of operational mergers, -
27% to 11%. <u>In other words, those who perceive Reform to be in crisis</u>
<u>are more willing to do something at both national and local levels,</u>
<u>although in one case it involves greater separation from the rest of</u>
<u>Judaism and in the other it involves greater cooperation.</u>

Rabbis themselves have little hope that a "community team rabbinate"
would work. Only 6% are pretty certain that it would, and 15% say
"probably." The rest are pessimistic.

Despite the fact that much more of the Reform rabbinate seems to be
opposed to a community rabbinical apparatus than those who are for
it, those who have spoken for such a mechanism have been exceedingly
articulate.

One <u>Reform</u> rabbi projects the idea as follows:

> It is about time we gave small pockets of serious Jews
> an opportunity to meet and to have professional rabbinic
> services - even if they can't afford them. The Jewish
> community as a whole can and should bear the financial
> burden of these, our 'saving remnants.'

A <u>Conservative</u> rabbi speaks to the same issue:

> What is needed instead is a commitment of Jewish leader-
> ship and communal service wherever Jews may be, not
> simply where they and their dues are conveniently col-
> lected. We have to be the leaders of the community, not
> the servants. We have to constitute a new community
> rabbinate. In other words, getting down from the lofty
> pulpit and getting dirty at the grass-roots, organizing
> groups, infiltrating others. Jewish education shouldn't

preach relevance; it should be relevant through interaction at the gut level of k'lal yisrael. There is a
tremendous untapped potential for Judaising, starting
from congregational meetings (where the action is, far
more than at services), including such twentieth century rituals as fund-raising dinners . . ., and even
circuit-riding 'missionizing' to the Jewish-in-name-only
camps, country clubs, student groups, hippie pads, etc.*

4. "The Crisis Index."

Taking material from the aforementioned data, and on the basis of a
selected sample of pressing Jewish issues that have been identified
in all of our findings to this point, we shall try now to summarize
what the rabbinate is telling us in terms of "crises." We are dealing now with issues that almost all rabbis had raised in interviews,
in written comments on the questionnaires that they had returned,
and at various meetings during the course of this study.

A statistical summary was formulated, and we shall call it "The Crisis
Index." The response pattern has been arranged on the basis of four
categories. Rabbis were asked to identify each issue as "extreme
crisis," "considerable crisis," "some crisis," or "hardly any crisis."
Table 30 presents these findings.

---

*Ben Hollander, "Some Radical Proposals for a Community Rabbinate,"
   The Jewish Digest (Condensed from Response), June, 1970, p. 36.

Table 30:

CRISIS IN JUDAISM AS VIEWED BY REFORM RABBINATE:

"THE CRISIS INDEX"

Rabbis who have identified themselves as follows:	Extreme Crisis (N=128) %	Considerable Crisis (N=129) %	Some Crisis (N=169) %	Hardly any Crisis (N=189) %
1. Satisfied with their own careers.	25	32	39	58
2. If starting career now, would still choose to be rabbi.	35	45	61	64
3. Crisis in Judaism lies in growing anxiety within the rabbinate and congregations as to their true roles:				
a. Rabbis' anxiety concerning themselves.	37	20	2	0
b. Rabbis' anxiety concerning their congregations.	46	28	10	0
4. Regarding unaffiliated Jews, rabbis should go out to get to know these people and try to get them into the synagogue.	19	19	13	9
5. Jewish communities should set up mechanisms (possibly through local rabbinical organizations, or through Jewish Federations), to reach these people in hospitals, convalescent homes, and in their own homes, in order to ascertain their needs and to provide for such needs in terms of practical procedures.	59	47	42	37

#	Statement				
6.	Reform should remain a separate branch of Judaism, but should incorporate something more of traditional Judaism in its theology and practice.	34	43	45	48
7.	Reform should remain a separate branch of Judaism, but veer away even more from tradition, if necessary, and possibly more toward humanism.	39	30	25	25
8.	Great uncertainty about the future survival of Judaism in general.	45	26	12	4
9.	Great uncertainly about the future survival of Reform Judaism in particular.	49	20	9	0
10.	"Strongly agree that while Reform Judaism may be the most satisfactory arrangement for many Jews in the modern western world, it depends nevertheless for its ultimate survival on the continued existence of Orthodox and Conservative Judaism."	22	20	10	11
11.	Strongly agree that Reform Judaism should spend more energy on proselytizing, but only among Jews.	8	13	7	6
12.	Strongly agree that Reform Judaism should spend more energy on proselytizing not only among Jews but among non-Jews as well.	2	10	11	8

What doesn't show directly in "The Crisis Index" is the component of faith. But a high and positive correlation seems to exist on one point. Those rabbis who identify the present scene as being in "extreme" crisis, are usually also those who identify themselves as non-traditional believers in God. Almost all who identify themselves as agnostics or atheists are included in this category. To be sure many traditional believers also see "extreme crisis," but often it is not a personal identification with them. It is more an observation of what they see around them that is viewed by them as crisis.

Table 30 informs us that rabbis who are satisfied with their careers are saying, over two-to-one, that there is "hardly any crisis." Of those in the rabbinate who see an "extreme crisis," only 35% would choose the rabbinate if they were starting all over again. Rabbis who feel anxiety concerning themselves and their congregations are the rabbis who see "extreme" or "considerable" crisis in Judaism. Rabbis who see "extreme crisis" also see a need for "community rabbinates" much more so than those who see "hardly any crisis." Those who see "extreme crisis" tend to veer away from traditional forms and lean toward or embrace humanism.

Excerpts from two selected interviews may help to clarify things:

Interviewer: How do you look at the concept of faith?

Rabbi: No two professors (HUC-JIR) ever defined the concept of faith the same way, so what is faith? A man can have faith in his wife until he is given reason not to . . . (so now) he no longer has faith in her. He gets a divorce and remarries. Now he has faith in his second wife. In this sense I can understand faith. Faith in God means a different type of faith. I just don't know . . . (To many) it means you do (believe in God) or you don't . . . this 'do or don't,' what does it mean? Do and you'll be saved, don't and you'll be damned? You know better than that. For a Jew to examine faith is not so easy.

Interviewer: Do you see a connection between the role
of faith, and the crisis that we were talking about a
few minutes back?

Rabbi: What has one thing got to do with the other?
The crisis goes beyond Reform . . . The Conservatives
are having their problems too. Look what's happening
in Catholicism. Obviously Western religion hasn't
made it. We, in Reform, will have to make some serious
changes.

Let us look at the other side of the picture. The next excerpt is from
an interview with a rabbi who had started his own congregation a little
over fifteen years ago.

There is a crisis and there isn't. I think many rabbis,
like many professors, students today . . . (and others)
from all walks of life are having a crisis within themselves, and they then see this crisis all around them,
almost like they want it to be there. When I see this
happening then I have to admit there is a crisis. . . .
in Judaism, all Judaism, not just with us. There can
only be one crisis, a crisis in faith. Everything else
can be manipulated. Of course, we all wonder at times.
And that's when I'm at my worst . . . But I have never
really wavered . . . I firmly believe that God is the
majesty of majesties.

Let us see how some of our non-Jewish religious bodies are expressing
themselves today on the same subject.

The Vatican last week announced that all Catholic priests
would henceforth be asked to make an annual public af-
firmation of their vows of celibacy and obedience . . .
the proposal was a nervous, defensive papal response to
a more enduring crisis: the most notable mass defection
of priests (and nuns) from the service of the church
since the Reformation.*

---

*"Priests and Nuns: Going Their Way," Time, Feb. 23, 1970, p. 51.

In a recent radio address on the Catholic crisis, Rev. Richard P. McBrien (Associate Professor of Theology, Boston College), noted it as follows:*

> There is a crisis of faith in the Church today . . .
> . . . .
> . . . One after the other, longstanding Catholic practices were shunted aside, and the Church began to look much different; we could take solid foods until three hours before Holy Communion; Lent was no longer a season of obligatory fast and abstinence; Catholics could eat meat on Fridays; Mass could be celebrated at a mixed marriage, and Sunday Mass in the evening (even on Saturday); and sisters could wear lay clothes and assume greater responsibility for the conduct of their own lives.
>
> And now they're saying, 'You've made it all too easy!' That's why you're not getting people to come to Church. What's the use? If it doesn't really matter that much, why bother at all?
>
> Unless I have completely misread the present pastoral situation, this latter charge is widely expressed and even more widely believed. The Catholic Church started going downhill when it began relaxing its discipline and turning its back on its own venerable traditions.

---

*"The Changing Church In a Changing World," Catholic Communication Foundation, <u>Guide Lines</u>, N. B. C. Catholic Radio Program, April 11, 1971.

And the Protestants:

> We propose that, during the coming three years, the Na-
> tional Council of Churches be given a mandate by her
> constituent churches to develop, both nationally and at
> the grass roots, a movement of those within and outside
> of existing congregations for the confrontation of exist-
> ing impediments to the reform of church and society . . .
> <u>The coming years will be ones of crisis for the insti-</u>
> <u>tutional churches</u> . . .*

> The Unitarian Universalist denomination, along with all
> others, is trembling and reeling in the shock waves of
> societal change.**

Compare the previous statements with the following comments from concerned Jews:

> The current panic about Jewish survival and commitment
> is like a suburban householder's despair when the elec-
> trical wires are down. Judaism, the ancient source of
> power is there but the wires are broken. Jews feel dis-
> connected, uncertain about their Jewish identity, unsure
> of their commitments.***

---

*National Council of Churches Triennial Assembly, 1971.

**Dept. of Ministry, Unitaritian Universalist Assn. and Board of
  N. Y. State Universalist Convention (Ministerial Shift
  Study), Spring, 1969.

***Sylvia Rothchild, "Jewish Identity Crisis and Commitment,"
   Council Woman (National Council of Jewish Women),
   Jan.-March, 1970, p. 7.

We badly need some carefully-constructed behavioral
research on working rabbis. It is one measure of the
depths of the trouble the rabbinate is in that no such
studies exist. And there are indications that many
rabbis need to resist the carrying out of such studies,
to judge by debates in the CCAR.*

Jewish life has taken on 'schizophrenic' patterns that
'fragmentize rather than integrate us into a whole
people.'**

If the picture of American Judaism today is a very
dismal one - and I believe it is - if the future of
American Judaism looks very grim - and I think it
does - that is in great part due to the fact that we
live in an essentially hostile environment.***

5. The Reform Rabbi Speaks His Mind.

Possibly the best way to end our story on the Reform rabbinate is to
let the rabbis speak for themselves. Many have already been quoted,
and will yet be quoted with regard to other sections of this study.

---

*Eugene E. Lipman, "The Changing Self-Image of the Rabbi,"
    Dimensions, Spring, 1970, p. 27.

**Rabbi Mordecai Kaplan, B'nai Brith Triennial Convention Address,
    New York City, as quoted in The New York Times, October 17,
    1971, p. 36.

***Philip Klutznick, Loc. cit.

The following excerpts have all been chosen at random from a host of
interviews, written comments, and from some of the contemporary literature.

> We must see visions, dream dreams. They may produce re-
> sults . . . Thank you for helping me focus on some pro-
> blem areas constructively. (Reference is made here to
> the questionnaire.)

> Reform Judaism ought to accept that aspect of Reconstuc-
> tionism which will somehow succeed to make the purely
> ethnic Jew comfortable in our ranks.

> In filling out this study I realized that I enjoy being
> a Rabbi, teacher, administrator very much . . .

> What we need are new ways of organizing Jewish exper-
> ience - new proto-institutions. They may be forming
> now - but I doubt that Reform rabbis will have much to
> do with them.

> The all-pervading unhappiness of the profession seeps
> through - and is disappointing.

> My complaint is that the criteria of placement are
> askew. The most qualified do not always get the best
> pulpits.

> Some of this thought has not been my concern. I have a
> checkered career. I have survived and am about to retire.
> I am not smug about the Jewish future nor indeed about
> America, Israel, or the future of the planet. There were
> those who tried to help me at H.U.C. - but congregants
> are alrightniks and our best efforts lead nowhere.

I would like to comment concerning myself as a rabbi. I
guess that on the whole I am a 'happy rabbi.' I see the
huge pitfalls of any human endeavor - and certainly of
the rabbinate. I am not without anxiety or a sense of
inadequacy in certain areas - but on the whole am very
gratified by my work.

The sense of unhappiness in the rabbinate is due to the
sense of frustration and futility as far as accomplishment is concerned and confusion in goals and objectives.
After 35 years in the active rabbinate one has the feeling that one's labors have been in vain.

I have found in the American rabbinate . . . a ruthless
competitiveness, concern with status, little concern
with the individual and his needs. This includes the
little man in congregations needing counseling and help.
Rather (I have found) a concern with prestige, getting
one's name in the paper, etc., promotion, community recognition, the favors of the powerful within or without
the congregation, and a pursuit of personal ambitions
that make the other person into an 'It.' The only exception has been in Reconstructionism, Mordecai Kaplan
being the example for its disciples.

The UAHC is nothing but an impersonal corporate structure - the CCAR is an irrelevant and dismal failure.
The Seminary is a petty dictatorship.

Jewish life is becoming increasingly secular. The gravest
danger to the future of Judaism is this growing secularization. The Reform rabbis,like their colleagues in the
other branches of Judaism,have unwittingly permitted this
secularization to increase. Often some rabbis are as deeply involved in secular Jewish affairs as in their own congregational family . . .
. . . .
. . . At a time when, for example, the Catholic church is
reconsidering some of its teachings and modernizing its
practices, the Reform movement seems to be moving in the
opposite direction. Latin did not hold the Catholics in
the fold nor will Hebrew save the Jews . . .

Strange as it may seem to some, the role and character
of the American rabbinate for the decades ahead, and
certainly for the coming century, still await formulation and definition. After four thousand years or more,
we are still in a transitional stage. Or perhaps this is
how it has always been and we have not had the experience
immediately, only the recorded impressions and images of
historical accounts.
....
But what of now? What of each day and year through which
we are passing? How do we relate to the uncertainties of
our times? . . .
....
The older generations still attached to the synagogue want
the rabbinate to be what they have grown used to thinking
it must be,- the priesthood, the pastorate, the comforting
agents of Judaism and of God to the individual Jew's
griefs and anxieties. The younger generations of Jews,
having moved far from the synagogue and being imbued with
the need for a better world lest this one destroy itself
in greed and evil, want the rabbinate to be the latter-day
Isaiahs, Jeremiahs, and Micahs.*

One factor tends to influence my responses strongly - I
am stuck off in a small town in a remote, mountainous area,
with no personal contact with my rabbinic colleagues. The
greatest personal problems that my wife and I have are:
    (1) living in a 'goldfish bowl' and
    (2) not having the opportunity to have any close
           friends of our own age and interest - our
           best friends, a couple from seminary, are
           almost 1000 miles away (we virtually grew
           up with them for five years at JIR).
        לֵב we have each other.
But with all the problems and frustrations, I'm glad I'm
a rabbi, and I hope I can keep growing as a Jew and as a
teacher of other Jews.

---

*Rabbi Joseph R. Narot, <u>Temple Israel Bulletin</u> (Temple Israel of Greater
    Miami), January 9, 1970.

I find that many Reform rabbis are acting as if they had
the right to <u>indoctrinate</u> or compel belief or action,
when in fact they have no such right (the traditional
bases for such a right have been undercut by the Reform
Jewish rejection of Bible and Talmud as binding author-
ities, and by the Reform Jewish tendency to pick-and-
choose according to what is subjectively found valuable
or meaningful) - many Reform rabbis are either acting
inconsistently or inauthentically. They, on the other
hand, don't seem to understand what I mean when I argue
for free religion. Therefore, while personally getting
on with my (older) colleagues, philosophically and theo-
logically we are poles apart . . . 'Pray' implies belief
in a personal God who listens. If God (however defined,
understood, conceived) is impersonal then there can be
no prayer - only words spoken by individuals and groups,
<u>for</u> these individuals or groups. This may be of much
value, but is not 'prayer.'

I went directly into Hillel rather than a congregation,
but even there I found that I was in for something of
a shock. I didn't expect quite what it was going to
feel like to be a rabbi. My six-year-old son wants to
grow up to be a garbage man these days. He knows as
much about what it's like to be a garbage man as I did
about what it's like to be a rabbi.*

Up until recently I've been a very happy and fulfilled
rabbi. I'm somewhat disenchanted with the organizations
of Reform Judaism. Not only the Union and the College
. . . take the Conference - the size, the bigness - the
control - the bureaucracy of our institutions . . .
Everybody, the younger rabbis, want these **privileges**
without having earned them - through a little invest-
ment of some time, some hard work, and maybe even a
little agony. It doesn't hurt any in the development
of a human being . . . The synagogue . . . is becoming
more and more of a social action center than it is of
a religiously oriented Jewish educational unit.

---

*Richard J. Israel, "On Being and Becoming a Rabbi," <u>Dimensions</u>,
    Fall 1970, p. 25.

There is a discontentment with the rabbis. The rabbinate
is an ill-defined profession. Things which are primary
to the rabbinate are secondary to the congregation and
vice versa.

I wear a tallith not a stole because a stole is a Protestant cop-out.

I think we're going to become more traditional. I think
we will see more tradition because people want more cer-
tainties, because of the uncertainties around. I'm not
too sure it will be a religious revival _per se_.

I have not answered Question 59 (in questionnaire) as
I am not aware of any crisis in Reform Judaism.

Judaism makes demands upon Jews to make demands upon society . . . (and) upon himself . . . We call that 'pos-
sessed by God.'

The matters raised in this research instrument are no
longer issues. Details of projected HUC-JIR changes
have long ceased to matter to anyone outside a rather
narrow little group. The Reform movement in Judaism
faced a formidable challenge in Post-War America, and
it lost. It offers little or nothing to American Jewry.
It hitches rides on the backs of whatever seems to be
moving at the moment,- otherwise it has neither wheels
nor feet. I rather regret my association with it.

It is my observation as one who has been in the rabbinate for a generation that the synagogue is of declining
importance in the minds of an increasing number of Jews.
The synagogue is no more appreciated than a fraternal
order, Jewish community center, etc. Jewish life is
becoming increasingly secular. The gravest danger to
the future of Judaism is this growing secularization.

The Reform rabbis like their colleagues in the other branches of Judaism have unwittingly permitted this secularization to increase. Often some rabbis are as deeply involved in secular Jewish affairs as in their own congregational family.

Many Reform rabbis have shown great courage in the field of social justice. But there seems to be lacking the courage to more radically modify past practices and create new forms of religious expression.

Reform Judaism has indeed undergone changes, as it should, but most of the changes in recent years have been a reversion to older traditional practices. I have a feeling that many Reform Jews and some rabbis have a guilt feeling,- for having forsaken the religious patterns of the previous generation. At times there seems to be little appreciation for the intellectual insights and creativity of the earlier generations of Reform leaders.

. . . The rabbinate is possible, even indispensable. without God and prayer - if some form of meditation with music, derived from Jewish literature, could be devised: not quite ethical culture nor humanism nor secularism but still very close to all three.

No one group can be an island unto itself and neither can Reform Judaism remain aloof from K'lal Yisrael - the totality of Jewish experience. A responsive, alive Judaism established throughout these United States planned and staffed accordingly, can be an example for the entire Free World Diaspora of how Judaism creatively survived in our technological society.

I am a man of prayer. This questionnaire forced that confession out of me. I pray that our Conference will face the findings of this research project intelligently, courageously, and always with the conviction that Judaism and the people who are its bearers must survive. It is with such a conviction that I faced each question.

The following excerpt was <u>not</u> chosen at random:

> . . . (Rabbi) Gittelsohn is pulling the Conference to-
> gether with ingenious craftsmanship . . . (and) . . .
> (Rabbi) Polish is of equal caliber . . . There's not a
> rabbi in the whole Conference who would not cherish
> either of these men as his own rabbi. If each of us
> could keep our own house in order and at the same
> time contribute so much not only to our own Movement
> but to Judaism in its far-flung reaches as these two
> gentlemen and scholars have done and are doing, we
> would all be very little lower than the angels . . .
> and we in the Reform movement would not be throwing
> the word 'crisis' into each other's faces.

6. Summary Highlights (What Lies Ahead?)

1) On the basis of responses to many questions concerning crisis
   in general, including Reform, over half of Reform rabbis say
   there <u>is</u> a crisis, but when asked if this has anything to do
   with possible anxiety that they might have concerning their
   <u>own</u> situations, only 14% say yes; only 19% say it involves
   any anxiety that resides within <u>their</u> congregations.

2) <u>Uniformities</u> to describe the crisis are not clearly ascertain-
   able. What is often crisis to one is not to another.

3) Three out of four rabbis do not wish to merge with Conservative and/or Orthodoxy (22% <u>are</u> in favor of merging with Conservative Judaism); there is a 60 to 40 split as to what direction to take.

4) Somewhat less than three-fourths of Reform rabbis want to retain a separate Reform movement; 43% want more tradition;
   29% want more humanism. These differences apply to rabbis
   across all age levels.

5) Based on #'s 3 and 4, above, and on other data, it is reasonable to conclude that over 60% of Reform rabbis would give
   serious consideration to merger with Conservative Judaism,
   providing the latter would liberalize. The Reform rabbis
   appear ready to accept more traditionalism.

6) Reform rabbis who would consider merging with Conservative
   Judaism feel that not many of their (the Reform) congregations
   would approve.

7) Reform rabbis are generally opposed to a Community Team Rabbinate; only 18% are "strongly in favor" of the idea.

8) Of those rabbis who are satisfied with their careers, two-to-
   one see "hardly any crisis" in Judaism.

9) Rabbis who see "extreme crisis," seek to veer away from tradition, and move more toward humanism.

10) Most rabbis who sense anxiety within themselves and within
    their congregations as to their true roles are those who tend
    to identify the present situation as being in "extreme crisis."

11) In many ways, what is being identified by many Reform rabbis
    as crisis in Judaism is also being so identified by Christian
    clergy concerning their own religious movements.

12) Reform rabbis give expression to many and varied satisfactions,
dissatisfactions, crises, stablizing forces:

(1) Some express total faith in God and man; others can't
define the term "faith."

(2) Some see Judaism as a failing institution to be the real
crisis; others see crisis only when they see their
colleagues "pressing panic buttons" for little or no
reason.

(3) Some express strong hopes and dreams; for others, God
and Judaism are already moribund.

(4) Some make specific complaints (e.g. inadequate placement
procedures); others see the total Reform establishment
as defective in many ways.

(5) Some are unfulfilled human beings and openly admit it;
some are very fulfilled and all's right with the world.

(6) Some submit incisive, analytical assessments of the
system and make constructive criticisms; others make
mass assaults against the system, but provide no alter-
natives.

(7) Some veer strongly toward traditionalism; others veer
strongly toward humanism.

(8) Some blame most of their ills on inadequate training and
preparation for the job of rabbi; others feel the seminary
did its share, other factors are to blame.

(9) Some blame what is happening outside of Reform for Reform's
ills (e.g., suburbanization, secularization); others
place the blame for their ills on what is happening within the Movement.

(10) Some want merger with Conservative Judaism; others want no God or prayer.

Uniformities are hard to come by. The situation can honestly be described somewhat in the manner of the two Frenchmen musing over a bottle that is exactly half-filled with wine. To one the world is cheery and well-worth living,- the bottle is half _full_. To the other, it is a sad day indeed,- the bottle is half _empty_.

PART III

T H E   R E F O R M   C O N G R E G A T I O N

This chapter deals with the responses of 984 randomly selected members
from 11 Reform congregations throughout the United States. The congregations themselves were carefully selected with respect to region,
size, and date of founding. The individual congregations will not be
identified in this report. While no claim is made as to the representativeness of the sample drawn, it can be said that the congregations cover the gamut of Reform life in the United States from large
urban East and West coast synagogues of long standing to small "rural"
congregations in the South to recently established ones in the sub-
urbs sprinkled throughout the country. A second point is worth
noting with respect to representativeness. Our analysis is more concerned with differences among Reform Jews with respect to certain
characteristics than with a purely descriptive statement. In sociological terms, we are interested more in the relationship between
variables, such as the relationship between one's religious background and attitudes toward Reform, than we are with simple descrip-
tion. The former, in addition to being more valuable, permits a
certain amount of flexibility in sample selection.

CHAPTER 11: SOME DEMOGRAPHIC CHARACTERISTICS OF REFORM CONGREGANTS

1. Age, Marital and Family Profiles.

Our respondents range in age from 20 to over 80, with the modal age
in the 40-44 year bracket (Figure 29). Fifteen percent are under

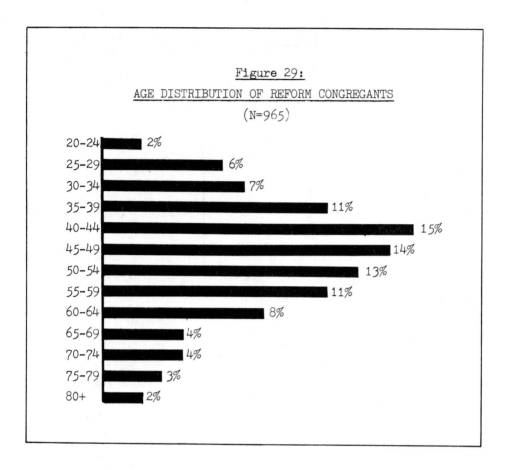

Figure 29:

AGE DISTRIBUTION OF REFORM CONGREGANTS

(N=965)

Age	Percent
20-24	2%
25-29	6%
30-34	7%
35-39	11%
40-44	15%
45-49	14%
50-54	13%
55-59	11%
60-64	8%
65-69	4%
70-74	4%
75-79	3%
80+	2%

35 and 41% are under 45. Almost a third are between 50 and 64, and less than 15% are over 65. The relatively small number of members under 35 does not necessarily suggest that Reform congregations are about to go under from lack of new blood. It is more likely due to the fact that many Jews in America today, Reform being no exception, often join congregations in their own right only when their children are ready for religious school. Subsequent data support this hypothesis.

The respondents in our sample were reached by mail questionnaires,
with a request that they be filled out by the male head of the
family. As a consequence, 85% of our respondents are males and
only 15% are females (presumably most are heads of families with
no male present).*   The responses we will be examining, then, are
overwhelmingly those of men. No breakdowns by sex will be offered
in this report, since preliminary comparisons indicate no substantial
differences between the sexes on most major issues.

Most respondents (85%) are married, with small numbers of widowed,
separated, or divorced. A bare handful, 3%, are single, again suggesting that membership is very much tied to family considerations. This
interpretation is borne out further by the finding that 90% of the
respondents have children. Family size is rather small, the modal
number being 2, although 36% have 3 or 4 children per family unit.
The fact that almost two-thirds of the respondents have less than
three children is probably related to the age distribution already
noted. There may be a trend under way toward smaller-sized families,-
a popular pattern a few years ago, but the more likely explanation is
that many of the family units represented have not yet been "completed"
(Figures 30 and 31).

Two out of three respondents have at least one child living at home
and 41% have at least one child living away from home. This again is
an indication of the relative youth of our respondent group. They tend
on the whole to be the parents of pre-adult children. This is seen more
directly in the finding that 43% of the respondents have children enrolled in elementary school, while only 28% have children enrolled in
high school. One out of four is the parent of a college student and
one out of ten has a child enrolled in graduate school.

---

*It should be noted that a few women sent in letters objecting to our
 presumption that the male was the head of the family, and thus
 were invoking their prerogatives to complete the questionnaire
 themselves. Less than a dozen made this known to us. Possibly
 more felt that way. It is a note not to be by-passed.

213

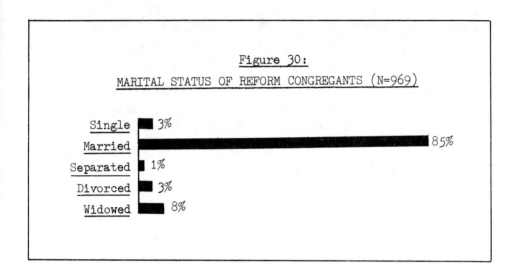

Figure 30:

MARITAL STATUS OF REFORM CONGREGANTS (N=969)

Single 3%
Married 85%
Separated 1%
Divorced 3%
Widowed 8%

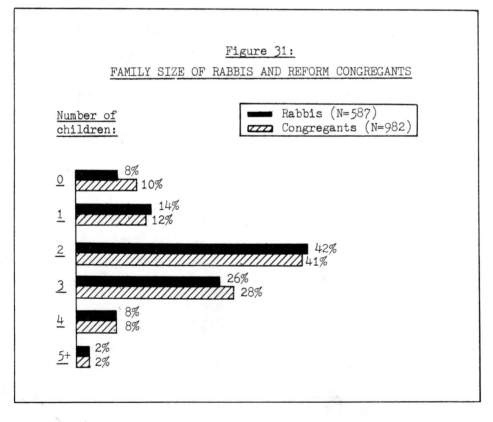

Figure 31:

FAMILY SIZE OF RABBIS AND REFORM CONGREGANTS

Number of
children:

Rabbis (N=587)
Congregants (N=982)

0 8%
   10%
1 14%
   12%
2 42%
   41%
3 26%
   28%
4 8%
   8%
5+ 2%
   2%

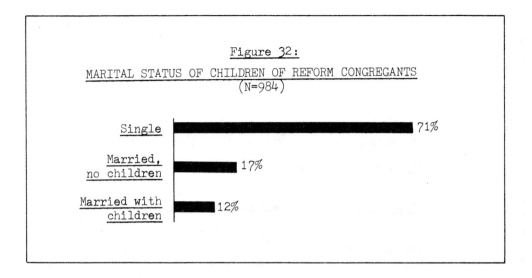

Figure 32:

MARITAL STATUS OF CHILDREN OF REFORM CONGREGANTS
(N=984)

Single   71%

Married, no children   17%

Married with children   12%

In a similar vein, 71% of the respondents have children who are still unmarried, and 17% have daughters- or sons-in-law. Only one in ten is a grandparent (Figure 32).

Generally speaking then, the members of the 11 Reform synagogues in our sample are on the younger side and tend to be the heads of young families.

The relationship between synagogue membership and the religious education of the young is revealed in Figure 33. Almost all (95%) of the children in the elementary school population are enrolled in religious school, two-thirds of those who could have been confirmed, were confirmed, and better than one-third of those who could have been either Bar or Bas Mitzvah were.

Almost 60% of the questionnaires returned by congregants contained comments regarding religious school. Virtually all were expressions

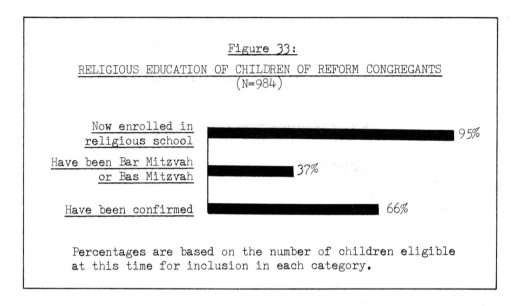

Figure 33:

RELIGIOUS EDUCATION OF CHILDREN OF REFORM CONGREGANTS
(N=984)

Now enrolled in religious school — 95%

Have been Bar Mitzvah or Bas Mitzvah — 37%

Have been confirmed — 66%

Percentages are based on the number of children eligible at this time for inclusion in each category.

of dissatisfaction, although a goodly number still felt compelled to add something akin to this thought, "It is still not a complete waste of time and our kids have to know they're Jewish." And some additional randomly selected comments from parents read as follows:

Religious school has made no impact on our children as far as we can judge. Our oldest child married a non-Jew and practices no religion. The others hated attending religious school and want no part of its youth programs and refuse to join us in attending services. They seem to exist totally in a world that identifies neither Jew nor Gentiles . . . However we're glad we are temple members (although inactive ones) and that we gave our children the opportunity to belong too.

Maybe we didn't do such a good job with our children at home . . . at least they didn't learn from us to question the existence of God. Thanks to our religious school, for our children at least, there is no God . . .

It only takes one bad parent or one bad teacher, to
ruin a child. Parents can't be changed, but teachers
can. They can be replaced, but not by our Rabbi.

Most of the Sunday School teachers are pure fakes.
They are ill-prepared to teach in a Jewish religious
program. They make no bones about it . . . It's an
economic thing with them, and our loss.

. . . one of us tries to take them to all the High
Holy Day Services as well as many of the Friday night
services. I want them to be fully exposed to their
religion in the hope that they will be proud of their
heritage and be familiar with their religion and in
time make better Jews than my wife and myself.

Sunday school has not been organized in a manner to
stimulate the children. Our Sunday school is taught
by professionals who do not seem to capture the interest or imagination of the children.

We live 70 miles from X City - we have been taking
our children to Religious School in X City for 13
years.

I often think the minimum requirement for a teacher
to teach in our Sunday School is that he or she
should have a positive Jewish attitude. I would
settle for this even if our kids learned nothing
. . . (which) is about all they do learn.

2. Intermarriage and Mixed Marriage.

The overwhelming number of Reform Jews are the children of two
Jewish parents (Tables 31 and 32). Only 4% are the offspring of
mixed marriages (where one spouse is non-Jewish and non-converted),
1% are converts from non-Jewish homes, and 1% identify themselves
as non-Jewish (probably the non-converted spouse of a Jew who

---

Table 31:
PRESENT LEGAL JEWISH STATUS OF REFORM CONGREGANTS
(N=980)

Both parents Jewish———94%

Mother only ——————— 2%

Father only ——————— 2%

Converted ———————— 1%

Not Jewish———————— 1%

Table 32:
PRESENT LEGAL JEWISH STATUS OF SPOUSE (RE: TABLE 31)
(N=937)

By birth——————————— 89%

By conversion——————— 6%

Not Jewish————————— 5%

---

responded in his or her place). Where 98% have (or had) parents who were either born Jewish or had converted, 95% are married to spouses who are Jews by birthright or conversion. Some 89% are married to Jewish spouses and another 6% have spouses who converted. Table 33 informs us that the intermarriage rate and the mixed-marriage rate have increased in the younger age congregants as compared to their older counterparts. More than one in three Jewish respondents aged 20 to 24 is now married to a spouse

who was born non-Jewish. One in four of this age group is married
to a spouse who has not converted. This is a very recent development. The figures for the 25-29 age group are not much different
from those in older brackets. To be sure, the sample involved is
rather small, and possibly not a completely reliable base for per-
centaging. So it may turn out to be a false alarm. A larger
data base is urgently needed to verify the trend. On the other
hand, the finding is consistent with some other research findings
on the subject.

While we are on the subject of mixed marriages, we have some interesting data with respect to some family life patterns with regard
to religiosity (Table 34).

Table 33:

AGE OF CONGREGANT AND RELIGION OF SPOUSE

Age categories of congregants:

RELIGION OF SPOUSE ↓	20-29 (N=68)	30-39 (N=175)	40-49 (N=177)	50-59 (N=228)	60-69 (N=108)	70-79 (N=54)	80+ (N=13)
	%	%	%	%	%	%	%
Born Jewish	82	89	87	90	93	87	100
Converted	9	6	8	4	4	3	0
Not Jewish	9	5	4	6	4	7	0

TABLE 34:

SOME FAMILY RELIGIOUS PATTERNS

INVOLVING MIXED MARRIAGES

			N:
1.	Married by a rabbi.	41%	(44)
2.	Children attend (or have attended) Jewish religious school.	81%	(32)
3.	Children attend (or have attended) non-Jewish religious school.	30%*	(30)
4.	The non-Jewish spouse participates in synagogue activities (e.g., Sisterhood, etc.)	63%	(43)
5.	The non-Jewish spouse attends Reform religious services.	69%	(43)
6.	The non-Jewish spouse attends his or her own church services.	33%**	(43)
7.	Children attend church services with their non-Jewish parent.	29%	(34)

* The fact that Item 2 and Item 3 add up to more than
100% is not explainable by any data at our disposal.
Is it possible some children attend or have attended
both Jewish and non-Jewish religious schools? Is it
possible that children from the same family attend
different religious schools? Or has a child attended
Jewish and non-Jewish schools at different times?

** Items 5 and 6 go beyond 100%. Again, no explanation.
(Possibly a little ecumenicism.)

The reader is reminded once again of the small sample involved. But if the mixed marriage rate as described in Table 34 is an increasing trend, these last figures may possibly suggest the new profile of the Reform family, with 3 of our 10 children attending church and receiving non-Jewish religious instruction.* Another finding, not from this study, but appropriate to it is the fact that "more than 42% of the spouses who had contracted inter-faith (inter- and/or mixed) marriage were themselves offspring of a mixed marriage."**

3. Educational Attainments.

If Jews are the most highly educated of religious groups in the United States, Reform Jews most likely make up its most highly educated segment (Figure 34). Only 11%, a mere one in ten, have not attended college, and only three in ten have not graduated from a college or university. Moreover, of those who have graduated, more go on to acquire at least one additional degree beyond a Bachelor's degree than those who do not. Some 35% of our respondents have advanced degrees. Spouses (amost all women),

---

* Census data have indicated that 58% of Jews who intermarry or mix-marry do so with Protestants, and that 42% do so with Catholics. ("Religion Reported by the Civilian Population of the United States, March, 1958" Current Population Reports: Population Characteristics, U. S. Bureau of the Census: Series 20, No. 79, February 2, 1958). (Several sociological studies have also found that Jewish males intermarry and/or mix-marry almost three times as often than do Jewish females.)

** Alfred J. Prince, "A Study of 194 Cross-Religion Marriages, Family Life Coordinator," January 1962, p. 4.

don't do badly either. The figures show that 38% have had some
college experience, 32% are college graduates, and 13% have advanced
graduate or professional degrees. Since the national figure for
white female graduates is in the neighborhood of 8%, the figure of

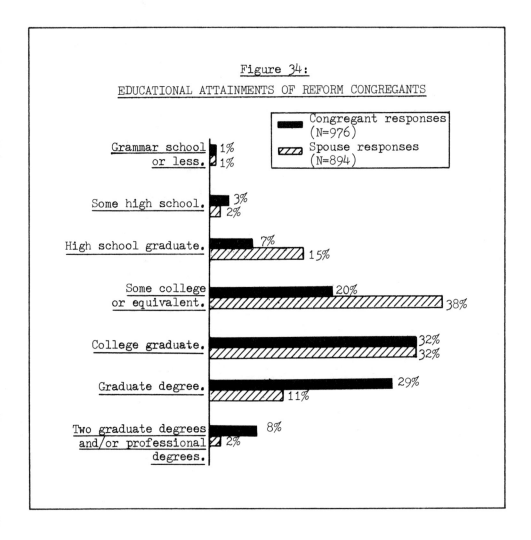

Figure 34:

EDUCATIONAL ATTAINMENTS OF REFORM CONGREGANTS

Table 35:

COMPARATIVE OCCUPATIONAL DISTRIBUTION

OF CONGREGANT AND SPOUSE

	Respondent (N=888)	Spouse (N=884)
	%	%
Professional	47	20
(Self-employed	24)	3)
(Salaried	23)	17)
Executive	29	3
Merchant	14	3
White collar	7	8
Blue collar	2	2
Not in labor force	10*	64

* Although 10% of the congregants are retired,
  their occupations prior to retirement are
  included in the above data.

32% representing our female congregant sample is nothing short of
an eye-opener! Some 69% of male congregants and 45% of female
completed four years or more of college. The national average
for those who have completed four years or more of college is 14%.**

4. The Occupational Picture.

And just as Reform Jews are highly educated, they also hold jobs
at the top of the occupational ladder. Table 35 and Figure 35 tell

** "Educational Attainment in 30 Selected Standard Metropolitan Areas:
    1970," Current Population Reports: Population Characteristics,
    U. S. Dept of Commerce, Bureau of the Census, Series P-20,
    No. 277, November 1971, p. 9.

this story.   Again a phenomenal story about American Reform Jews.
As Figure 35 shows, almost one in four is a self-employed professional person, and almost half are either professional or managerial,-
clearly on top of the occupational ladder for the country as a whole.
The occupation that was once the chief mainstay for the American
Jew - the merchant - is now the occupation of only 14% of our entire
sample of Reform congregants.   The working class labor force is
represented by **only** 9% of Reform congregants,- 7% white collar, **and**
2% **blue collar.**

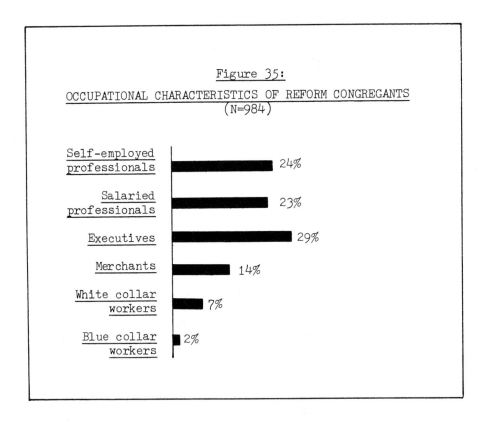

Figure 35:
OCCUPATIONAL CHARACTERISTICS OF REFORM CONGREGANTS
(N=984)

Self-employed professionals   24%
Salaried professionals   23%
Executives   29%
Merchants   14%
White collar workers   7%
Blue collar workers   2%

224

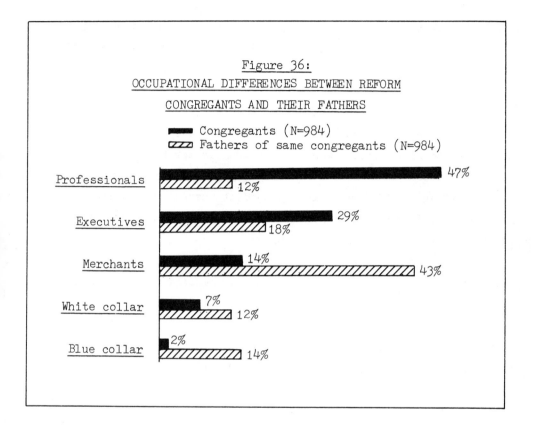

Figure 36:
OCCUPATIONAL DIFFERENCES BETWEEN REFORM
CONGREGANTS AND THEIR FATHERS

■ Congregants (N=984)
▨ Fathers of same congregants (N=984)

Professionals — 47% / 12%

Executives — 29% / 18%

Merchants — 14% / 43%

White collar — 7% / 12%

Blue collar — 2% / 14%

Moreover, 20% of the spouses are professionals, the majority of these
(17%) are salaried and are mostly teachers or social workers. All
in all, 36% of the spouses have jobs. After the salaried professionals,
come white-collar job-holders (8%).

The occupational differences between fathers and sons are striking
(Figure 36). Although Reform Jews are upwardly mobile, it is clearly
not a case of rags to riches. If only 26% had working class fathers,
then we have a clue to the incredible educational and occupational
distribution of the sons. Even assuming that their fathers sacrificed
more and that the sons worked harder than their respective non-Jewish
counterparts to get where they are today, they still had an obvious

competitive advantage over most young non-Jewish men and women during their formative years, coming as they did from the then comparatively small Jewish middle class.

But if the story is not out of Horatio Alger, it _is_ one of "making it." It should be noted that 51% of the professionals in our sample had fathers who were either owners, managers, or merchants, and 49% of all our respondents have higher prestige occupations than did their fathers. Only 8% of all respondents have lower prestige jobs than their fathers had. Some of these may well be young men who have not yet made final job decisions.

5. Income.

With such high educational attainments, and with such equally high occupational levels, it should come as no surprise to note the affluence of Reform congregants. (Please refer to Figure 3, p. 26.)

By way of some additional highlights, let us note the following:

1. Only 9% of our congregant sample earn less than $10,000 annually.

2. Only 21% earn less than $15,000.

3. Some 40% earn over $30,000.

4. Over 20% earn $50,000 or more.

There is no question that Reform Jews occupy an enviable place indeed in American society. And with this comes, as we shall see later, a certain amount of conservatism on social and political matters. And while Reform Jews may still be more liberal than their non-Jewish counterparts, nevertheless it should not be overlooked as a possible source of strain and tension between affluent and complacent laymen, who like things just as they are,

and the younger members of the rabbinate, who are increasingly
questioning the "status-quo" life-styles of so many Jewish leaders
and Jewish organizations, and especially with so many of their
own congregants.

6.   Summary Highlights (Reform Congregants: Demography).

1) Modal age of Reform congregants is in the 40-44 bracket;
    85% are married; 90% have 2 to 4 children, most of whom
    are either in religious school, or have been Bar/Bas Mitzvah
    and/or Confirmed.

2) Most parental comments regarding religious school are
    negative.

3) More than one in three Jewish respondents aged 20 to 24
    are now married to a spouse who was born non-Jewish; one in
    four of this age group is married to a spouse who has not
    converted. The overall sample is small.

4) Intermarriage and mixed marriage appear to be increasing.

5) Concerning mixed marriages (based on a small sample): 41%
    were married by a rabbi; 81% of their children attend Jewish
    religious school; 30% attend non-Jewish religious school
    (some overlapping); 69% of non-Jewish mates attend Reform
    services; 33% of non-Jewish mates attend Church services
    (overlapping); 29% attend Church services with the non-
    Jewish parent.

6) Reform Jews are highly educated; 32% of male and 32% of female congregants are at least college graduates (over twice as many as for national white population); 37% of male and 13% of female congregants hold one or more graduate and/or professional degrees.

7) Some 47% are professionals, as are 20% of their mates; 29% are executives; 14% merchants; only 2% blue collar. Most working spouses are teachers or social workers.

8) Some 9% of our congregants earn less than $10,000 annually; 21% earn between $10,000 and $15,000; 9% earn between $15,000 and $30,000; 40% earn over $30,000; another 20% earn $50,000 or more.

CHAPTER 12: RELIGIOUS AFFILIATION PATTERNS OF REFORM CONGREGANTS

1. Parents' Religious Backgrounds.

Only 34% of the members of the 11 congregations studied were themselves brought up in Reform homes. Two out of three, in other
words, come from other backgrounds (Figure 37). We see, then, that
many Reform Jews come from a non-Reform background. This does not
mean, however, that the 66% who shifted actually had belonged to
other (Orthodox or Conservative) congregations in their own right.
Quite the opposite, in fact. Only 23% had ever actually belonged
to a non-Reform congregation. Some 6% were Orthodox and 17% were
Conservative. Defection, therefore, is not the big source of new
membership in Reform congregations. If only 34% are Reform Jews
by upbringing, and 72% have never belonged to anything but a Reform
congregation, then it follows that the remaining 38% had either
shifted to Reform or their present affiliation with a synagogue
may be their first affiliation. The 19% who do not identify their
parent's religious backgrounds include many different possibilities.
Primarily, of course, most are from intermarriage and/or mixed-
marriage families where no religious practices were observed, or
where one or two different religious backgrounds were known to be
existent, but only dormantly so. The important thing is that the
congregant had no clear identification with any religion.

One congregant writes:

> My father's mother was Jewish, and although he
> considered himself Jewish, he never practiced it.
> My mother was born a Baptist, and we actually be-
> longed to the Baptist church, but only nominally
> . . . I did attend Sunday School. There was no
> other church - and no Temple. My wife came from a
> Conservative Jewish family, and I converted -

I don't know from what, . . . But it wasn't comfortable growing up not belonging. My Judaism is now one of my best feelings. . .

2. Affiliation with Reform.

We note (Figure 38), that of those from Reform backgrounds, 23% had joined in their own right while they were still single, while only 8% of those from non-Reform backgrounds did so at that time. And while 19% of those with Reform backgrounds joined when it was time for their oldest child to enter religious school, the figure for those from non-Reform backgrounds was 34%.

Finally, there are differences in the affiliation patterns (Table 36), of those who had come from other religious affiliations. Of those congregants who had never belonged to any other but a Reform

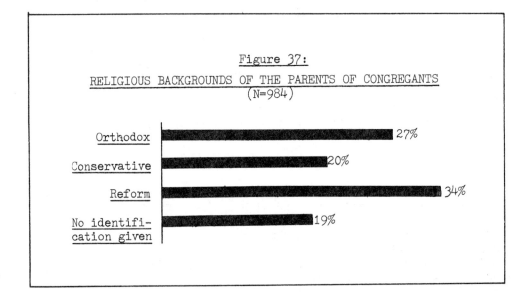

Figure 37:
RELIGIOUS BACKGROUNDS OF THE PARENTS OF CONGREGANTS
(N=984)

Orthodox 27%
Conservative 20%
Reform 34%
No identifi-
cation given 19%

230

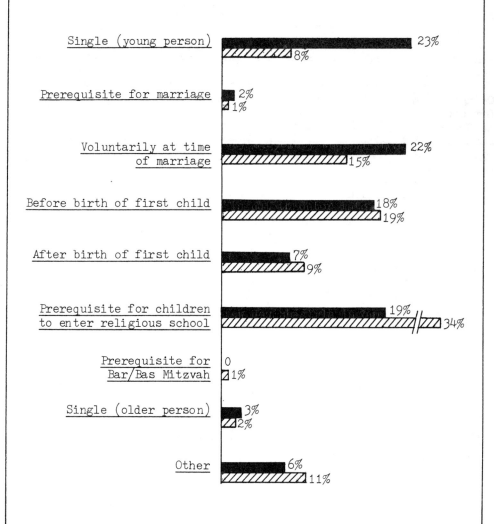

Figure 38:

REFORM AND NON-REFORM BACKGROUNDS AT TIME

OF FIRST SYNAGOGUE AFFILIATION

Congregants from Reform background only (N=318)
Congregants not from Reform background (N=666)

Single (young person) — 23% / 8%

Prerequisite for marriage — 2% / 1%

Voluntarily at time of marriage — 22% / 15%

Before birth of first child — 18% / 19%

After birth of first child — 7% / 9%

Prerequisite for children to enter religious school — 19% / 34%

Prerequisite for Bar/Bas Mitzvah — 0 / 1%

Single (older person) — 3% / 2%

Other — 6% / 11%

Table 36:

AFFILIATION PATTERNS OF REFORM CONGREGANTS
AND EARLY RELIGIOUS BACKGROUND

CONGREGANT'S AFFILIATION PATTERN	Father's affiliation:			
	Reform	Orthodox	Conservative	Unaffiliated or non-Jewish
Reform only. (N=695)	45%	19%	15%	21%
Changed from Orthodox to Reform. (N=63)	-	86%	3%	11%
Changed from Conservative to Reform. (N=172)	-	-	38%	62%
Changed from unaffiliated or non-Jewish* to Reform.(N=39)	-	-	-	100%

* The non-Jewish (non-converted) spouse of a mixed marriage.

congregation, some 19% have (or had) Orthodox fathers, 15% have (or had) Conservative fathers, and 21% have (or had) unaffiliated fathers. Congregants who have shifted to Reform from previous personal affiliations with Orthodox congregations had grown up in households where the affiliation was 86% Orthodox, 3% Conservative, and 11% unaffiliated or non-Jewish. Congregants whose first personal affiliation was with a Conservative congregation and who subsequently shifted to Reform came from homes that were affiliated with a Conservative congregation in 38% of the cases, or were unaffiliated or non-Jewish in 62% of the cases.

The reader is again asked to note the three different variables that are treated in Table 36: (1) The branch of Judaism in which the congregant had been reared, (2) The congregant's own first affiliation, and (3) The congregant's shift pattern to his present Reform affiliation. In many cases, of course, the congregant has been in Reform all his life, and no shift has taken place.

3. Summary Highlights (Reform Congregants: Religious Affiliation Patterns).

1) Only one-third of Reform congregants (based on our sample), come from Reform homes.

2) Only 23% of Reform congregants had previously been affiliated with a non-Reform congregation.

3) Of those who are affiliated with Reform, 19% joined in anticipation of the first-born child; 29% joined when their oldest child entered religious school.

4) Religious backgrounds of parents of Reform congregants are 34% Reform; 20% Conservative; 27% Orthodox; 19% no identification given.

5) Of those congregants who were <u>always</u> Reform, 45% come from Reform backgrounds, 15% from Conservative backgrounds, 19% from Orthodox backgrounds, and 21% from unaffiliated or from non-Jewish backgrounds.

CHAPTER 13: HOW JEWISH ARE REFORM JEWS?: JEWISH CONSCIOUSNESS

1. Jewish Consciousness.

How do Reform Jews see themselves vis-à-vis the rest of the world?
How concerned are they with maintaining a specifically Jewish
cultural and religious heritage that is distinct from that of
their neighbors?

To begin with, congregants were asked to look at eight reasonably
common components of Jewishness (Figure 39), and to rate the amount
of importance they place in each. The response pattern clearly
indicates that whereas almost everyone stresses the importance of
being ethical, only about half respond that belief in God is very
important. Indeed, "Jewish identification" is in second place,
with 62% endorsing it. While it may come as little surprise to
some that only one in five think of Jewish study or synagogue worship
as being very important, it may be a big surprise to note the relatively small number who mention charity as very important, particularly since social action is slightly more favored as very important.
Finally, about half think that support of Israel is important. These
are considerably less than those who talk about Jewish identification.

An intensive study of the response patterns and priorities which
have come forth on this one battery of questions may yield significant insights to the major trends of contemporary American Reform
Judaism.

It needs to be noted here that most of the written comments which
accompanied this question, and there are many, emphasize how unimportant and unnecessary attendance at services are in terms of being
"good Jews." A substantial number of respondents seem to focus

on the role of the children on this point. It is a "for the
children's sake, we go" type of theme.

Many such comments were forthcoming. With few exceptions, most are
variations of the same theme. Rationalizations abound.

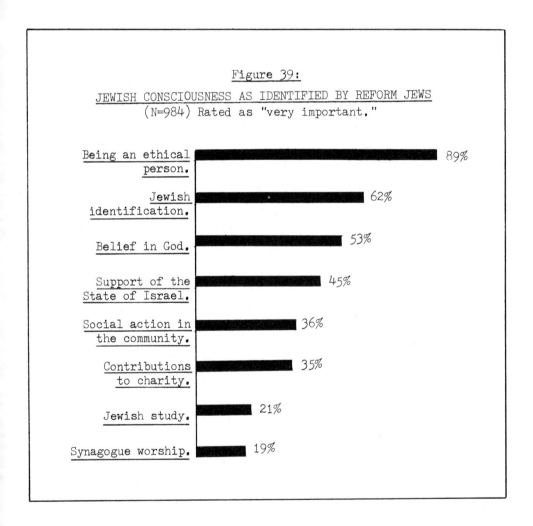

Figure 39:

JEWISH CONSCIOUSNESS AS IDENTIFIED BY REFORM JEWS
(N=984) Rated as "very important."

Being an ethical person. 89%

Jewish identification. 62%

Belief in God. 53%

Support of the State of Israel. 45%

Social action in the community. 36%

Contributions to charity. 35%

Jewish study. 21%

Synagogue worship. 19%

We are new members from an Orthodox Congregation
. . . I joined because I hoped my teenagers would
become active in religious school and youth group.

Now our daughters are finished with religious school
there is a lack of interest in temple activities.

. . . of course we were active for our children's
sake. We even went to services . . . but now let
some of the younger mothers (parents) take our place
. . . they have children to think of. Our children
are no longer with us . . .

And here is an interview excerpt with a woman who came with some
Sisterhood friends to a Regional Biennial:

Going to Temple is hard . . . we send our children
to Sunday School and they have services for them
there . . . of course we go on Rosh Hashanah and
Yom Kippur and our children know they're Jewish . . .
Would they (the children) be any more Jewish if we
(the parents) went to Temple every week?

Interviewer: How . . . would your rabbi answer this
question, if you asked him?

Congregant: You know what he would say . . . He
would want us all to come. He's right, of course
. . .(but) he once said the Jewish home is even
more important than going to services. And we
have a Jewish home. (Then a brief interval of con-
versation on many topics-)

Interviewer: Incidentally, do you have a Sabbath
Service at home?

Congregant: We do when we can. Of course, it's
basketball time now, so our two older boys can't
wait for that (the games are on Friday nights at
the high school). Otherwise it's other dates, you
know . . .

Interviewer: Do you kindle the Sabbath candles?

Congregant: No, we do it in our temple.

Interviewer: Does your temple distribute Hanukkah candles and little metal menorahs to the students in religious school?

Congregant: I don't think so. They used to bring home pictures, you know, of Queen Esther . . .

2. Jewish Identification.

Why does "Jewish identification" rank so high as a Jewish concern to Reform Jews? The term was not defined for the respondent when the question was asked. Hence each respondent needed to define it for himself as he confronted the term. How do our congregants define the term for themselves as they respond to it? We see that it is important not only from responses to the attitude battery in Figure 39, but from other data as well. Thus, despite what we have seen of the relative indifference on the part of many congregants to religious matters, we note that nearly two-thirds give as a "very important" reason for joining a congregation such responses as "desire for formal Jewish education of children," and "we want children to remain within the faith." Is it "faith" or "the faith?" Or is it something else? Let us look at some pertinent questions which were asked, and to which our congregants indicate a "strongly agree" response pattern.

We need to study the five statements which are presented in Table 37. They are significant in themselves even without the responses. They are statements (slightly paraphrased), made to the writer by men who are trustees from five different Reform synagogues in vastly different parts of the country. This was how these synagogue trustees identified "Jewish identification." If, as trustees, these lay leaders are holding something in trust for

Table 37:

CONGREGANTS EXPRESS THEMSELVES ON "JEWISH IDENTIFICATION"

		PERCENT EXPRESSING AGREEMENT
1.	When you get right down to it, the differences among the three major religions are not very great. I remain a Jew because it is simply the most convenient thing to do.	11% (N=940)
2.	It's not important which religion you belong to, just as long as you maintain membership in one of the faiths.	25% (N=934)
3.	I feel that any attempt to identify ourselves with and as a "Jewish community" is undesirable and does us more harm than good, inasmuch as we don't live in isolated solidarity, and are subject to the same authority as the general society.	28% (N=947)
4.	I really see no meaning to "Jewish community" in my life. I am an American with my basic commitment to my country. I may or may not have more to do with Jewish people, but even if I do, I don't see where this makes us any separate "Jewish community."	34% (N=947)
5.	People who think that American Jews are primarily Americans are mistaken. Basically, Jews are different from other Americans and Judaism is different from other religions.	28% (N=935)

their fellow-Jews, what is it that they are holding in trust?
Certainly it does not appear that our overall sample of Reform
congregants is endorsing in an overwhelming manner the beliefs
of these five trustees. Yet, the memberships of five different
synagogues have democratically elected these men to serve them
as their leaders in their immediate world of Judaism.

In a comment quoted earlier regarding the religious school teacher,
it will be recalled that a congregant had expressed himself as
follows:

> I think the minimum requirement for a (Religious
> school) teacher . . . is that he or she should have
> a positive Jewish attitude . . .

The implication of the congregant who uttered the above words is
that the Rabbi is responsible for this. After all, it is the
Rabbi who hires or at least must approve of those who teach under
him in the religious school. Let us assume that this congregant
is reasonably representative of most of his fellow-congregants on
this particular point. One wonders, then, if this same congregant
holds himself and his fellow-congregants equally responsible that
a trustee should also hold a positive Jewish attitude as a minimum
requirement as a trustee? And who is responsible for having
elected the person if he does not possess this minimum requirement?
Hardly the rabbi.

As for the views of the rank and file of Reform congregants with
regard to "Jewish identification," the responses itemized in Table
37 speak for themselves, - both for the elected trustees who expressed
their views, and for a goodly number of congregants as well.

3. "Particularism-Universalism Index."

By taking the responses on <u>consciousness</u> and <u>identification</u>, and a few others, a combined index was produced which we shall call the "Particularism-Universalism Index." We shall regard those who score high at one end of the continuum to be persons whose primary loyalties are to Jews, Judaism, Jewishness and Jewish culture. They may even be viewed, in effect, as people who deny that all Americans are the same and opt for a cultural pluralist definition of the situation. At the opposite end are the people who represent what used to be regarded by many as the standard Reform position,- that American Jews were Jewish Americans, or, as viewed by some,- Americans of the Mosaic faith. On the basis of these definitions, Figure 40 portrays how our congregants are distributed along the particularism-universalism continuum.

The importance of this formulation lies not so much in the exact numbers in each category (the cutting points could have been different, thus yielding different distributions). Rather, it is in the <u>differences</u> between those who score high and those who score low with respect to <u>background characteristics</u> on the one hand and various <u>attitudes</u> on the other. In other words, the important question is not how <u>many</u> people score high on an arbitrary scale, but <u>who</u> these people are and how are they different from others? This is the procedure throughout this section, and indeed throughout the study.*

---

* See Charles S. Liebman, "A Sociological Analysis of Contemporary Orthodoxy," <u>Judaism: A Quarterly Journal of Jewish Life and Thought</u>, Vol. 13, No. 3, Summer Issue, 1964, for a reasonably similar break-down of Orthodox Jews into four categories on the basis of background characteristics and attitudes. (Professor Liebman does not deal with quantitative data in the formulation of his categories.)

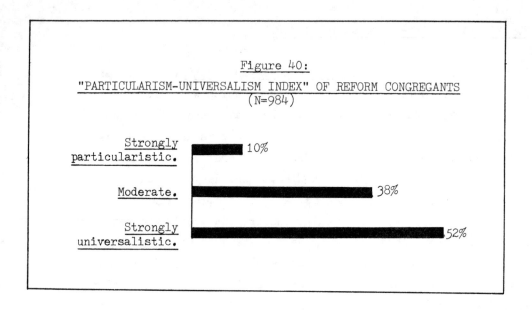

Figure 40:
"PARTICULARISM-UNIVERSALISM INDEX" OF REFORM CONGREGANTS
(N=984)

Strongly particularistic. 10%

Moderate. 38%

Strongly universalistic. 52%

Having said this, let us look at some of the differences. Differences in age, for instance, will provide many readers with a surprise. There is a fairly steady increase in particularism as we move from older to younger members. Many of these younger members, it should be recalled, are the very ones who are most likely to marry non-Jews, yet the same cohort scores highest on feelings of Jewish separateness and uniqueness. Admittedly, the absolute number is not very high, but it is twice that of the oldest age groups among Reform congregations (Figure 41). In other words, there is a suggestion here that younger Reform Jews do not share to the same extent the attitudes and behaviors of many of their parents and grandparents that Jews should pursue a non-conspicuous life-style. On the other hand, almost half of even the youngest members endorse the universalistic mode.

As one might expect, Reform Jews from Orthodox backgrounds are more
likely than those from Reform backgrounds to have particularistic
views (14%). As expected, those from Conservative homes are some-

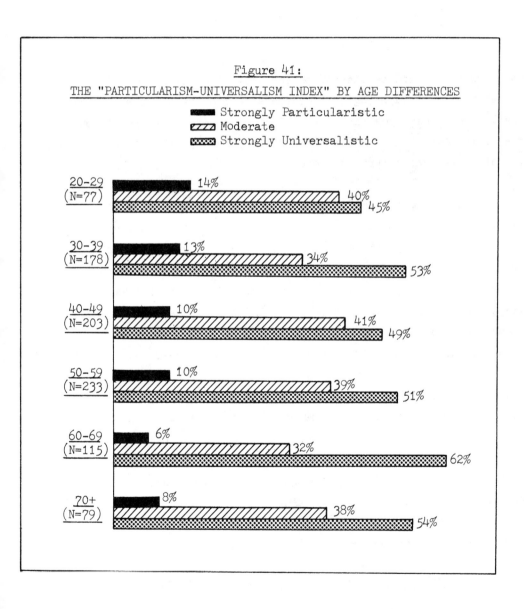

Figure 41:

THE "PARTICULARISM-UNIVERSALISM INDEX" BY AGE DIFFERENCES

■ Strongly Particularistic
▨ Moderate
▥ Strongly Universalistic

20-29
(N=77)
14%
40%
45%

30-39
(N=178)
13%
34%
53%

40-49
(N=203)
10%
41%
49%

50-59
(N=233)
10%
39%
51%

60-69
(N=115)
6%
32%
62%

70+
(N=79)
8%
38%
54%

where in the middle (11%). Those from Reform backgrounds are least
particularistic (7%). This may be due to a greater degree of
emphasis on Jewish culture and nationality that might be expected
from Orthodox and Conservative backgrounds. It may be due, also,
to the fact that many Reform members from Orthodox and Conservative
backgrounds are more likely to be first-generation, or at most
second-generation Americans.

Even more to be expected is the potentially stronger relationship
between a person's upbringing in respect to Zionism and particularist
views. The percentages range from 21% for those coming from strongly
pro-Zionist parents to 2% for those whose parents were strongly anti-
Zionist. Nothing surprising here.

There are some regional differences as well. Reform Jews are somewhat more likely to be particularistic if they grew up on the Pacific
coast (14%). Other regional distributions are Middle Atlantic (12%),
abroad (12%), or the North Central region (11%). Jews are very low
on particularism amongst those who were raised in the Southeast
(4%), or South Central states (6%). This in large measure reflects
the much greater pressure on conformity to majority group values
in the South, particularly in the presence of a white-black dichotomy.

So much for a few background characteristics as they are related to
the cluster of values that by common definition would be labelled
particularistic. Now we need to look at the attitudinal and
behavioral correlates of this value cluster. In the following pages
we have tried to summarize a vast amount of data concerning Jewish
attitudes and behaviors in terms of our "Particularistic-Universalistic
Index." It is an unusually long table of statistics, and it is
interspersed with commentary.

Table 38:

ATTITUDES AND BEHAVIORS OF REFORM JEWS:
"THE PARTICULARISTIC-UNIVERSALISTIC INDEX"
(N=984)

SP - Strongly particularistic (N=98)
M - Moderate (N=374)
SU - Strongly universalistic (N=512)

(Percent indicating "very important" as reason for affiliating with Reform)	SP	M	SU
1. They wanted their children to remain in the faith.	81%	65%	49%
2. They are religious Jews.	27%	17%	12%
3. They want their children to be Bar/Bas Mitzvah.	40%	30%	18%
4. They want their children to be confirmed.	38%	36%	29%

The smaller spread with respect to confirmation as opposed to Bar Mitzvah is an indication of those who consitute the largest number of universalists, viz., those with earlier Reform backgrounds and/or orientations.

(Yiddish and Hebrew)	SP	M	SU
5. Speak Yiddish reasonably well.	14%	11%	7%
6. Read prayerbook Hebrew very well.	22%	9%	5%

The data tell us that one out of four particularists cannot read Hebrew at all. Approximately half of the universalists cannot read any Hebrew. Among the

Table 38 (continued)
SP - Strongly particularistic
M - Moderate
SU - Strongly universalistic

universalists the rate is <u>five in one hundred.</u> Here we may
have a rather realistic clue why some Jews feel the need to
affiliate with Reform. It, of all groups, makes the least
demand on its members with respect to reading Hebrew at
worship services. Even those who have no reading ability of
Hebrew can attend Reform services with dignity and self-
assurance that they are indeed Jews worthy of their heritage.

(Memberships in organizations)	SP	M	SU
7. Belong to at least one Jewish organization.	81%	72%	64%
8. Belong to at least <u>four</u> Jewish organization.	29%	9%	8%
9. Membership in non-Jewish organizations.	62%	59%	62%

Neither the particularists nor the moderates can be accused
of being "a bunch of joiners." Universalists and particularists
are equally involved in non-Jewish organizations. It also
means that, while particularists are more likely to belong
to Jewish groups as befits their greater concern and involvement, they do not ignore the larger community around them.
And both groups give of themselves to such organizations as
Community Chest, Red Cross, Girl Scouts, housing, and senior
citizen activities. Politics, too.

Table 38 (continued)

SP - Strongly particularistic
M - Moderate
SU - Strongly universalistic

Let us now look at ritual observance behaviors of our
three groups of Reform Jews.

(Ritual observances: Jewish and non-Jewish)	SP	M	SU
10. Attend Friday night services (usually).	24%	18%	12%
11. Observe the High Holy Days at home with dinner, candles, blessings.	81%	65%	50%
12. Fast all day on Yom Kippur.	57%	42%	29%
13. Have a family dinner on Thanksgiving Day.	86%	84%	82%
14. Have a Christmas tree at home.	2%	10%	22%
15. Exchange Christmas gifts.	20%	30%	48%
16. Exchange gifts on Hanukkah.	84%	75%	57%

Even though there are striking differences between particularistic and universalistic Reform Jews in the area of ritual
observance with all of the differences in the expected direction,
even the most particularistic do not identify themselves as
extravagantly observant. When only 24% attend Friday night
services, one is forced to conclude that the degree of fit
between particularism (as we have measured it), and religious
behavior is not very great.

Now comes the matter of belief. It was pointed out earlier
that particularists are more likely to call themselves "religious"
Jews. Yet when we ask the question about belief in God, we

<u>Table 38</u> (continued)

SP - Strongly particularistic
M - Moderate
SU - Strongly universalistic

<u>do not find any startling differences between particularists
and universalists.</u>

(Belief in God)	SP	M	SU
17a. Traditional belief in God.	16%	19%	16%
17b. Modified traditional belief in God.	54%	50%	48%
17c. Agnostic or Atheist.	13%	11%	10%

But if religious <u>beliefs</u> do not discriminate among the types
of Reform Jews under discussion, other religious attitudes do.

(Marriage, Intermarriage, Mixed Marriage)	SP	M	SU
18. Insist that a chuppa should <u>always</u> be used at weddings.	29%	20%	8%
19. Insist that the glass <u>should always</u> be broken.	30%	19%	7%
20. <u>Disapprove</u> of rabbis officiating at mixed marriages where no conversion has taken place.	31%	14%	6%

It is obvious that the marriage ritual, ranging from disapproval
of mixed-marriages, to the inclusion of the traditional chuppa
and glass, are <u>considerably</u> more of concern to the particularists
than to the universalists.

Table 38 (continued)

SP - Strongly particularistic
M - Moderate
SU - Strongly universalistic

	SP	M	SU
21. Intermarriage and mixed marriage are <u>very</u> important sources of the crisis in Reform Judaism.	38%	29%	4%
22. Intermarriage and mixed marriage are "<u>great threats</u>" facing American Judaism.	44%	26%	10%

In general, <u>particularists are more likely to perceive</u>
<u>Reform Judaism</u> (and American Judaism generally), <u>as facing</u>
<u>a number of crises.</u>

(Percent who see each of the following
as being a "great threat" to Reform
Judaism:)

	SP	M	SU
23. Antisemitism.	38%	32%	27%
24. Black militancy.	26%	26%	19%
25. Generally weak religious school.	49%	38%	19%
26. Changes in traditional Jewish family structure.	36%	27%	16%
27. Insufficient demands made by Reform on its lay members.	27%	18%	10%
28. Poor rabbinical leadership.	42%	39%	32%

It is significant, that while our particularists point to
"poor rabbinical leadership" as a crisis in Reform, they are
nevertheless not very insecure about their own lay capacities.
<u>Particularists are most likely to identify poor lay leader-</u>
<u>ship as a crisis in Reform Judaism.</u>

Table 38 (continued)

SP - Strongly particularistic
M - Moderate
SU - Strongly universalistic

(Lay leadership)	SP	M	SU
29. Poor lay leadership.	35%	30%	24%

(Stress the IMPORTANCE of)	SP	M	SU
30. Jewish identification.	84%	75%	48%
31. Support for the State of Israel.	77%	55%	32%
32. Jewish study.	59%	22%	12%
33. Social action in the general community.	55%	37%	32%

Only some basic pertinent comments have been interspersed
with all the data that are contained in Table 38. Many more
observations can be made from the various findings that have
been presented. A case in point, for instance, would be the
relationship between the findings of Numbers 7, 8 and 9
(regarding organizational memberships), with the "Lay Leadership Index" in Chapter 15.

By way of summary, then, while particularists are most
concerned with maintaining Jewishness as they know it, with
the threats stemming from antisemitism, and from intermarriage, and mixed marriage, and from black militancy, they
are nevertheless more willing to work in the community. One
may conclude, then, that their "Jewishness" is not particularly
religious or observant, but it is in keeping with another
rather old ethnic tradition which calls for involvement in the
world.

Of course, one might look at our detailed particularistic-
universalistic break-down of Reform Jews in contemporary America,
and come away with this conclusion:

> Particularism and universalism, it's called now; but
> it's the age-old Jewish dilemma, - assimilation or
> apartness, etched more starkly by the threat to Israel,
> the pressures on all American society. For some Jews,
> it breaks down into either Aliyah, or going along with
> the diaspora, America my homeland . . . For my own
> interpretation of particularism and/or universalism,
> I choose Rabbi Hillel's 2,000-year old code: 'If
> I am not for myself, who will be for me? And if I
> am only for myself, what am I? And if not now,
> when?'*

And that's precisely what our Particularism-Universalism Index
is all about, - only with some <u>factual data</u> as to how it applies
to contemporary American Reform Judaism.

4. Summary Highlights (Reform Congregants: Jewish Consciousness).

1) Jewish consciousness is identified by most Reform Jews (92%)
   in terms of being an ethical person; belief in God rates
   third; charity rates 6th; Jewish study 7th; synagogue worship 8th and last.

2) "Jewish identification" rates very high as an item of
   Jewish concern, second only to "being an ethical person."
   However, two-thirds of Reform congregants say they remain

---

* Gerald Astor (Look Senior Editor), "The Agonized American Jew,"
     <u>Look</u>, April 20, 1971, p. 19.

Jews "because it is simply the most convenient thing to
do"; 25% feel it's unimportant what religion one belongs to;
28% feel that "any attempt to identify ourselves with and
as a 'Jewish community' is undesirable"; 34% "see no meaning
to 'Jewish community'."

3) There is a fairly steady increase in particularism as we
move down from older to younger members. (The tendency to
marry non-Jews by the latter denies some of this particularism in them.)

4) In terms of data on Jewish consciousness, Jewish identification, and other items, Reform congregants can be viewed on
a particularism-universalism scale as follows: 10% strongly
particularistic; 38% moderate; 52% strongly universalistic.

5) Reform congregants from more traditional backgrounds tend to
be more particularistic. Those from Reform backgrounds are
least particularistic (7%).

6) Almost half of the universalists cannot read prayerbook
Hebrew.

7) Universalists and particularists are equally involved in
non-Jewish organizations.

8) Even the most particularistic are not very observant. More
have a family Thanksgiving dinner (86%), than observe the
High Holy Days at home (81%); almost as many exchange Christmas gifts (20%), as attend Friday night services (24%). The
observance rated highest by most (84%) is the exchange of
Hanukkah gifts.

9) When it comes to belief in God, little difference exists between particularists and universalists. Both show high majorities who <u>qualify</u> their belief "in terms of my own views of what God is and what He stands for."

10) Particularists, five-to-one over universalists, disapprove of rabbis who officate at mixed-marriages; 29% to 8% say <u>chuppa</u> should <u>always</u> be used; 30% to 7% say breaking of the glass should always be part of the wedding ritual.

11) Particularists <u>much</u> more than universalists see the following as crises in America today: antisemitism, black militancy, poor religious education, breakdown in Jewish family, poor rabbinical leadership.

12) Particularists, almost three-to-one over universalists, say Reform congregants make insufficient demands on their lay leaders, while universalists, more than three-to-one over particularists, complain of the poor quality of Reform <u>lay</u> leadership.

13) Particularists over universalists stress the importance of Jewish identification 84% to 48%; support of the State of Israel 77% to 32%; Jewish study 59% to 12%; community social action 55% to 32%.

14) Overall, while particularists stress <u>Jewishness</u> more than universalists in terms of several more traditional be-havioral practices, the latter do not appear to be, necessarily, expressions of <u>observant religiosity.</u>

CHAPTER 14: HOW JEWISH ARE REFORM JEWS?: RELIGIOUS BELIEFS

1. Belief in God.

There are at least two questions one can ask about religious beliefs:
(1) What is believed, and (2) the perceived importance of these beliefs. As to the first, the story is rather clear. Some 17% of our
Reform congregants (Table 39) say they "believe in God in the more
or less traditional Judaic sense," and an additional 49% claim to
hold to this belief, but qualify the statement by choosing a response

Table 39:
BELIEF IN GOD:
RESPONSE PATTERNS FROM REFORM CONGREGANTS
(N=984)

Believe in God in the more or less traditional Judaic sense.	17%
Believe in God in the more or less traditional Judaic sense "as modified in terms of my own views of what God is, and what he stands for."	49%
"Non-traditional" believers.	8%
Total who believe in God.	74%
Agnostic.	21%
Atheists.	4%

that includes the following: "as modified in terms of my own views
of what God is, and what he stands for." And additional 8% are
non-traditional believers, thus bringing the total believers in
some sense of the word to 74%. One out of four of our congregants
identify themselves either as agnostics (21%), or as atheists (4%).

Here are a few random comments from congregants on the subject of
belief:

> That there is a God, and that He is the God of our fathers,
> I have never questioned, and never will. Non-believers
> can out-argue me with words . . . but they can never take
> away from me what is in my heart . . . (because) that's
> where He is.

> I am an athiest. I lost my belief in God many years
> ago but I believe that the study of Torah and Mishna
> - and other works are helpful.

> Religion is something that I accept now only for its
> moral, ethical, and cultural teaching. The prayers
> and the gods should disappear as most superstitions do.
> Truth and enlightment are the true guiding lights.

> We have a rabbi who is to say the least - not very in-
> spiring . . . Perhaps my fault but maybe the services
> could be more inspiring . . . At times when I am alone
> on a lake fishing I get close to God thanking him for
> letting me be a part of this world.

> One of my children at 15 joined the local Ethical
> Culture group because it offered sympathetic under-
> standing of her viewpoints.

> I belong to a congregation which I helped to found
> because we felt the need to teach our children
> Judaism without nationalism . . . I have become

disenchanted with the organization of religion; it
gets itself too involved with the forms and rituals
and forgets or ignores the basic teachings of
humanism.

2. "Religiosity Index."

When our congregants were asked to rate a number of areas of
"Jewish concern," some 89% (as close to unanimity as is normally
obtained in survey research), cite "being an ethical person,"
another 62% rate "Jewish identification" as very important, and
53% (a bare majority), list "belief in God." In short, about 78%
identify themselves as having some sort of belief in God, but
only 53% consider belief in God as a "very" important part of
being Jewish (Figure 42).

These two responses ("belief in God" and "being an ethical person"),
were formulated into a "Religiosity Index" and it is this Index
that will be discussed for the rest of this section. The basic
distribution of our congregant sample in terms of religious
commitment (at least as they themselves identify it), is portrayed
in Figure 43.

3. Who are the Believers?: Selected Characteristics.

By and large, the strongest believers are the oldest congregants
(Figure 44). Where 73% of those aged 70 and over are religious
by our "Religiosity Index," (a composite of their self-evaluations
on "belief in God" and "being an ethical person"), the same is
true for only 40% of those in the 30-39 year bracket. It applies
to 41% of those between 40 and 49 years of age. Generally speaking,
then, it would appear that the parents of religious school children
identify themselves least as having any marked religious feelings.

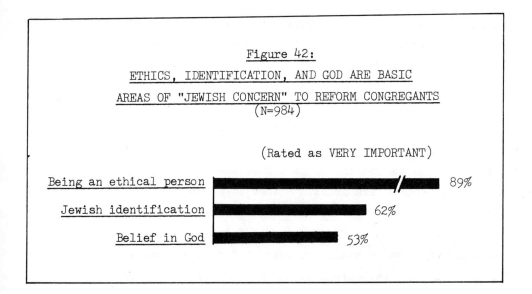

Figure 42:

ETHICS, IDENTIFICATION, AND GOD ARE BASIC

AREAS OF "JEWISH CONCERN" TO REFORM CONGREGANTS
(N=984)

(Rated as VERY IMPORTANT)

Being an ethical person — 89%

Jewish identification — 62%

Belief in God — 53%

And, we shall see later that it is this group of least religious Jews who are most critical of the rabbi's role in the religious school, and most critical of the rabbi's leadership with his Temple Youth Group.

Before leaving the matter of age, however, it is worth noting that the "Religiosity Index" identifies the youngest group of our congregants, those between 20 and 29, as slightly more religious than their older fellow-congregants. It is risky to comment on a 5% difference, but it is a possible straw in the wind, particularly in view of the current revival of interest in religion on the part of young people generally.

Moving on to other background characteristics (Table 40), we find among Reform Jews some of the same patterns which are to be found in many other religious groups. Women express their religiosity more than men, - in this case by a substantial 20%. This is not due to the fact that the women in our sample are some-

what older than the men. The general finding holds at every age
level for our women congregants. Much has already been written
on this phenomenon and we will not go into the matter here. Single
persons seem to be considerably more religious than married ones,
which invites the possible interpretation of sublimation and related
psychological behavior. However, we did not elicit data in this
study with which to test this particular proposition. Part of
the difference may be due to the fact that the single members
are among the youngest age group. A more important reason for
the difference, however, may be that single members are more
likely to join a synagogue for reasons of faith rather than for
"life-style fit." We have already seen, and we shall see again
shortly, that synagogue membership would probably be very small
indeed were it not for the apparent desire on the part of parents
to give their children a Jewish education. But this desire is
quite obviously not generated from within. If it were, we would
not have found the difference just reported. Nor would we find

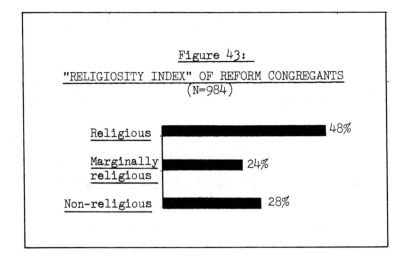

Figure 43:

"RELIGIOSITY INDEX" OF REFORM CONGREGANTS
(N=984)

Religious _____ 48%

Marginally _____ 24%
religious

Non-religious _____ 28%

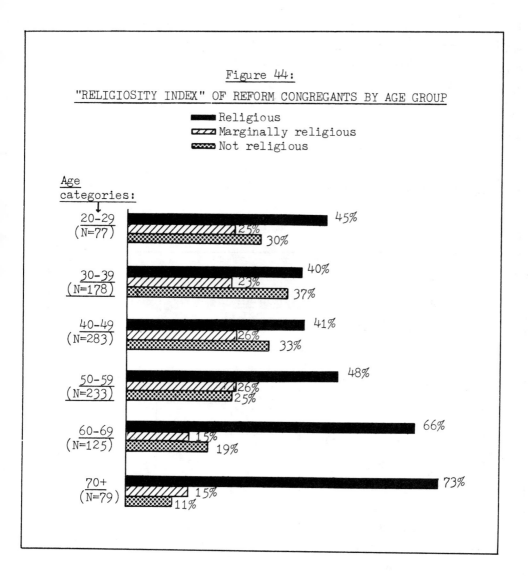

Figure 44:

"RELIGIOSITY INDEX" OF REFORM CONGREGANTS BY AGE GROUP

■■■ Religious
▨▨ Marginally religious
▧▧ Not religious

Age
categories:

20-29
(N=77)
45%
25%
30%

30-39
(N=178)
40%
23%
37%

40-49
(N=283)
41%
26%
33%

50-59
(N=233)
48%
26%
25%

60-69
(N=125)
66%
15%
19%

70+
(N=79)
73%
15%
11%

that the <u>more children in the family, the less religious is the head</u>
<u>of the household</u>! It is difficult to come up with a cogent explana-
tion for this finding. Students of the sociology of religion
have long considered religion to be, among other things, a cele-
bration or observance of group values, a way of symbolizing the
unity and cohesiveness of the group. Similarly, it could be assumed

that members of large families should be, other things held constant, more religious than those from small ones. Not so in this study. One tentative interpretation might be that Reform makes fewer demands, doctrinally or ritually, on its members compared with Orthodox and Conservative standards. If this assumption is reasonably accurate, then it follows that it might fail to supply some of them with the kinds of symbols that could then become part of an individual's way of expressing his place in the social world, such

Table 40:

"RELIGIOSITY INDEX" OF REFORM CONGREGANTS

BY SEX, MARITAL STATUS AND FAMILY SIZE

	Religious	Marginally religious	Not religious
	%	%	%
Male (N=800)	45	24	31
Female (N=145)	65	18	17
Single (N=32)	69	22	9
Married (N=797)	47	24	30
Children: 0 (N=99)	62	21	17
1 (N=115)	60	20	20
2 (N=402)	48	23	28
3 (N=274)	42	27	31
4+ (N=92)	35	22	43

as membership in a large and close-knit family for example.
Instead of that, many Reform Jews have presumably found other
ways of symbolizing that cohesiveness. This matter deserves
long and careful study. It might just throw a more penetrating
beam on what appears to be an important and possibly critical
situation.

In an examination of Figure 44 and Table 40, relative to the
religiosity of older congregants, we find that there appears to be
a breaking point immediately before and immediately after children
are all or almost all married or on their own. The religiosity
of the parents appears to start in early adulthood, probably as
the first child enters religious school, since this also represents the peak time for synagogue affiliation. To be sure, as
Table 40 shows, there is a decrease in religiosity as they get a
little older and more children come into the family. Possibly
the mother is kept very busy with her household at this point,
and possibly the husband is also working extra hard to attain
his stride in his business or profession about the time that the
third and fourth children start coming into the picture. We
notice, however, in Figure 44, that as the parents start moving
through their 50's, religiosity starts to increase again, and
continues to do so for the rest of their lives. One explanation
that suggests itself here is that the children start to emancipate
themselves when the parents are going through their 50's, and
furthermore the husband's professional or business situation has
just about reached some equilibrium. Thus, more time is now
available for synagogue attendance, and more time (and money,
perhaps), is also available for other involvement in synagogue
and allied Jewish affairs. Whether this explanation is accurate
or not, there still remains the inconsistency between the data
registered in Figure 44 and the data in Table 40. Figure 44 tells
us that religiosity steadily increases with age, and Table 40 tells
us that religiosity tends to decrease as the number of children

per family unit increases, meaning, of course, that age is
also increasing. *

4. "Religiosity Index" Applied to Intermarriage and Mixed Marriage.

Reform Jews with two Jewish parents are less religious (47%), than
those with one non-Jewish parent (77%). To be sure, the latter
percentage is based on a comparatively small number (Table 41),
but the finding is not inconsistent with some other findings in
this study. One interpretation might be that non-Jews who are
married to Jews are more religious than their spouses and more
religious than their Jewish counterparts.

At any rate, we find that Reform Jews who are married to converts
are themselves more religious than those married to fellow-Jews
(Figure 45). Of 834 who married fellow-Jews, 46% identify themselves as religious (in terms of the "Religiosity Index"). And
to top it off, the remaining figures show that those whose spouses
are not converted, are even more religious than those with converted spouses! What do these findings mean? One possible interpretation is "psychological compensation." Exposure on an intimate
and long-run basis with persons from different cultural or
religious backgrounds may produce a heightened self-consciousness
which is reflected in part by greater compliance with the normative
demands of one's religion. We say this may produce such a result.
We have no notion from our quantitative data of how many Jews are
lost to Judaism when they marry non-Jews. All we can say is
that those who intermarry or mix-marry, and stay, tend to be more
religious ritualistically than those with spouses who were born
Jewish.

---

* The comments that have been made in the foregoing paragraph are
    generalizations that may or may not apply to the same persons
    throughout their respective lives. We are speaking of differ-
    ent age groups. Nor can we take for granted that families
    with more children are older families.

TABLE 41:

CONGREGANTS IDENTIFIED AS "RELIGIOUS" BY "RELIGIOSITY INDEX:"

RELIGIOUS COMPOSITION OF PARENTS AND SPOUSE

	Congregants identified as "Religious"
I. RELIGION OF PARENTS:	
Both parents Jewish———————————	47% (N=925)
One Jewish parent—————————	77% (N=30)

Some sociologists indicate that it is nearly impossible for one to
mix-marry if he (or she) doesn't mix-date. It is almost inconceivable to marry someone in today's society whom we haven't dated
first. If one wishes to prevent mixed marriage either for himself
(or herself) or for his (or her) children, then it would appear
that the most feasible approach is not to enter into a mixed-
dating arrangement of any making, including blind dates.

Many congregants do not see it this way. Their comments are often
something like "It's all right to date others (non-Jewish persons),
but not to marry ...," or "The few Jewish girls in our area
don't appeal to my son ...," or "My three children are all
married now, and only one intermarried, but she (the daughter-in-

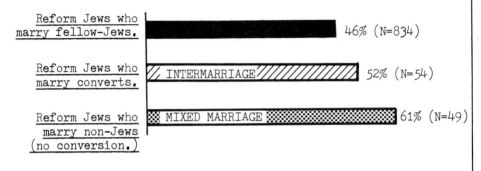

Figure 45:

CONGREGANTS WHO INTERMARRY OR MIX-MARRY
TEND TO BE MORE RELIGIOUS THAN THOSE MARRIED
TO FELLOW-JEWS

(Percent Identifying Themselves as Religious by "Religiosity Index")

Reform Jews who marry fellow-Jews. — 46% (N=834)

Reform Jews who marry converts. INTERMARRIAGE — 52% (N=54)

Reform Jews who marry non-Jews (no conversion.) MIXED MARRIAGE — 61% (N=49)

law), has since converted. If they didn't date non-Jewish girls, they wouldn't have dated. Although we have many Jewish families, you know how it is with the boys . . ."

5. Earlier Religious Affiliations and Current Belief Patterns.

Figure 46 provides us with some meaningful information regarding present day religious patters of Reform Jews in terms of their religious affiliations in earlier years. Of 226 Reform Jews whose backgrounds are Orthodox, 56% identify themselves as "religious." This is followed closely by those with roots in Reform (52%). Puzzling to some, may be the smaller number from Conservative homes (43%). But what is even more intriguing is the pattern that emerges when we control for past affiliation on the part of the

congregant, himself, where such existed (Figure 47). Present
Reform congregants, who originally came from Orthodox homes, <u>and</u>
<u>prior to joining Reform were first affiliated with Orthodox or</u>
<u>Conservative synagogues in their own right as adults,</u> are
even more likely to be religious (61%), than those who had affiliated
with Reform directly from Orthodox homes (55%).

Many congregants submitted comments concerning the relationship
between their earlier <u>home</u> environments and their present religious
outlook:

> Speaking as one who was brought up in a very ultra
> Reform home - the following might be helpful to you
> . . . My belief in Judaism stems totally from the
> home environment and with the love and warmth shown in
> my early years by my parents. Find a way in Judaism

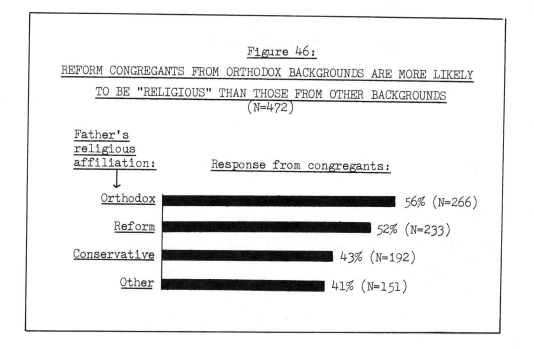

Figure 46:

REFORM CONGREGANTS FROM ORTHODOX BACKGROUNDS ARE MORE LIKELY
TO BE "RELIGIOUS" THAN THOSE FROM OTHER BACKGROUNDS
(N=472)

Father's
religious
affiliation:

Response from congregants:

Orthodox — 56% (N=266)
Reform — 52% (N=233)
Conservative — 43% (N=192)
Other — 41% (N=151)

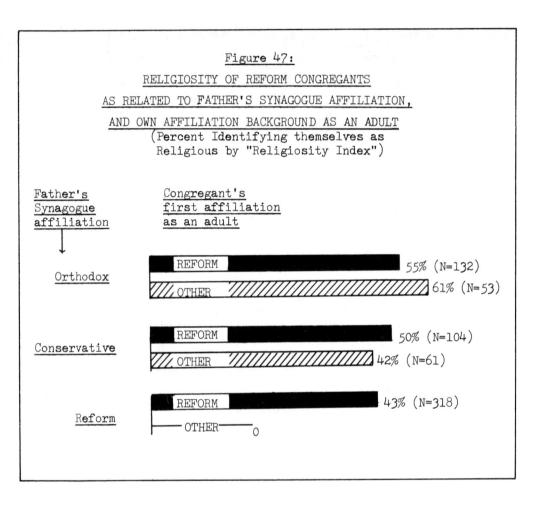

Figure 47:

RELIGIOSITY OF REFORM CONGREGANTS

AS RELATED TO FATHER'S SYNAGOGUE AFFILIATION,

AND OWN AFFILIATION BACKGROUND AS AN ADULT
(Percent Identifying themselves as
Religious by "Religiosity Index")

Father's
Synagogue
affiliation

Congregant's
first affiliation
as an adult

Orthodox
REFORM 55% (N=132)
OTHER 61% (N=53)

Conservative
REFORM 50% (N=104)
OTHER 42% (N=61)

Reform
REFORM 43% (N=318)
OTHER 0

for 'the family with love and affection' for each other
and religion will live.

I'm of the older generation, reared by Reform Jewish
parents who loved their religion and attended services
regularly - but had few home observances (no Sabbath
candles, home prayers, etc.). Therefore I did not
practice this in rearing my child ... I feel this
was a lack in my religious upbringing and in my
ability to so train and rear my son. I hope such
home practices will be stressed and encouraged much
more strongly now and in the future.

6. Socio-Economic Status, Regional Differences, and Religiosity.

The level of religiosity varies inversely with socio-economic status. The better educated (Figure 48), and the more affluent (Figure 49), are considerably less religious than those at the other end of the respective scales. As Figure 48 shows, of the 42 congregants who are non-high school graduates, 76% are identifiable as "religious" (by "Religiosity Index"). Of the 74 who hold two or more graduate and/or professional degrees, only 30% are identifiable as "religious."

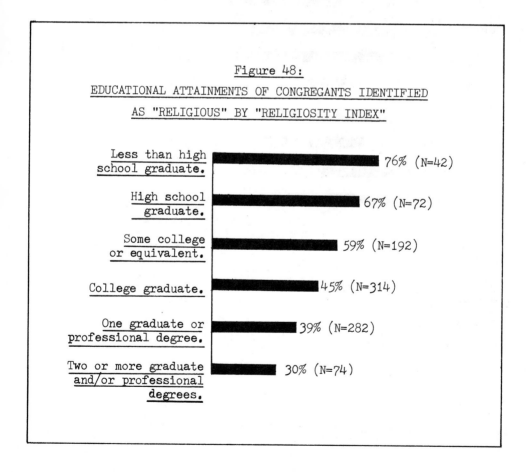

Figure 48:

EDUCATIONAL ATTAINMENTS OF CONGREGANTS IDENTIFIED
AS "RELIGIOUS" BY "RELIGIOSITY INDEX"

Less than high school graduate. — 76% (N=42)

High school graduate. — 67% (N=72)

Some college or equivalent. — 59% (N=192)

College graduate. — 45% (N=314)

One graduate or professional degree. — 39% (N=282)

Two or more graduate and/or professional degrees. — 30% (N=74)

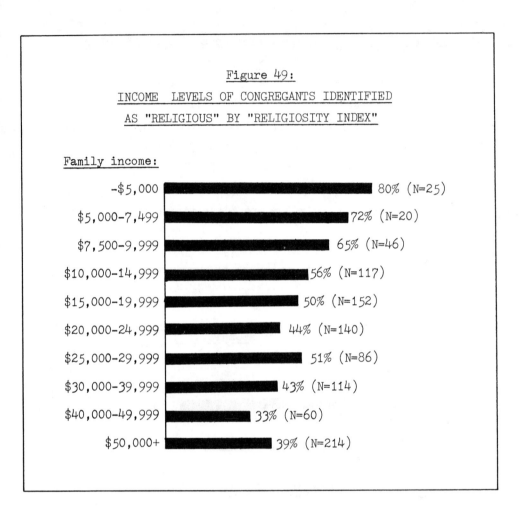

Figure 49:

INCOME LEVELS OF CONGREGANTS IDENTIFIED
AS "RELIGIOUS" BY "RELIGIOSITY INDEX"

Family income:

-$5,000	80% (N=25)
$5,000-7,499	72% (N=20)
$7,500-9,999	65% (N=46)
$10,000-14,999	56% (N=117)
$15,000-19,999	50% (N=152)
$20,000-24,999	44% (N=140)
$25,000-29,999	51% (N=86)
$30,000-39,999	43% (N=114)
$40,000-49,999	33% (N=60)
$50,000+	39% (N=214)

It should be recalled that earlier data pointed out rather markedly
that Reform congregants, as a whole, are easily identifiable as
highly educated and highly affluent. What we have here now is
virtually a textbook example of the usual data which are used for
demonstrating the strong inverse relationship between social position and religiosity. As we note in Figure 49, of those who earn
less than $5,000, 80% are "religious" (in terms of "Religiosity
Index"), whereas those who earn over $50,000, only 39% are

"religious." (For some reason, the least religious fall into the
$40,000 - $50,000 interval, - 33%).

A variable that perplexes many a clergyman is the role of higher
education as it affects the religiosity of young people. Many a
youngster has gone off to college presumably as a reasonably committed
person to his or religion. After a year or two confronting the
sciences and the humanities, he begins "to question" things. Sometimes it is truly a genuine confrontation with new knowledge and
new ideas that brings serious questions and well-considered doubt.
Sometimes it is simply a substitution of a professor's personal
"gospel" for the previous "gospel" of a clergyman. In short, it is
possible that the youngster was only presumably committed in the
first place.

And it appears that many congregants fall in line with this possibility.
As education increases, the percentage who see themselves as religious
decreases. (Figure 48). However when one looks at all of those who
show a high religiosity, we find the following: 7% did not complete
high school; 10% graduated high school; 24% had some college experience; 30% were college graduates; and 29% had at least one graduate degree. These percentages are quite close to those of the
educational attainment of all congregants (Figure 34). This is
an indication that those who show high religiosity are a repre-
sentive cross section of the congregants, at least with respect to
educational attainment.

There is finally the matter of regional differences. Southern-
reared Jews are far more likely than their northern counterparts to be religious. This may be due, in part, to the fact that
they are more likely to have been brought up in towns or small cities.

Generally speaking, however, it may well be that Southern Jews are
no different from southern non-Jews when it comes to religion.
Southerners in general are more religious, and this generates a
"climate," a normative situation that makes it as "normal" for the
southern Jew to believe in God as it is "normal" for the one from
the north to regard such a question as moot. As Figure 50 shows,
of the 86 congregants whose origins are from New England, 30% have
been identified as religious (by "Religiosity Index"). Of the 369
who were reared in the Middle Atlantic states, 44% are identifiable
as religious by the same criteria.

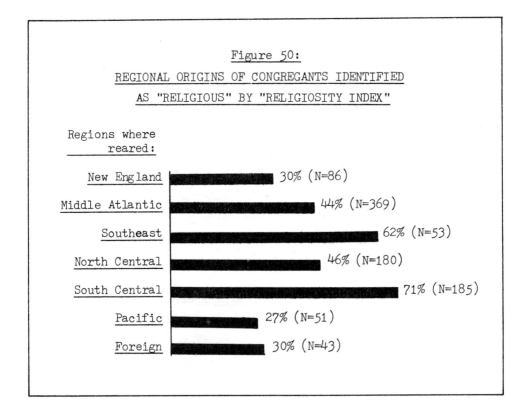

Figure 50:

REGIONAL ORIGINS OF CONGREGANTS IDENTIFIED
AS "RELIGIOUS" BY "RELIGIOSITY INDEX"

Regions where
reared:

New England — 30% (N=86)

Middle Atlantic — 44% (N=369)

Southeast — 62% (N=53)

North Central — 46% (N=180)

South Central — 71% (N=185)

Pacific — 27% (N=51)

Foreign — 30% (N=43)

7. "Religiosity Index" and Time of Affiliation with a Reform Synagogue.

A rather expected finding was the fact that religious persons were more likely to join their respective congregations at an early stage than those who identified themselves as least religious (Figure 51). Only 22% of the more religious group had joined when it was time for their first child to enter religious school. Of the less religious category, some 41% give this as the time of first affiliating with a synagogue. This tends again to underscore an interpretation of motives. It would appear that non-religious or less religious people join synagogues for functional need purposes, or at least such appears to be the case with our congregant sample.

If those who have a more or less traditional belief in God are termed more religious than those whose beliefs are either non-traditional, agnostic, or atheist, does it follow that the members see themselves that way? When asked, for instance, to indicate the importance of various possible reasons for joining their respective congregations, only 27% of the people whom we call "religious" gave "I am a religious Jew" as a very important reason! To be sure, only 1% of the least religious gave such an answer. This is not surprising. What is significant is that even those who "believe" appear to be hesitant to identify themselves strongly as such. It is obviously one thing for a congregant to believe, quite another for him to think of himself as a religious Jew. This could be interpreted in a number of ways. If such a large number of congregants recognize the "credence gap" between themselves and some ideal-typical religious Jew, then it might be hoped that some at least will be concerned with closing that gap. If that were the correct interpretation, it follows that more intensive religious experiences would be in order for Reform members who want to get closer to God. If, on the other hand, the finding

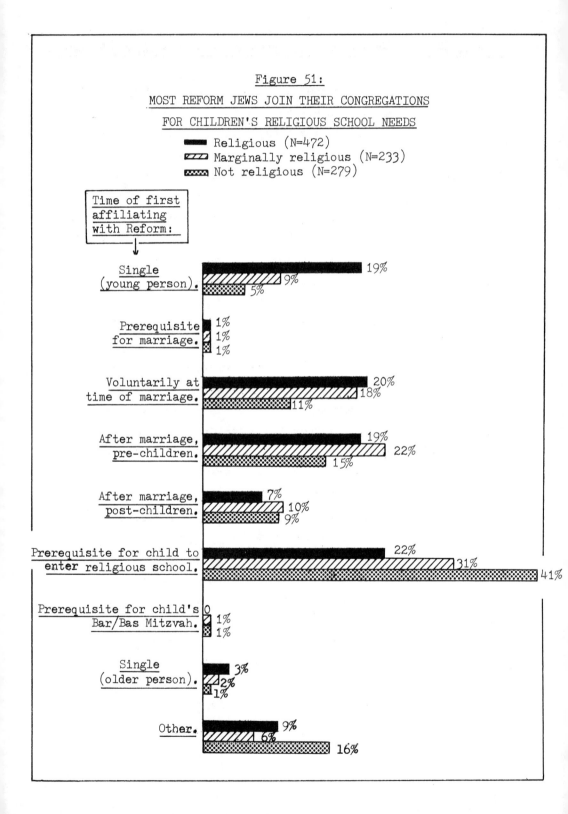

Figure 51:

MOST REFORM JEWS JOIN THEIR CONGREGATIONS

FOR CHILDREN'S RELIGIOUS SCHOOL NEEDS

▬▬ Religious (N=472)
▨▨ Marginally religious (N=233)
▦▦ Not religious (N=279)

Time of first
affiliating
with Reform:

Single
(young person).
19%
9%
5%

Prerequisite
for marriage.
1%
1%
1%

Voluntarily at
time of marriage.
20%
18%
11%

After marriage,
pre-children.
19%
22%
15%

After marriage,
post-children.
7%
10%
9%

Prerequisite for child to
enter religious school.
22%
31%
41%

Prerequisite for child's
Bar/Bas Mitzvah.
0
1%
1%

Single
(older person).
3%
2%
1%

Other.
9%
6%
16%

means that Reform Jews are comparing themselves not so much with what they think they ought to be or would like to be, but rather with "other kinds" of Jews, particularly Orthodox ones, then we may be dealing with a wall, not a gap. Possibly the Reform congregant is making an unfair demand of a Reform synagogue when he expects it to provide him with something that he "remembers" as Orthodoxy.

From the interviews even more than from written comments, one strong uniformity makes itself known regarding the Reform Jew's self-image regarding his religiosity. When a Reform Jew is asked, "Are you religious?" or "Do you consider yourself a religious Jew?," the answer is usually some form of negative response. Most often he equates religiosity with Orthodoxy.

The following interview excerpts are reasonably typical:

(After the congregant had expressed pride in the fact that he probably had the most Jewish home in his congregation, "with the exception of the Rabbi's.")

Interviewer: In light of all this, would you say you are a religious person?

Congregant: Well, to a Gentile I would be. They come to our house and join in our Passover and Hanukkah . . .

Interviewer: Do you consider yourself a religious person?

Congregant: A religious person maybe yes, a religious Jew, that's another thing.

Interviewer: How do you mean?

Congregant: Well you know, you don't have to ask.

Interviewer: Could you explain that please?

Congregant: How should I explain it? I'm not a religious Jew by Jewish standards. Of course not.

Neither is my rabbi for that matter. He does not observe Kosher, and I don't. He doesn't observe the
Orthodox rituals anymore than I do. We're Reformed.

Interviewer: Do you consider yourself a religious
Jew by Reform standards?

Congregant: (Following a burst of laughter) What
standards? I just told you my rabbi doesn't observe any standards, didn't I? That's what Reform
is. We are Jews by tradition, and we are required
to only observe the holiest requirements, like Rosh
Hashanah and Yom Kippur.

Interviewer: Well, can any Reform Jew be a religious
Jew?

Congregant: Then he wouldn't be Reform . . .

Interviewer: If you are not a religious Jew, how
different would you have to be before you would
consider yourself to be religious?

Congregant: When I said I wasn't religious, that
doesn't mean I don't consider myself a good Jew.

Interviewer: How do you mean that?

(Congregant proceeded to talk of rearing his children
in a positive Jewish manner and his Jewish identification.)

Interviewer: Then why don't you consider yourself
religious?

Congregant: To any Orthodox rabbi, I am a goy.

Interviewer: But you don't claim to be Orthodox,
so why do you judge yourself by Orthodox standards?

Congregant: I don't but they (Orthodoxy) do.

Interviewer: Suppose you kept the Sabbath and observed all Orthodox rules for being a religious
Jew, but still belonged to a Reform synagogue, would
you then consider yourself a religious Jew?

Congregant: That's a hard one. Why would I want to
be Reform in that case . . . Anyways I think I
would consider myself religious but they (Orthodoxy)
still wouldn't, would they?

(Asked of a prominent community leader in Jewish and
non-Jewish affairs, formerly president of his Reform
congregation - who also happens to hold membership in
the only other synagogue in his city, a small
Orthodox congregation -)

Interviewer: Do you feel that a Reform Jew who is
committed and devout could call himself a religious
Jew?

Congregant: Not in a million years, . . . maybe
by Reform standards, which is still unclear to me
after 35 years, but not by any stretch of the imagination. You see, we read from the Torah, but we
are not bound by it except to be an ethical person.

Interviewer: You said after 35 years you are not
clear what Reform requires of you. How do you mean
that?

Congregant: I take it back. I am clear, and this
sounds bad but I don't mean it that way. Reform
requires that I be a good human being. This is the
Reform religion . . . This is what I try to be.

Interviewer: But every religion requires that. . .

Congregant: Yes, but Judaism tells us how specifically,
like giving to charity, helping the underprivileged
to be tolerant etc.

Interviewer: Well, if a person is all these things,
can't we consider him to be a religious person?

Congregant: Yes, of course, but as you said, the
Protestants and the Catholics have the same requirements, so you can be a religious person, and be a
Protestant or a Catholic, but that still doesn't
mean you're a religious Jew.

Interviewer: What is a religious Jew?

Congregant: Well by the Orthodox it's one thing,
still another by the Conservatives, and by us still
another thing altogether.

Interviewer: As you understand Reform, - and you
have considerable experience, - you've been an

officer, - the president of a Reform congregation, in
your opinion what does it take to be a <u>religious</u> Jew
in Reform Judaism?

<u>Congregant</u>: (After a little thought and a slight
smile-) Pay your dues.

So it goes with many Reform congregants when depth interviews are
employed. The above are only excerpts. But the theme is similar
throughout the entire interview. Somehow, Orthodox tradition
hangs heavy, and imposes itself on the congregant's self-image
in terms of <u>religiosity</u>.

Even from third and fourth-generation Reform congregants, where
the person has little or no knowledge of Orthodoxy, and has a long
background in Reform Judaism, somewhat similar responses tend to
come forth.

(From a fourth-generation congregant-)

Yes, I consider myself a religious person, not as
religious as I'd like to be maybe, but I don't hesitate
to say I am religious . . . and by this, I don't
mean by Orthodox or Conservative rules. I mean I
even consider myself <u>more</u> religious than many of my
Orthodox and Conservative friends.

<u>Interviewer</u>: How do you mean that?

<u>Congregant</u>: We go to Services regularly. We are
proud of our Jewishness. My daughter is completing
her Junior year in Israel . . . (the congregant went
on with many other Jewish activities in which his
family is involved.)

<u>Interviewer</u>: I suppose you have a few Orthodox
and Conservative friends who are involved in most
of these activities . . . How does this make you
possibly <u>more</u> religious than them?

<u>Congregant</u>: Well there's a big difference. They
don't observe what they are supposed to believe in.

There are very few real observant Jews. I know them
well. They're wonderful people. But the rest do not
observe, but they claim to be Orthodox or Conservative.
Isn't this being not religious?

Interviewer: You use the word "observe." What does
a Reform Jew observe to qualify him as a religious
Jew?

Congregant: You miss the point . . . and in Reform
we don't believe in these rituals. We believe in
the ethics that Judaism teaches us. That doesn't
mean that all Reform Jews are ethical people more
than Orthodox or Conservative. I'm just answering
your original question. By what Reform requires, I
consider myself to be a religious person.

As can be noted, these and most other expressions on the subject
of religiosity include the whole range of defensiveness, appre-
hensiveness, concern, satisfaction, disregard and sometimes even
irony. One thing is certain, - religiosity means very different
things to different people.

Two selected diverse examples from Reform congregants are the
following:

Because I and my family are very active members of
a Unitarian Fellowship and I have not been able to
interest them in the Temple, you may want to separate this questionnaire from your tabulations.

Judaism is a beautiful Religion. Members should
attend Temple more often.

We could go on with over 200 additional comments, written and
oral, on the subject, and they are all reasonably similar to one
which recently appeared in a colleague's publication:

'We think we ought to light Friday night candles
regularly, but we're lax about some of the things
we talk about doing,' said another businessman,
also minimally observant. And an active ORT leader
admitted: 'We could have Jewish records or go to
services Friday night or put up a sukkah. We don't
because we're not that interested.'*

8. <u>Summary Highlights (Reform Congregants: Religious Beliefs)</u>.

1) Some 17% of Reform congregants believe in God "in the more
    or less traditional sense of the term"; another 49% qualify
    with "in terms of my own views of what God is, and what
    he stands for"; 8% are non-traditional believers. Thus
    a total of 74% believe in God; 21% are agnostics; 4%
    atheists.

2) Congregants rank items of "Jewish concern" as follows:
    ethical behavior 92%; Jewish identification 63%; belief
    in God 54%.

3) A "Religiosity Index" (constructed on the basis of response
    patterns to "belief in God" and "being an ethical person"),
    depicts the following distribution: Reform congregants
    who are "religious", 48%; "marginally religious," 24%;
    "non-religious", 28%.

4) On a percentage basis, women are more religious than men
    (65% to 45%); single persons more than married (69% to 47%).

5) The <u>more</u> children in a family, the greater trend toward
    <u>less</u> religiosity (belief patterns).

---

* Marshall Sklare <u>et al</u>., <u>Not Quite at Home</u>, American Jewish Committee,
    Institute of Human Relations Press, 1969, p. 40.

6) In terms of above "Religiosity Index," between 40% and 45% of Reform congregants between ages 20 to 50 can be categorized as "religious"; from ages 50 upward the numbers increase from 48% (ages 50-59); 66% (ages 60-69); 73% (70 and over).

7) Marriage patterns (based on <u>small</u> <u>sample</u>), are as follows: Reform Jews with two Jewish parents are <u>less</u> religious (47%), than those with one Jewish parent (77%); those married to converts are <u>more</u> religious than their Jewish counterparts; 46% of Jewish spouses are identified as "religious"; converted spouses who are so identified are 52%; non-Jewish spouses, 61%.

8) In terms of "Religiosity Index", Reform Jews whose fathers are (were) Orthodox, 56%; Reform, 52%; Conservative, 43%; no answer, or non-Jewish, 41%.

10) There is almost an inverse proportion between religiosity and income.

11) Southern Reform Jews are more "religious" (by "Religiosity Index") than those from other geographical regions.

12) Approximately 20% of "religious" Reform congregants join a congregation as single young adults; another 20% at time of marriage; another 20% shortly after marriage (pre-children); another 20% in order to enter the oldest child in religious school.

13) Some 30% who are "marginally religious" and 41% who are not religious did not affiliate with their congregations until it was time to enroll their oldest child in religious school.

CHAPTER 15: THE LAY LEADERSHIP

1. The "Lay Leadership Index."

Almost all organizations, synagogues included, have members who
spend a considerable amount of time and energy in its affairs, and
it is therefore important to know something about them and what
they stand for. In this study <u>leaders</u> are defined as people who
1) are or have been officers in their respective congregations,
2) belong to other Jewish organizations, and 3) have always been
members of a religious congregation. People with all three of
these characteristics, it is assumed, are likely to play more of a
leadership role than those with two or one of these. Based on our
raw data, we are able to identify four congregant types, in terms
of the <u>leadership</u> component. These range from what we call
<u>strong leaders</u>, all the way to those who seem to be relatively
inactive. The distribution is as follows: strong leaders (most

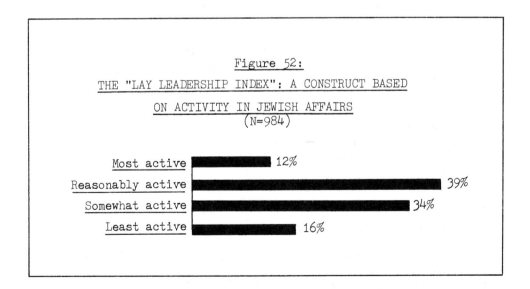

Figure 52:
THE "LAY LEADERSHIP INDEX": A CONSTRUCT BASED
ON ACTIVITY IN JEWISH AFFAIRS
(N=984)

Most active 12%
Reasonably active 39%
Somewhat active 34%
Least active 16%

active), 12% reasonably active, 39% somewhat active, 34% least active, 16%. We shall identify this as our "Lay Leadership Index" (Figure 52). To be sure, any measurement of performance that is based on quantity of activity alone is not fully satisfying. But the measurement of quality of performance is beyond our questionnaire capabilities. At any rate, it is not altogether out of order to hypothesize that there is at least a reasonable relationship between quantity and quality when we consider that our data do separate those who are involved, regardless of how minimally, as against those who are not involved at all, or almost not at all. It is hypothesized that the "most active" (Figure 52), are the most probable leaders in most congregations without denying that those from the next category, the "reasonably active," surely contribute some effective leadership in some specific ways. It is rather difficult to accept the last two categories as leaders. It is altogether possible that many individuals in these two categories are leaders in other spheres, but by their own responses they do not identify themselves as active leaders in their respective congregations.

2. Who are the Leaders? Some Descriptive Characteristics.

In brief, the stronger (most active) lay leaders are the people who can most often be identified by the following characteristics:*

1. They are usually men.
2. They are usually fathers.
3. They are usually affluent.
4. They are usually less well-educated.
5. They are usually from Reform and Orthodox backgrounds.

That men in our sample should provide more leadership than women is not particularly surprising. But even then, the differences are not very great. Men who qualify as "most active" on our

---

*These conclusions are ascertained by the total number of congregants, not by percentages in Table 42 (following page). N=809

Table 42:

"LAY LEADERSHIP INDEX" OF REFORM CONGREGANTS:

SEX, MARITAL STATUS, AND FAMILY SIZE PATTERNS

"LAY LEADERSHIP INDEX"

	Most active	Reasonably active	Somewhat active	Least active
	%	%	%	%
Male (N=809)	13	35	35	17
Female (N=145)	8	54	30	8
Single (N=32)	13	28	38	22
Married (N=797)	12	37	35	17
Children: 0 (N=99)	8	33	40	18
1 (N=115)	8	45	31	16
2 (N=402)	11	37	37	15
3 (N=274)	16	39	30	15
4+ (N=92)	9	43	33	16

"Lay Leadership Index" constitute 13% of our male congregant sample (Table 42). Women who qualify as "most active" by the same criteria constitute 8% of our female congregant sample.

Fathers are more active than non-fathers. It comes as little surprise. They are older and have presumably been around longer, and thus would tend to have more background and experience in the

leadership roles. Also, they seem to be more interested in the
affairs of the congregation, possibly because most have children
of religious school age.

And when did the affluent not play more of a leadership role? The
Jewish gvir is after all truly a strong man and has played a dis-
tinctive role throughout Jewish history. As a man of affairs, he
is indeed able to give valuable advice on a number of critical

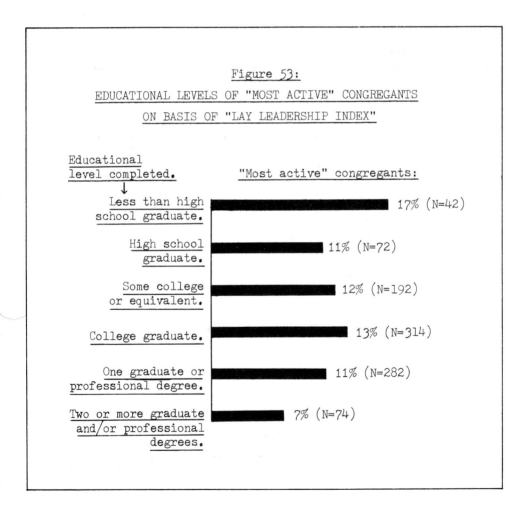

Figure 53:
EDUCATIONAL LEVELS OF "MOST ACTIVE" CONGREGANTS
ON BASIS OF "LAY LEADERSHIP INDEX"

Educational
level completed.
↓

"Most active" congregants:

Less than high
school graduate.   17% (N=42)

High school
graduate.   11% (N=72)

Some college
or equivalent.   12% (N=192)

College graduate.   13% (N=314)

One graduate or
professional degree.   11% (N=282)

Two or more graduate
and/or professional
degrees.   7% (N=74)

matters, from putting up a building to dealing with local officials
in the matter of zoning regulations.

But the activists in this case do not happen to be the best-
educated (Figure 53). The differences are not great, but there
is some tendency on the part of those with the most training and/
or education to stay out of the leadership ranks. To the extent
that businessmen are oriented toward "results" and "getting things
done," they may be best suited to deal with things "head on."

From some of the written comments, but more during the course of
interviews, a rather strong position makes itself known by many
congregants with regard to their respective Boards of Trustees.
The theme here is that the Boards (or at least "influential
members" of the Boards), in many cases are suppressing their
respective rabbis from speaking out freely, especially in community
activities that focus on certain social action movements.

Here is how some of our congregants tell it:

>Congregant: Look at the ministers and the priests.
>They're all over, in and out of . . . (the community
>and the nation) . . . doing things. Our rabbi can't
>do these things. The Board won't let him. I know he
>would like to, but he can't.
>
>Interviewer: How do you know he can't?
>
>Congregant: If you knew our Board, you'd know the
>answer.
>
>Interviewer: Has the Board announced any policy on
>this? Has any one Board member said anything on this
>to you?
>
>Congregant: They don't have to. They're too smart.

Interviewer: Has your rabbi ever indicated to you
or to anyone else that he would like to speak up or
do something that the Board won't allow?

Congregant: I've certainly gotten that impression from
him several times . . . and besides, actions speak loud-
er than words. He (the rabbi) has taken no action on
anything in the (several) years he's been here. Last
year (1969), when our rabbi gave a sermon where he
compared Black Militantism with the underground fight-
ers . . . The Palmach who fought for the freedoms
(the creation of Israel) . . . (and with) the American
Revolution, . . . the Trustees sat on him so hard, he
never said a word since.

Interviewer: How do you know what the Trustees actually did?

Congregant: I know them all. I talk to them. I
have lunch with half of them every day, but I don't
share their views. Sure they (Black Militants)
could break my (store) windows too . . . I don't
like what they're doing either, but to stop the rabbi
from speaking up from the pulpit on some pretty
rotten things that are happening in this country
. . . (isn't right).

There's always a few k'nockers ('big shots') on the
Board who have to push the rabbi around. On this
civil rights things, one of them told me himself
that he made it clear to the rabbi that if he (the
rabbi) ever marched in a group with Negroes and
hippies, he (the Trustee) would see to it that the
rabbi would never have his contract renewed.

Trustees on the Board like the status quo and put
pressure on the rabbi not to speak on social and
moral questions.

This is not quite the same story the writer had gotten from Board

members, or from the rabbis themselves.

Of several Board members interviewed, only one response actually

makes it plausable to accept what some of the congregants are

saying:

Do you know where the action is? It's right here in
our Temple. It's in our religious school. It's in
adult education . . . It's in . . . giving good sermons that uplift us. This is where the action is, or
at least it should be for those of us who belong to
Temple _____. It's not in Selma, Alabama!

To be sure, using trustees as self-informants with regard to
such behavior is a questionable research procedure. But three
questionnaires from the rabbis brought forth comments to indicate
that a Board of Trustees had actually stopped them from continuing
or starting something in this arena of action. Of course, there
were individuals on and off the Board who may have expressed
themselves differently, but only three rabbis reported any official
action, or any other concerted pressure having been taken to
stop them. This does not preclude the possibility of the existence
of subtle pressures that may very well be operative in this matter.
Interviews with rabbis on this issue do not tend to verify in a
substantial way the generalized position taken by many congregants
that their rabbis are not permitted to speak up or to act in
behalf of current civil liberties' movements. Exceptions do prevail. Interestingly, many more rabbis say that their Boards fully
support them when individuals or groups of congregants raise objections about some of their actions.

Appropriate to all this is a comment from one rabbi who stated
his thoughts as follows:

I know where my Trustees stand . . . and, if necessary,
I can work things out personally with one or two of
the frightened ones . . . so what bothers me sometimes is where some of my members stand . . . this
is a big congregation (over 600 families), and
(many of them) have had bad experiences . . . (a
race riot had done damage to some retail estab-
lishments of members). I must be sensitive to their

feelings as well as the bigger issues involved . . .
sometimes I wonder if they like what I'm saying, or
if they're making trouble behind my back . . . this
can easily happen in a large congregation and the
rabbi is the last to find out.

It is not intended here to render harsh judgment on anyone. The
important thing is to obtain the necessary knowledge about the
strong leaders that might help us to understand two things: 1)
How may they be identified from among those who are not presently
serving their synagogues so that opportunities for leadership
might be opened up to them?, and 2) By obtaining a more intimate
glimpse into some characteristics about their personalities, we
might be in a better position to understand the anatomy of synagogue
policy and synagogue administration, and particularly the dynamics
of Board-rabbi interaction. Table 43 (soon to follow) will address
itself to these issues.

The first piece of data that we have is that the leaders are
usually more religious than the non-leaders. They also _perceive_
themselves as more religious. They attend Sabbath (Friday
night) services more regularly, and are somewhat more likely
than the non-leaders to have some Sabbath ritual at home as well.
They do not differ much with regard to fasting on Yom Kippur,
exchanging Hanukkah gifts, or having a Christmas tree at home.
Significantly, the leaders are somewhat _more_ likely to exchange
Christmas gifts than the rest of the congregant sample. From
an interview with a businessman-trustee of a suburban 400-family
synagogue regarding the practice of exchanging Christmas gifts
within his home, a unique explanation came forth:

We had always exchanged Christmas gifts when I was
a kid . . . (classical Reform home), and I don't
think it ever made me less Jewish. It's part of our

business world. Why shouldn't I give to my family the
nice things I give to my employees and to several of my
preferred customers every year?

Still, strong leadership appears to be stronger on values (albeit
not necessarily all-Jewish values), than on performance. At the
same time, they are most likely to blame poor rabbinical leadership for a crisis in Reform Judaism, and while many are critical
of lay leadership as well, the rabbis are selected as the chief
objects of criticism. One wonders what "crisis" these leaders have
in mind? One wonders if it is the same crisis that the rabbis
have in mind. Indeed, this disparity may be a very meaningful issue
not only in the Reform movement, but one that is not unknown to
Orthodoxy and Conservatism, and to other religious groups as well.

In order to really dig into these and many additional serious
areas of Jewish concern, the reader is directed at this point to
a few specific pages of statistics. Here we get some of the
keenest insights into what constitutes the heart of the Reform movement, for here we see what we are all dealing with in Reform, - how
the lay leadership - from the strongest to the weakest - feels,
thinks, and acts on a variety of Jewish areas of life, some more
important, some less important. The attitudes and behaviors that
have been itemized for this purpose were designed to represent a
reasonably accurate cross-section of the ingredients that constitute
the routine (and some not so routine) dynamics of American Jewish
life today. The response patterns provide us not only with some
specific answers, but more important, they should provide us with
clues as to where the Reform laity identifies its present posture
and possibly its future direction. So before we go on, let the
reader please examine in detail Table 43. Let it be noted that only
the first column ("Most Active"), represents those congregants who
qualify according to the three criteria that are set down in the
opening paragraph to this chapter. (These constitute 12%.)

Table 43:

REFORM LAY LEADERSHIP:
ATTITUDES AND BEHAVIORS REGARDING A
CROSS-SECTION OF AMERICAN JEWISH LIFE

"LAY LEADERSHIP INDEX"

	Most active (N=115)	Reasonably active (N=380)	Somewhat active (N=336)	Least active (N=153)
I. Dangers facing American Judaism:				
(Percent reporting "GREAT THREAT")				
1. Anti-Semitism.	30%	35%	26%	27%
2. Intermarriage.(*)	22%	23%	19%	11%
3. Black militancy.	17%	28%	22%	14%
4. Changes in traditional Jewish family structure.	24%	23%	22%	18%
5. Weak religious school education.	37%	30%	29%	21%
II. Jewish survival depends on such factors as:				
(Percent reporting "VERY IMPORTANT")				
1. Jewish identification.	72%	68%	57%	51%
2. Jewish study.	26%	22%	21%	13%
3. Social action in the community.	43%	39%	32%	32%
4. Support of the State of Israel.	51%	51%	43%	32%

(*) Includes mixed marriage.

(Table 43, continued)

"LAY LEADERSHIP INDEX"

	Most active (N=115)	Reasonably active (N=380)	Somewhat active (N=336)	Least active (N=153)
III. Attitudes toward Israel:				
(Percent reporting "AGREEMENT")				
1. Should exist as a Jewish state.	67%	73%	71%	69%
2. It is <u>not the</u> Jewish homeland.	23%	13%	13%	16%
3. It is not a nationality.	9%	11%	13%	13%
IV. "I remain a Jew because it is simply the most convenient thing to do." (Percent reporting "AGREEMENT")	11%	10%	10%	11%
V. Should Reform rabbis officiate at mixed marriages (one spouse not converted)? (Percent reporting "DISAPPROVAL")	17%	13%	12%	6%
VI. Should the chuppa (canopy) be included in the wedding ritual? (Percent reporting "It should be left to the discretion of the bride and groom.")	78%	67%	69%	80%

(Table 43, continued)

"LAY LEADERSHIP INDEX"

	Most active (N=115)	Reasonably active (N=380)	Somewhat active (N=336)	Least active (N=153)
VII. Should the breaking of the glass be included in the wedding ritual?	(Percent reporting "It should be left to the discretion of the bride and groom.")			
	78%	65%	66%	80%
VIII. If there is a crisis in Reform Judaism, how important are the following factors?				
	(Percent reporting "VERY IMPORTANT")			
1. Poor rabbinical leadership.	45%	39%	32%	26%
2. Poor lay leadership.	37%	29%	29%	14%
3. Mixed marriage.	21%	18%	16%	12%
4. General decline of religious feeling.	56%	47%	47%	45%
5. Reform makes insufficient demands for commitment on the part of its lay members.	17%	17%	13%	11%

(Table 43, continued)

"LAY LEADERSHIP INDEX"

	Most active (N=115)	Reasonably active (N=380)	Somewhat active (N=336)	Least active (N=153)
IX. Ability to speak Yiddish reasonably well.	(Percent reporting "WELL")			
	12%	12%	7%	5%
X. Ability to read prayerbook Hebrew.	(Percent reporting "WELL")			
	32%	26%	21%	17%
XI. Membership in Jewish organizations (other than synagogue).	(Percent reporting 4 or more)			
	23%	16%	7%	0%
XII. Membership in non-Jewish organizations.	(Percent reporting "YES")			
	79%	68%	55%	41%
XIII. Attendance at Sabbath (Friday night) Services.	(Percent reporting "USUALLY")			
	34%	15%	14%	8%
XIV. The Sabbath (and Festival) candles are kindled in the home.	(Percent reporting "USUALLY")			
	31%	30%	24%	18%
XV. Head of household fasts on Yom Kippur.	(Percent reporting "USUALLY")			
	38%	40%	37%	27%

(Table 43, continued)

"LAY LEADERSHIP INDEX"

	Most active (N=115)	Reasonably active (N=380)	Somewhat active (N=336)	Least active (N=153)
XVI. Exchange gifts on Hanukkah.	(Percent reporting "USUALLY")			
	61%	67%	67%	69%
XVII. Christmas tree is decorated in home.	(Percent reporting "USUALLY")			
	17%	13%	15%	19%
XVIII. Exchange of Christmas gifts.	(Percent reporting "USUALLY")			
	45%	34%	40%	36%
XIX. How important was each of the following as a reason for affiliating with your present congregation?				
	(Percent reporting "VERY IMPORTANT")			
1. Want our children to remain within the faith.	66%	67%	52%	42%
2. I am a religious Jew.	31%	20%	9%	5%
3. For Bar Mitzvah.	26%	28%	21%	24%
4. For confirmation.	51%	41%	24%	19%

Table 44:

CONGREGANT LAY LEADERS AND NON-LEADERS:

ATTITUDES AND BEHAVIORS ON SELECTED JEWISH ISSUES

	Lay leaders (N=115)	Non-leader congregants (N=153)
	%	%
Stress the importance of Jewish identification.	72	51
Stress the importance of social action in the community.	43	32
Stress the importance of Jewish study.	26	13
Critical of inadequacy of religious school education program.	21	20
Support of the State of Israel.	51	32
Fear of anti-Semitism.	30	27
Anxiety over black militancy.	17	14

3. Some Comparisons Between Strong Lay Leaders and Congregants in General.

As to more general matters touching on Judaism, leaders can be compared with non-leaders on a number of religious and social issues. As Table 44 points it out, we see that while there are background and situational differences in the characteristics of people who become comparatively active in lay affairs, the evidence indicates that the active members are somewhat more involved in the religious aspects of Reform than are the inactive ones. This might be explainable by the fact that those who are active in synagogue affairs tend to be more in interaction with the rabbi(s), and thus more religion may "rub off" on them.

As one active Men's Club member put it,

> . . . and these Sunday mornings have been a good religious education for me . . . (Men's Club sponsors Sunday morning breakfasts). It's impossible to come Fridays. The store is open and it's a busy shopping night . . . But this is better than the sermons and everything . . . The rabbi is informal and we have good discussions after our lox and bagel. I've learned a lot of Judaism. . . . we have chapel services before breakfast. I like it.

4. Summary Highlights (Lay Leadership).

1) In terms of leadership, congregants can be identified as follows: 12% most active; 39% reasonably active; 50% almost inactive.

2) Lay leaders are mostly affluent fathers; not the best educated in the congregation; usually from Reform or Orthodox backgrounds.

3) Many congregants feel their Boards often suppress the Rabbi's freedom to speak out and to engage in social action in the wider community. They give some evidence. Rabbis, generally, deny this. Some agree with their congregants.

4) "Most active" lay leaders are two-to-one against intermarriage and mixed marriage over the "least active" congregants.

5) "Most actives" are only slightly more fearful than "least actives" with respect to anti-semitism, black militancy, Jewish family break-down as threats to Judaism.

6) "Most actives" almost two-to-one over "least actives" are concerned about the weakness of poor religious education, and consider Jewish study to be a very important requirement for Jewish survival.

7) "Most actives" much more than "least actives" consider the following as contributing factors in the making of crisis in Reform Judaism: poor rabbinical leadership; poor lay leadership; mixed marriage.

8) "Most actives" twenty-to-one over "least actives" belong to Jewish organizations; two-to-one belong to non-Jewish organizations; over three-to-one attend Sabbath services.

9) When asked if being a "religious Jew" was a "very important" reason for affiliating with their present congregations, some 31% of the strong lay leaders say "yes"; only 4% of the "least active" congregants say "yes".

10) Overall, strong lay leaders show greater concern over non-leader congregants not only of "inside" and "outside" threats to Reform, but to Judaism in general.

CHAPTER 16: AS CONGREGANTS VIEW THEIR RABBIS

1. General Assessment.

Generally speaking, Reform rabbis are well-thought-of by the
majority of their respective congregations. In response to a
question as to whether their rabbi should be in some other occupation instead of serving in the pulpit, two out of three (65%) reply
that he should remain a rabbi. An additional 12% think that he
might be more comfortable and more successful as a college professor.
While some congregants might mean this in a derogatory sense, it is
unlikely that very many in such a highly educated group would mean
this. Quite the contrary, it might suggest that they consider him
too good for the congregation. But this is only a neutral conjecture.
One congregant (a dentist), inserted such a comment during the course
of an interview, when he said,

> Rabbi _____ is a fine man, maybe too fine for some of
> the things he has to put up with (as a congregational
> rabbi) . . . He's a thinker, and here he has to be a
> doer mostly . . . He should be a college professor,
> and he'd be a good one.

It is particularly interesting to note that not only do 12% of our
congregants feel that their rabbis would be better off as college
professors, it will be recalled that 12% of the rabbis had also
indicated this for themselves.

2. Expectations and Performance: As Congregants View Their Rabbis.

But to get a more accurate picture of laymen's views, it is necessary
to become more specific. The questionnaire presented a list of

rabbinical activities in a number of areas. The congregants were
asked to indicate the extent to which a rabbi should perform each
activity (expectations), and next to each answer to then indicate the
extent to which he feels his rabbi (the senior rabbi if more than
one), actually does this activity (performance).

Table 45 includes all 16 rabbinical activities, and shows how Reform
congregants address themselves to each role. The list is rearranged
from the order in which it appeared in the questionnaire. Items
appear now on the basis of a rank order arrangement in terms of the
response pattern relative to expectations.

The first thing that Table 45 tells us is that, on a specific role
basis, "a great deal" more is expected of their rabbis than the
performance that they feel he gives in most of these activities.
As one compares the responses to expectations (a great deal), with the
responses to performance (a great deal), only in four activities do
performance scores exceed expectation scores. What is more, when
performance figures exceed expectation figures, it is by only one or two
percentage points in three of the four activities (#'s 9, 11, 12).

The second general assessment we can make of the data in Table 45 is
that in at least seven rabbinical activities (#'s 1 - 7), the figures
are 50% or over for those who expect "a great deal."

It should be noted again that these figures are by no means a
qualitative assessment. The expectations figures are based only on
what congregants feel a rabbi should do, and performance figures
reflect congregants' responses in terms of the amount of his performance.
There are some possible pitfalls attached to such a body of data.
Asking congregants to speak about their rabbi's performance

Table 45:
CONGREGANTS VIEW THEIR RABBIS IN TERMS OF
EXPECTATIONS AND PERFORMANCE
(N=984)

	Expectations		Performance*	
	A great deal %	Little %	A great deal %	Little %
1. "Priestly" roles (weddings, funerals, etc.)	78	1	70	2
2. Religious teacher.	68	3	43	11
3. Representative to Jewish community.	67	3	47	8
4. Rabbinical scholarly achievement.	62	3	58	5
5. Counselor on personal problems.	59	3	35	10
6. Preacher.	59	6	54	8
7. Visiting sick/bereaved.	59	5	43	10
8. Adult education teacher.	48	6	35	12
9. Representative to non-Jewish community.	45	6	47	6
10. Youth group leader.	38	13	21	22
11. Social action leader.	32	15	33	15
12. Work with synagogue auxiliaries.	24	20	21	19
13. Administrator.	19	19	21	18
14. Writer of books and articles primarily of Jewish subjects.	10	28	18	18
15. Radio and television speaker.	8	33	14	22
16. Fund raiser.	5	31	9	25

* Based on what congregants say their own rabbis actually do.

is not too unlike asking college students to evaluate the faculty.
Some students are more perceptive than others. Some have more
experience and background with college courses and professors. Some
never miss a class. Factors such as these may apply to congregants
as well. How often it it heard where one congregant is highly pleased
with a given sermon, and another congregant is highly displeased.

Having said this, let us return to the data. The only activity where
there appears to be near concordance between congregants' expectations
(78%) and congregants' recognition of performance (70%) on the part of
their rabbis is in the area of "priestly" roles (officiating at life-cycle
events). This shouldn't come too much as a surprise. A Conservative
rabbi recently conveyed to the writer, that in his opinion, both Conservative and Reform rabbis are slowly becoming more and more "life-
cycle officiators" and "family counselors," and surmised "there is
great possibility that this might become 80% to 90% of the rabbi's
duties in the future in Conservative and Reform congregations." And
possibly this gives us a clue for interpreting the close and high figures
between expectations ("a great deal"), and performance ("a great deal").
It is in the performance of his "priestly roles," that the rabbi is
probably closer to the congregant and his family than at any other time.
It is a personal affair for the congregant. Whether it be a simcha or
the opposite, it is an occasion when the rabbi is all his. He is not
sharing his rabbi with the rest of the congregation. The rabbi's
personal touch is psychologically very meaningful during these life-
cycle events.

Let us look at another activity. All sorts of comments were made,
written and oral, regarding the rabbi's role in his "work with synagogue
auxiliaries" (#12). Many rabbis tell us that this area can be and
often is a very time-consuming task. Other rabbis take the position

that they simply don't have the time for it, and still others say the
auxiliaries should run their own affairs. Several auxiliary officers
who were questioned also provide different versions of what the rabbi's
role should or should not be in these matters.

Here are two selected excerpts that are appropriate to the situation:

Interviewer: How do you explain such success (on the
part of your Sisterhood)?

Sisterhood Program Chairman: Before I became program
chairman . . . (it) wasn't always that way. But now
. . . it's different. (Our new rabbi) looks in on us
. . . but he's not a meddler. His wife is a doll . . .
She's there but she minds her own business.

A rabbi views it from the other side of the fence:

Rabbi: How little they know . . . If you really let
them go, . . . they'd have a circus here . . . Right
now the Men's Club is planning their program . . .
They've already got three sports figures lined up
. . .

Interviewer: How do you handle this, Rabbi?

Rabbi: It's a Temple program, not a Rod and Gun
Club, but they tell me unless we do this (have
sports figures), the men won't come. This is true.
Some won't come. But what are they coming to?
What are they coming for?

Interviewer: So you feel a rabbi has to be ac-
tively involved in the planning programs of the
synagogue auxiliaries?

Rabbi: Without a doubt. I don't give as much time
as I should . . . (because) there just isn't enough
time.

From Table 45, we can only say that apparently about one-fourth of our congregants are asking a great deal, and that the figure for performance (of a great deal) seems to be reasonably similar to expectations, at least regarding rabbis and the auxiliaries.

The only pair of items that might be somewhat difficult to understand are those dealing with scholarship. It will be noted that 67% expect a great deal of their rabbi by way of "rabbinical scholarly achievement (#3), but only 10% expect a great deal of him as a "writer of books and articles primarily on Jewish subjects." (#14). Surely to many readers the two statements are intertwined. Yet, there just might be a message here. It will be recalled that Reform congregants are, generally speaking, a very highly educated group of people. Because of this, there is the possibility of a very sophisticated distinction between the two activities as congregants confronted them. Is it possible that congregants want their rabbi to be scholarly in his synagogue activities, for them (the congregants), more than for out of the synagogue, for others? A scholarly journal article might impress the rabbi's colleagues, but does it make for a more erudite sermon or a more scholarly adult education lecture? Perhaps we're stretching a point. Perhaps not. The hard fact is that only 10% of Reform congregants are saying they expect "a great deal" of scholarly writing from their rabbis, and almost three times as many congregants say they expect "little" of this from their rabbis.

3. With Focus on Rabbis as Pastors, Community Leaders, and Scholars.

Three areas (Figure 54), are chosen for specific assessment at this point: (1) the rabbi's role as a pastor, (2) his role as community leader, and (3) his role as scholar.

<u>Figure 54:</u>
<u>REFORM CONGREGANTS (N=984) ASSESS THEIR RABBIS:</u>

I. As pastors
II. As community leaders
III. As scholars

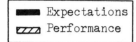
■■■ Expectations
▨▨▨ Performance

I. AS PASTORS:

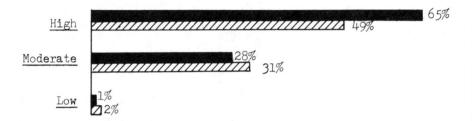

II. AS COMMUNITY LEADERS:

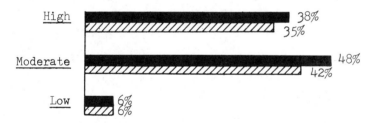

III. AS SCHOLARS:

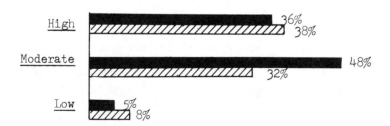

(Percentages do not total 100% because responses of "can't decide" and "no answer" are not included.)

The three role assessments are based on a statistical composite of congregants' ratings based on the following rabbinical activities (as derived from Table 45):

As pastor:
1. Counselor on personal problems.
2. Visiting sick/bereaved.
3. "Priestly" roles (weddings, funerals, etc.).

As community leader:
1. Representative to Jewish community.
2. Representative to non-Jewish community.
3. Social action leader.
4. Radio and television speaker.

As scholar:
1. Rabbinical scholarly achievement.
2. Writer of books and articles primarily on Jewish subjects.

We note in Figure 54 that congregants who have high expectations of their rabbis as pastors do not feel that the performance matches these expectations. Expectations and performance are not too far apart on community leader. Those who have high expectations of their rabbis as scholars are somewhat more than satisfied with the performance in this role.

So much for those with high expectations. Let us look at the other extreme. The striking thing is that those who have low expectations seem to feel that low performance is all they are getting from their rabbis. This type of finding is not uncommon in other areas of human behavior. We need to keep in mind, however, that the same respondents, may not necessarily be involved in any of these response patterns.

4. Five Selected Statements Concerning Reform Rabbis: Congregants Agree and Disagree.

When congregants are asked to express their degree of agreement concerning a list of selected statements on Reform rabbis (Table 46), we find some interesting results. Congregants are about equally divided with respect to whether they believe their rabbi's position of leadership is more important than is enjoyed by rabbis in Orthodox and Conservative congregations. Far more agree than disagree, 41% to 13%, that their rabbis believe in a personal God. Very few (9%) agree that their rabbi gives the impression that he is more concerned with salary, vacation, and fringe benefits than with developing a strong Jewish life in his congregation. In fact an overwhelming 76% disagree with that statement.

There seems to be a healthy respect for the rabbinate of all of Judaism on the part of the 32% who disagreed with the statement on the rabbi's position of leadership. But almost the same number seem to be saying that Reform rabbis enjoy a better status in Reform congregations. If some Reform Jews feel they hold their rabbis in greater esteem in their congregations than do other congregations vis-à-vis their rabbis, that is certainly their privilege.

Almost two-thirds disagree that the rabbi likes to plan the synagogue's

Table 46:

FIVE SELECTED STATEMENTS CONCERNING REFORM RABBIS:
CONGREGANTS AGREE AND DISAGREE
(N=984)

STATEMENT	AGREE	DISAGREE
1. The rabbi's position of leadership in MY congregation is more important than the positions of Orthodox and Conservative rabbis in THEIR congregations.	29%	32%
2. My rabbi believes in a personal God.	41%	13%
3. Many of my rabbi's sermons are devoted to public and social issues like Viet Nam, the drug problem, the racial problem and such.	70%	15%
4. My rabbi gives the impression that he is more concerned with salary, vacation and fringe benefits than with developing a strong Jewish life in his congregation.	9%	76%
5. My rabbi does not involve members of the congregation in planning program activities. He likes to do it himself.	10%	65%
6. Viet Nam, the drug problem, the racial problem and such are not Jewish issues; I wish my rabbi would preach on Judaism rather than these topics.	16%	68%

program activities by himself. In fact only 10% believe that he does not involve members of the congregation in such activities. One last and interesting point. While we find that some 70% of the congregants agree that many of their rabbi's sermons are devoted to public and social issues like Viet Nam, the drug problem, the

racial problem and such, 68% of such congregants disagree that their
rabbis usually preach on Judaism rather than these topics. Thus we
may find a rather good concordance between what the congregants like
and what they get with regard to sermon topics. The question here is
to determine if this is what the rabbi wants, or if this is what the
congregant wants. It is more than likely that this is at least
acceptable to congregants, or the rabbi would be a displeasure to
them and would very likely come to know this. Now then, does it mean
that in some cases rabbis are simply catering to the wishes of their
congregants? If, of course, the sermon is on Judaism as Judaism
addresses itself to social issues of the day, that is one thing.
But it may be something else again, if the focus is truly on some
sociological, political, or psychological issues, per se. This, in
most cases, would be out of the rabbi's province of competence.

Here is a comment from one congregant on this issue:

> . . . as a psychiatric social worker, it gives me much
> discomfort to listen to a sermon that even I would
> hesitate to present to an educated group of men and
> women. I don't know why he (the rabbi) doesn't stick
> to a Jewish or Israeli topic, or at least something
> allied. To speak on the psychology of race relations
> is simply 'not his bag.'

Some pertinent questions on this point may be in order. Is the
rabbi simply giving his congregants what they want and without realizing it is he holding them at their current level of Jewish knowledge?
If this is so, is it possible that he could shift his emphasis if
he chose to do so, so that more Jewish content and perspective could
be effectively taught from the pulpit? It appears to the writer
that these are questions that only the rabbi, himself, is qualified
to answer. In the last analysis, it is the rabbi who determines the

religious teaching that comes forth or does not come forth from his
pulpit. It is his pulpit.

5. Congregants Speak Their Mind.

We have, thus, a complicated picture. In terms of general platitudes,
congregants say they like their rabbis. In answer to more specific
questions certain qualifications set in, so that a more refined
measure of satisfaction yields a somewhat lower level.

Possibly the best way to complete this section is to let the congregants
have the same opportunity as was given to the rabbis in the preceding
section, - to speak for themselves.

The statements are excerpts from interviews, from letters to the writer,
and from written expressions that were included in the returned questionnaires. These are all randomly selected.

First let us see what congregants are saying about their rabbis:

> If our Rabbi would not work so hard, we'd all feel more
> relaxed. I come from a large Temple in (a large city)
> ... Our former Rabbi never worked so hard ... I'm glad
> we're only a hundred families for the Rabbi's sake.

> I feel the HUC-JIR is wasting the talents of its re-
> sources (physical and professional) in the education
> of young men who do not wish to enter the Rabbinate
> for service to Congregations ... In my humble opinion
> the 'undedication' of the newly ordained Rabbis from
> the HUC-JIR is one of the main threats to Reform
> Judaism in the United States today.

> The rabbi should be more concerned with his congrega-
> tion in a pastoral sense and more emphasis should
> be placed on emotionalism and less on intellectualism
> in Reform Judaism. More ritual would add this factor.

Our rabbi does not encourage activities in
the Temple. He disbanded the Men's Club as
unnecessary. He brags about how small the
Temple's utilities bills are instead of
realizing how little our huge building is
used. He refuses to call on the 'shut-ins.
Our congregation is small and the rabbi
could easily see the few shut-ins in our
community.

In my opinion, graduates in Reform Judaism
have been exposed to 'degrees' in philosophy, etc., etc., etc., but are not dedicated to religious Judaism and consequently cannot and do not teach, and/or
instill Judaism to congregants.

I strongly resent the disinterest of our
long-time Rabbi in the religious school
now that he has an associate Rabbi who
is in charge of the school.

... Our Senior Rabbi devotes so much of his
time to us and our well being that I feel
I am doing everything for him and not just
the Temple.

I believe that we are very lucky to have
our rabbi and his wife as our religious
leaders.

Our rabbi is not committed to the belief
in God, the value of prayer, or the
necessity for organized religion. He is
humanistically oriented. He conveys these
doubts to the youth of the congregation,
so that intermarriage is rampant in our
Temple. We have become so disillusioned
with his lack of religious leadership that
we are about to resign.

The following statement was not selected randomly. It is included
here because it is a rather special statement, and very possibly
speaks for many more congregants who may not have spoken up but
may share similar feelings about their respective rabbis. Like
democracy and fresh air, - only when these are threatened and
polluted do we speak up. When all is well, we are prone to
take things for granted.

> If only there was some way our Rabbis could
> realize how much they mean to us ... how much they
> do for us. My wife and I are average Jews. But
> we have that good feeling of security about our
> Rabbi. He has done so much for our children,
> not just by way of Jewish learning, but as a
> model human being... Even though our children
> don't care for religious school too much, they
> respect the Rabbi, and through him, they re-
> spect Judaism in a deep sense. It's hard to
> put into words, but without him (the rabbi)
> we would be lost. We live in a small town
> and all around us are small towns and ours
> is the only Temple. Our community Seder
> makes me proud of the little share that
> our little (Jewish community of) over 100
> families is doing to continue our heritage
> of 3000 years. It is the one man (the
> rabbi) who is holding us together and we are
> honored by his presence. He is a man of
> God ... I could write pages ... Thank you
> for the opportunity to say these few words...

And what do our congregants say about the synagogue and Judaism?

> The American Synagogue tends to be parochial,
> self-centered, poorly organized. Each con-
> gregation has more concern for its own sur-
> vival than for the varied needs of Jewish
> people and Judaism.

We have been in the process of examining
Reform Judaism for the past two years and will
be formally converted within the next two
months. The three youngest are being raised
as Jews (7, 8 & 10 years) - the older children
(13, 16, 18 & 19) were raised as Catholics.
The older ones have been encouraged to follow
their own convictions. We find Judaism very
relaxing ...

I feel uninspired by the general Judaic
religious concepts and ritualism - also confusion and general ineptitude of Rabbi and
staff. I still support a Reform congregation
by dues-paying, but have no interest in the
religious program. I, and wife have been
attending Christian Science services regularly for five years (weekly) and have found
religious experience.

My wife and I were converted in 1967 after
35 years of marriage. We were both raised in
the Christian church and brought our children
up there but became disenchanted and hadn't
gone to church for about 8 years. My wife's
grandmother was Jewish as was her father, aunt
and uncle so after all these years we converted
and are very happy we did.

I thank you for the opportunity to respond to
this range of questions; it shows me how confused I am ...
....
... Raised anti-Zionist, I have, after a year
of study in Israel, become something of a
Zionist - at least as part of a new concern
for Jewish peoplehood ... Jewish institutions
should help the part of the Jewish people
that they serve to join in restoring our
awareness and action in this effort.

Perhaps in our search for the answers to many
natural phenomena, we have sacrificed something of the mystical that once was a part
of the Synagogue and religious ritual.

Because of my disenchantment with Reformed
Judaism as I saw it practiced in the local
Temple, I recently resigned and sent the
dues equivalent to the annual Allied Jewish
Appeal - added to my usual contribution to
Israel. The feeling of satisfaction was
great. It will be an annual occurrence. (The
respondent wrote "Allied" not "Combined"
or "United.")

The day the Jews decided by getting in the
'main stream' of the WASP world and become
totally integrated is the day Judaism began to fall apart in the U.S. They were so
anxious to be accepted by the Protestant
and Catholic world, they changed spots -
and fell heir to the non-Jewish problems...
....
While all the time, they could live as
Jews, with their own ethnic culture and still
be decent human beings with some semblance
of moral values. But Jews, God bless them,
when they do something they go all out, and,
walk right to the end of the plank, falling
into the sea of disintegration as Jews.
Please, God, put a safety net under the plank
and save them.

Things not done in Reform Temples which I
feel are important:

1) Wearing of Talles.
2) Wearing of Yamulka.
3) More prayer in Hebrew.
4) Teaching children to understand
        as well as read and write Hebrew.

Catholic, Protestant or Jew - we will find in
the 70's a surge toward spiritualism - out of
need - and hopefully resulting finally in some
unity of mankind. God was never dead. People
took a sabbatical from His teachings - but they
will return and so, perhaps, will religion.

Orthodoxy turns Reform for social acceptance
and to refute eastern European origins -
once in Reform they are basically unhappy and
try to turn ritual, thought etc. backwards
a century to Orthodoxy with a Reform label.
Forward we must go, not backwards - release
the past, - but keep that which proves the
test of time in behavior and civilization.

I feel our leadership in the Temple is very,
very poor as far as young are concerned.
I also feel we are raising our young to
believe in money as a "God," rather than
giving them the true values of Judaism.
We are losing our young to other religions
that seem to work to keep their youngsters
interested.

In (a large city) we belonged to a Temple
of over 1000 families. We didn't know
them all, but we knew enough families
with whom we had much in common. After
six years we moved to ... Here we have
been ... almost ten years. We have only
80 or 90 families. We know everybody,
but we know nobody. It's a cold feeling.
Most of the Jewish families have non-Jewish
families as their closest friends. Somehow the Temple is just another building in
town. The rabbi's best friend is a young
minister his age.

I'm trying to raise my children to be concerned, caring citizens and Judaism doesn't
have a whole lot to do with it.

There is a basic anomaly at the core of the
formalities of the Jewish religion which involves the concept of the brotherhood of man
and the injunction against intermarriage.
The fear that intermarriage will result in
the disintegration of Jewish group existence
is a by-product of this inconsistency. Perhaps the results of the foregoing questionnaire
will disclose the fallacy and, hopefully,
thus dispel the fear as evidenced by the following statement attributed to Rabbi Einhorn,
"Each intermarriage drives a nail in the coffin
of Judaism." If the ultimate objective of
"Judaism" is the brotherhood of man under the
fatherhood of God, then the position of the
Orthodox, Conservative, and apparently the
majority of the Reform rabbinate on the matters
of intermarriage and "conversion" are representative of the essence of hypocrisy.

To this day, when I enter our present, modern
(and beautiful) facility, there is to me an
atmosphere of cold pragmatism. The Temple I
remember (from youth) was uncomfortable but
I could not enter it without feeling the com-
manding presence of something greater than an
aggregate of individuals. Can the inspiration
that I miss be the same type of thing our
youth seeks today?

My view is close to that of the Reconstructionists.

As a family we have always been members of both
the Temple and Conservative synagogue - our son
was Bar Mitzvah in the synagogue and our daughter
confirmed in the Temple. Both children were
married in the Temple and are members of the
Temple. My husband and I always attended high
holy day services at the synagogue - we have
always felt that both temple and synagogue
had a definite place in our lives.

I do not feel that Judaism has much future in
the United States. This is an open society,
and the odds favor intermarriage. In addition,
we are not salvationists; we have no pie in
the sky when we die. I mourn at the grave
of my faith; what else can I do? We have
brought much that is good to the world; but
as a religion, I fear we are dying. I
read the Bible in Hebrew,- I not only can,
but I do so. My children do not read it at
all. As for Jewish leadership, it is poor.
However, what can you expect? You will understand that this is written in Cincinnati.
It is my opinion that most of the people who
go into the Reform rabbinate could not earn
a living elsewhere.

No such thing as 'Jewish new leftism' - it
is as old as the oldest Jew. Clear well
defined questions.

Questions seem to imply a vast cleavage between
Reform and other Jews. I am not aware of this
problem and do not recognize it as a problem.

(There is) a need for laymen to speak their
minds at the UAHC Regional conferences so that
rabbis can hear what we are thinking. We
moved a few years ago, and this is the second
experience with UAHC Regions. It's still mostly
the rabbis listening to themselves.

We have a nice little Temple ... 150 families,
but what we don't have is a good feeling of
togetherness. I think our Rabbi could do more
to bring us together but his best work is with
outside community, and we follow suit.

I am a 4th generation American - with a strong
mid-west background - and Jewish ...
....
... I attend the Unitarian Church nearby - since
it is convenient but mostly for the sermons of
the minister - who speaks more brilliantly
than any man I have ever heard - and seems
to make sense out of this confused world.
Our former Rabbi is a dedicated, sincere,
brilliant and dear man - I would not ever
want to hurt him - but just can't accept
Judaism any more - or Christianity.

I envy those who belong to 'live' Conservative Temples. Wish my town had one. I am
impressed by Rabbi Silverman's prayerbook
(and his son Hillel's jumping congregation).

And then there are the occasional comments (not selected at
random), that break up the day a bit:

I think a Rabbi should preach and run the
church (the respondent wrote 'church'), and
let the President run the country.

Our children are enrolled in a religious school
40 miles away... the Jewish community in this
town has been beautifully split by a Yenta.

Shemini Atzeres??

Only Reform Jews could have the time and curiosity
to fill out this questionnaire.

Sure was long. I'm tired. Good night.

6. Summary Highlights (Reform Congregants View their Rabbis).

1) Generally speaking, Reform congregants mostly speak well of
   their rabbis; 67% feel he had chosen the right calling; 12%
   feel he should have been a college professor. Hence 79%
   respect and regard the man as a professional person.

2) The data tell us that "a great deal" more is expected in
   most of the specific rabbinical roles than the extent to
   which the rabbis perform in these roles. This makes reference
   only to the amount of work they do, and makes no implication
   of a qualitative assessment.

3) The only activity where there is near concordance between
   congregants' expectations and congregants' recognition of
   performance on the part of their rabbis is in the area of
   "priestly roles."

4) By far, a majority of congregants expect "a great deal"
   from the rabbi in "priestly" roles, religious teaching, involvement in the Jewish community, rabbinical scholarship,
   counseling, preaching, and visiting the sick and bereaved.

5) On the basis of combining several activities into three
   categories (pastors, community leaders, and scholars), by
   far the greatest expectation that congregants have of
   their rabbis is in the pastoral role (65%).

6) Whereas 65% of the congregants have high expectations of
   their rabbis as pastors, only 49% say his performance matches
   his expectations.

7) Congregants' high expectations and high performance ratings
   are reasonably similar when they view their rabbis in their
   community leadership roles (38% to 35%), and in scholarly
   activities (36% to 38%).

8) Reform congregants who have low expectations seem to feel that
   low performance is all they are getting from their rabbis.

9) Some 41% of Reform congregants feel that their rabbi believes
   in a <u>personal</u> God; 13% disagree; the balance say they don't
   know.

10) Whereas 9% feel their rabbi is probably more concerned with
    salary and vacations than with developing a strong Jewish life
    in his congregation, 76% disagree; 15% don't know.

11) One in ten congregants feels that his rabbi "tries to run the
    whole show himself" when it comes to planning congregational
    activities; 65% disagree; 25% don't know.

12) Some 16% agree that their rabbis preach on social issues of the
    day and would prefer he preach on Judaism instead; 68% dis-
    agree; 16% don't know.

PART IV

T H E   S E M I N A R Y   S T U D E N T

Introduction.

Much concerning the seminary student has already been identified in
the section on the rabbinate in Part II.

The questionnaire to the seminary students purposely asks many of
the same pertinent questions for the purposes of comparative assessment. And we have already seen what these data say to us.

Other questions that were asked bring forth responses that substantiate much the same tone. There is an undeniable discontent on
the part of many of our seminarians. They seem to share little
of the strong, positive, and hopeful views that so many of the rabbis
feel and gratuitously express in their comments. Nor is the pessimism
supported by much substantive data. And this is all right, too.
One doesn't always use data to support emotions. But what we
have here is a coin where both sides seem to reveal the same malaise.
There are many rabbis who express malaise and chagrin, but even
here the manner of expression is in the form of questioning, rather
than in the form of acrimonious, hard and fast judgment. Not so
from a goodly number of seminarians. A few, very few, question.
But with regard to any positive, hopeful praise, there is little
that is forthcoming. The other side of the coin shows mostly the
firm expression of bitter conviction that things are almost all bad!
And it concerns almost everything, - religious belief, HUC-JIR, the
CCAR, Reform, Judaism in general, and by no means least, this study.
In 25 years of survey research, this writer had not been exposed

320

from <u>any</u> population sample, to the castigating and destructive comments
that even begin to be commensurate with the outpouring of criticism
that comes forth from close to 50% of our seminarian sample.

So let us go on now, and let us try to understand this. To have the
aforementioned information (and it is presented here merely as data,
with no implication of any evaluation), is important, but it is more
important to understand how it comes to pass, and where it is going.
Again, the reader is referred to the section on the rabbinate for considerable raw data and comment concerning the seminarians. A case in
point is Figure 25, page 160 and accompanying comment.

Possibly the reader should be reminded at this point that the responses
in this chapter are based primarily on a 30% return rate*, that no
questionnaires were processed at the New York school, and that the
differences in population size at the other two schools are so marked
(Cincinnati 132, California 15), that most of what we are being told in
this chapter is based on data from the Cincinnati campus.

---

* See pp. 10 and 11.

CHAPTER 17: SOME DEMOGRAPHIC CHARACTERISTICS OF SEMINARIANS

1. Educational Backgrounds.

Seminarians are better educated than their predecessors. Again, it
is obvious why 98% should have at least a B.A., as opposed to 83%
in the case of ordained rabbis. More of them (77% of the seminarians compared with 70% of the rabbis), entered seminary directly
from college.

2. Fathers' Occupational Backgrounds.

Our future rabbis (13%) are somewhat more likely to have come from
rabbinical homes than did their predecessors (10%). They are
definitely more likely to have professional and managerial fathers
(41% compared with 33%). Self-employed merchants and white collar
personnel who were fathers to 52% of the older rabbis have now
reduced to 44% for seminarians' fathers. At any rate, rabbis continue to be middle- or upper-middle-class, and very likely to have
grown up in a highly-educated household.

3. Jewish Backgrounds.

One of the things that greatly distinguishes rabbis from congregation
members (Parts II and III), is the fact that the rabbis (while coming
from a similar class background), grew up in a more Jewish milieu.
This same kind of milieu seems to have made a difference in the case
of seminarians, and practically in the same proportions. Some 57%
report that the parental atmosphere was pro-Zionist. The new rabbis
are less likely to come from Orthodox homes than did many of their
older colleagues. Thus there continues a trend that we had already

identified in Part II. Some 6% claim to have Orthodox fathers, and 24% identify their parents as Conservative. And, for the first time, Reform is really beginning to produce its own. Almost six out of ten seminarians have Reform parents.

4. Marital and Family Status.

Almost six out of ten (57%) of our seminarians are married, although very few have children. Although no accurate figures are available for graduate students elsewhere, this distribution would seem about par for the course. The trend suggested by the data is that the majority of our seminarians, whose average age is just under 25, tend to marry within a year of ordination.

5. Religious Beliefs of Seminarians.

Let us turn our attention to religious belief (Figure 55). It is very simply told. Belief even in a qualified version of God is much lower among seminarians, much lower even than among rabbis who were ordained in the last five years. The slack is not taken up, it should be noted, by a non-traditional belief in God either. Instead virtually all of the shift has been in the direction of agnosticism. It applies to 43% of the seminarians, as compared with 19% of the most recently confirmed rabbis, as compared with 14% for all rabbis. Is this an epidemic of theological doubt? It is not something that is likely to go away next year or the year after, and it is quite obviously related to the whole range of questions and issues - and proposed solutions - that are part of what Roszak calls the "counter-culture," Reich calls "the greening of America," and Peter Berger calls the "blueing of America." Assuming this is true, does it suggest that we might then expect that a substantial number of

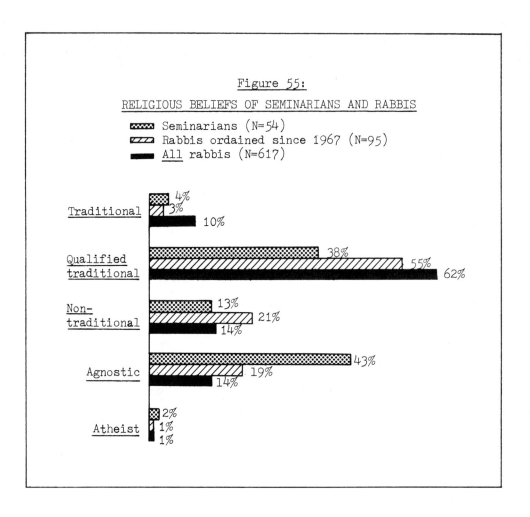

Figure 55:

RELIGIOUS BELIEFS OF SEMINARIANS AND RABBIS

Seminarians (N=54)
Rabbis ordained since 1967 (N=95)
All rabbis (N=617)

Traditional — 4% / 3% / 10%

Qualified traditional — 38% / 55% / 62%

Non-traditional — 13% / 21% / 14%

Agnostic — 43% / 19% / 14%

Atheist — 2% / 1% / 1%

these seminarians will be rabbinical dropouts once they have come into contact with their first suburban congregation? And it is these young seminarians who may well be among the most precious people that have ever been attracted to Reform. That is part of the dilemma. Possibly this is why one HUC-JIR administrator, during the course of an interview, stated, "We have great need for a

<u>demonstration</u> of commitment to Judaism (on the part of potential students), <u>prior</u> to their admission."

Here are some random comments from seminarians on the subject of <u>religious belief</u>!

> Being an agnostic is not being an atheist ... and it is not contrary to Judaism to search one's soul. Agnosticism means searching ... Incidentally I don't intend to be a pulpit rabbi, at least not for the present. When I first came here I didn't know there was anything else ... (other than for a rabbi to be a pulpit rabbi.) I sometimes do ask myself what I'm doing here with the College, and what the College is doing with me.

> ... There is no mention (in the questionnaire) of the crisis of beliefs that confronts Rabbis and/or students - neither know what they believe.

> If I had faith in God before I came here (HUC-JIR), and I'm not sure if I did or did not ... I was never confronted with it ... I lost it there soon enough. When a rabbi-relative of mine once asked me if my professors believe in God, I couldn't honestly answer him.

6. <u>Summary Highlights (Seminary Students: Demography and Belief)</u>.

1) Some 13% of our seminarians come from rabbinical homes; most have fathers in professional or managerial occupations.

2) Six of ten seminarians are married; few have children.

3) Belief in God, even in a qualified version, is lower than for rabbis as a whole, even lower than among rabbis who were ordained in the last five years; 43% are agnostic; only 4% are "traditional" believers; 38% say that they are traditional believers with some "qualification;" 2% are atheists.

CHAPTER 18: THE RABBINATE AS CAREER CHOICE:
SEMINARIAN RESPONSES

Let us now examine the seminarians' values and attitudes. Why
did they choose the rabbinate? Are they satisfied with their choice?
What kind of rabbis are they likely to become? Are they very
different from those who have gone before? Do they resemble
the more recently ordained rabbis? Is there a great gap between
the pre- and post-ordained groups?

1. Reasons for Choosing the Rabbinate.

When we look at reasons for choosing the rabbinate as a career,
some significant differences begin to show up between the pre-
and post-ordained groups. Table 47 points up these differences.

As we see, the rank order of responses from rabbis and from seminarians (Table 47), is identical. Both seminarians and rabbis
are most likely to mention self-fulfillment and serving people.
Both seminarians and rabbis are least likely to mention the
power component of the rabbinate as a reason. But there are
differences. Seminarians more than their elders stress self-
fulfillment and serving people. They are somewhat less likely
to stress scholarship and power. To put it another way, the
image of the rabbi seems to have shifted from that of unapproach-
able, deeply learned, father-figure to that of a more informal,
permissive, pastor type. As the novelists often put it, - "the
friendly village curate."

Is it of concern to the rabbinate, indeed to Judaism, that less

326

than 40% of the newer rabbis seem to view scholarship as almost
of secondary importance? We will relate this to their aspirations
as teachers a little later on.

Table 47:

WHY CHOOSE THE RABBINATE AS A CAREER?:

COMPARATIVE RESPONSE PATTERNS FROM SEMINARIANS AND RABBIS

	Seminarians	Rabbis
	%	%
"As an occupation it offered me the most opportunity to 'do my thing' in terms of my interests, needs, and general fulfillment."	74 (N=54)	61 (N=616)
"I like people and the rabbinate provided maximum opportunities to serve my fellow-man."	58 (N=54)	48 (N=616)
"My intense belief in God and in Judaism and my desire to continue one of its major traditions,--- to be a teacher unto my People."	44 (N=54)	44 (N=616)
"It was the image of the rabbi as scholar, teacher and community leader that attracted me most."	38 (N=53)	41 (N=616)
"When I saw rabbis in the pulpit, they seemed to me to represent significant, powerful figures."	8 (N=53)	18 (N=615)

2. How Seminarians View Rabbinical Roles.

If for example, we look at the way seminary students rate the
various rabbinical roles, in order of importance, and compare
these ratings with what rabbis have already told us, we find a remarkable degree of concordance. Leaving aside the numbers endorsing each role, and concentrating on rank order, Table 48
tells us that both groups (rabbis and rabbinical students) rank
religious teaching first. The third choices (priestly roles)
are also the same, although the rabbis nominate scholarly activities equally as their third choice.

There is similar agreement when it comes to ranking the least
important roles, viz., working with synagogue auxiliaries,
administration, being a radio or television speaker, or fund-
raising. On the whole, seminary students demonstrate a posture
that is reasonably similar to their elders of what it means to
be a rabbi. If these role definitions continue to conform to
those already entertained by their older colleagues, it means
that there should be little future discord within Reform
over these matters. There will certainly be disagreement
over others, but it is clear that Reform seminary students
accept the structural arrangement of the system.

Before leaving this topic, however, it is interesting to
note that rabbinical students consistently demonstrate a
greater preference than do rabbis in the following three areas:
(1) "priestly" roles, (2) counseling, and (3) pastoral
visits. Rabbis are equally likely to stress scholarly activities. This is completely in line with what we already saw

Table 48:

RABBINICAL ROLE EXPECTATIONS:

A COMPARATIVE RANK-ORDER ASSESSMENT

BY SEMINARIANS AND RABBIS

"WHAT RABBIS OUGHT TO DO."	Seminarians (N=54) %	Rabbis (N=620) %
Religious teacher.	92	82
Adult education teacher.	69	74
"Priestly roles" (weddings, funerals, etc.).	61	51
Counselor on personal problems.	59	44
Pastoral visitations.	54	30
Representative to Jewish community.	50	38
Preacher.	41	49
Rabbinical scholarly achievement.	39	51
Youth group leader.	28	14
Social action leader.	17	29
Writer of books and articles primarily on Jewish subjects.	11	14
Representative to non-Jewish community.	9	12
Work with synagogue auxiliaries.	9	17
Administrator.	9	6
Radio and television speaker.	4	5
Fund raiser.	0	1

in analyzing the motives for entering the rabbinate. Thus, while this is not likely to produce any major conflict within Reform, it is worth noting that there appears to be a trend toward personal service, helping people in trouble; a trend which is not new in the rabbinate, but a trend which is being given increasingly strong emphasis by our seminary students. There is a reflection of some rejection by the younger generation of intellectualism in terms of specific Jewish scholarship. We can also identify some rejection of rationalism and "authority." Although these phenomena may be viewed as distressing to some readers, it is not necessarily a discomforting picture when we view things in terms of the total cultural context. The picture seems to be strongly in line with our contemporary counter-culture. Whether this trend will grow even stronger in the future, no one can say. But with all due respect, one can at least ask a question. If these young rabbis-to-be see the role of teacher (of Judaism) as most important, how can one be a teacher without being a scholar? Or if one can, how good is that which is being taught? Of course, as noted in previous pages, if the large majority presently pursuing graduate studies in non-Jewish institutions are concentrating in areas of Judaica, the question would be out of order.

3. Do Seminarians Want to Be Pulpit Rabbis?

As to plans for the future, most seminary students are by no means determined to become pulpit rabbis, at least not immediately upon ordination. Indeed, less than half definitely plan to do so. Table 49 gives a clear indication of things. Presumably, of the 19% who indicate graduate studies for the next step (after ordination), many hope to go into teaching, or so the

Table 49:

FUTURE PLANS OF SEMINARY STUDENTS
(N=54)

Definitely plan to become pulpit rabbis —— 46%

Intend to teach —————————————— 15%

Intend to pursue graduate studies ———— 19%

previous data would suggest. Some, no doubt, will become pulpit
rabbis. But it is noteworthy that 15% plan to enter teaching
immediately after ordination. The rest will either become Hillel
rabbis, engage in full-time writing, or in a variety of other
(unspecified) activities.

4. How Seminarians View the UNION PRAYER BOOK.

Up to now, some readers will have identified a crisis in faith on
the part of our seminary students, - our future rabbis. If so, is
this crisis in faith reflected in the different response patterns
regarding the Union Prayer Book?

Both rabbis and seminarians were presented with a passage from the
Union Prayer Book. They were then asked a few questions concerning
their reaction to this passage. It is not an untypical passage.
Several rabbis, seminarians, and a few steady synagogue-attending
laymen were in reasonable agreement that the verse in question is
typical in content, in tone, and in language to the rest of the

volume. The passage is stated in Figure 56. The lesson is
plain. Not only are seminarians generally more criticial of the
Union Prayer Book than are the rabbis, but seminarians are also
far less likely to respond positively to the verse in question.
It is the last that sets them apart from the rabbis, many of whom
are also critical of the Union Prayer Book. But the rabbis tend
to express their discontent, much more so than the students, from
something like a religious perspective.

What we have seen so far can be repeated for a large number of
items, all of which appear throughout the comparative findings
that are to be found in Section II. There is no need to discuss
them here again because they do not add or subtract from the
picture we have already obtained. It is basically this. Seminary
students resemble young rabbis, only more so. Their major motivation for becoming rabbis appears to be related to their interest
in staying away from the kind of segmental roles so typical of
industrial societies, in which relationships involving the whole
person are replaced by formal, bureaucratic ones. This is a wide-
spread phenomenon among young people in America,- indeed, throughout the industrialized countries of the world. Some portion of
this desire is romantic and sentimental, but not necessarily all
of it. At any rate, it remains to be seen whether the Reform
rabbinate will be a suitable setting for the kind of work these
young men want to do. One thing that will make things easier is that
their notion of the rabbi's work closely resembles that of the older
men with whom they will be working. The conflict, if there is to
be one, will come over religious beliefs, and between their expectations on the one hand, and on the fulfillment that they are
able to obtain from their congregations, on the other hand.

332

Figure 56:

A PASSAGE IN THE UNION PRAYER BOOK:
REACTIONS FROM SEMINARIANS AND RABBIS

"We gratefully acknowledge, O Lord our God, that Thou art
our Creator and Preserver, the Rock of our life and the
Shield of our help. We render thanks unto Thee for our
lives which are in Thy hand, for our souls which are ever
in Thy keeping, for Thy wondrous providence and for Thy
continuous goodness, which Thou bestowest upon us day by
day. Truly, Thy mercies never fail and Thy loving kindness
never ceases. Therefore do we forever put our trust in Thee."

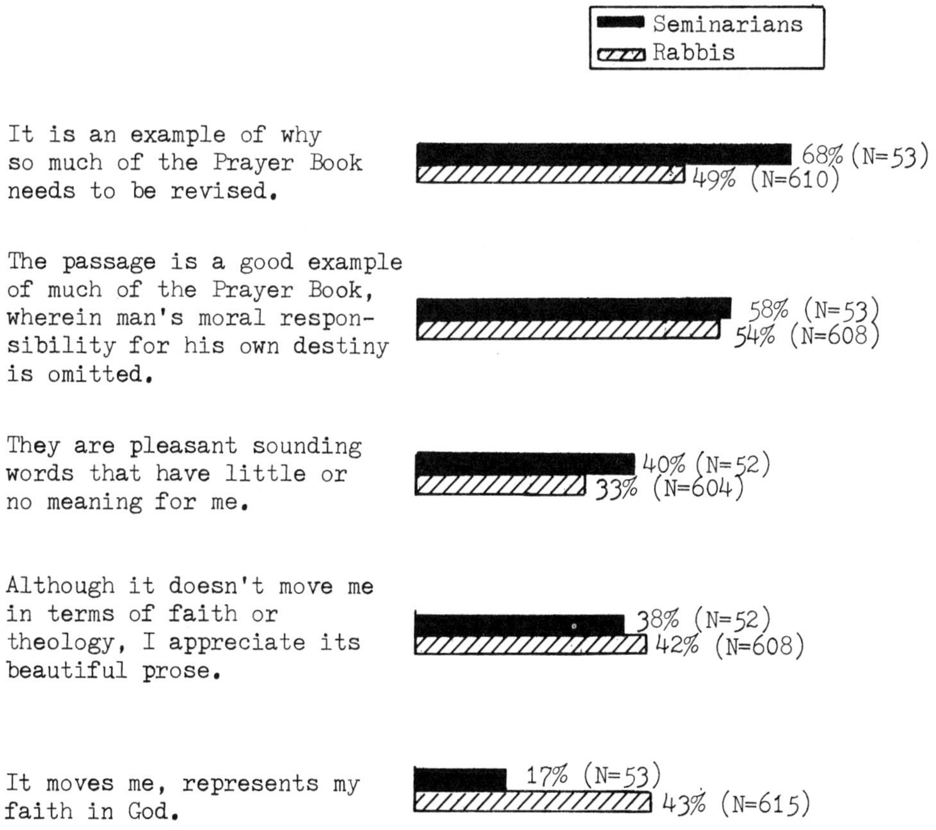

■ Seminarians
▨ Rabbis

It is an example of why
so much of the Prayer Book
needs to be revised.
68% (N=53)
49% (N=610)

The passage is a good example
of much of the Prayer Book,
wherein man's moral responsibility for his own destiny
is omitted.
58% (N=53)
54% (N=608)

They are pleasant sounding
words that have little or
no meaning for me.
40% (N=52)
33% (N=604)

Although it doesn't move me
in terms of faith or
theology, I appreciate its
beautiful prose.
38% (N=52)
42% (N=608)

It moves me, represents my
faith in God.
17% (N=53)
43% (N=615)

An HUC-JIR administrator who was interviewed stated it this way:

> There's a tug between the student's impatience to
> transform the world, and the institution who wants
> the student to be prepared to do so. ... We need
> to recreate a Jewish human being.

Students are professionally oriented, and, if only because they
want to measure themselves against other professionals and academicians, they want to spend the necessary time in training and
in receiving the appropriate degrees. It is significant that
from 20% to 40% of our student respondents want to see changes
of one sort or another. Some, however, say that the real crux
is the quality of students who are admitted to the seminary.
(See Chapter 10, Tables 25-27, pp. 166-73 for more on this.)

Let the seminarians speak their minds. Again a random selection
of excerpts:

> My own feeling is that we need better quality
> students: more dedicated, idealistic, committed,
> concerned with Jews, Judaism. Everything else, 4
> or 6 years, D.H.L. or Ph.D., etc., etc., is relatively
> unimportant.

> The training of rabbis can indeed be improved ...
> There may be some men who do not have the intel-
> lectual capacity nor the commitment to moral
> principles that enable them to function effectively
> as rabbis. The HUC-JIR should concern itself more
> with the psychological problems of its students and
> their motivations for becoming rabbis.

I have spent countless hours with students in all
classes at both the New York and Cincinnati schools
discussing some of the issues.
. . . .
To begin as frankly as possible I believe that there
is virtually no student who is satisfied with either
the religious atmosphere or the academic procedures
at HUC-JIR. In fact, most of us view it as a spiri-
tually debilitating, intellectually vapid ordeal
which has been set up as an obstacle in our path
toward intellectual and human growth. The general
picture of the attitude of students at New York
ranges from despair to bitterness and cynicism.
There is a general consensus that the school is a
pox on our existence from which we must rush to
escape at the end of the day.
. . . .
At Cincinnati there is an undetermined number of
students who have filed applications with the Reconstructionist Seminary in Philadelphia and considerably more than half have requested that they
be allowed to leave Cincinnati ... clearly arising
out of disenchantment with HUC ...
. . . .
The students at both schools are not morons and are
quite aware of the very low academic level required
in almost all classrooms ...
. . . .
There is a disappointing lack of the consciousness
of JUC as an institution engaged in the holy task
of passing down the tradition. I think some of
this consciousness could be regained with a greater feeling of connection with the rabbinical
community.
. . . .
I would add, finally, a word about one of the more
depressing realities about the life on the campus
of both schools. This is the sterile atmosphere
which is created at worship services and which
has in fact led to an attendance rate of less than
10% at New York and only slightly better at Cincinnati.

We are hopefully awaiting what we understand
to be a reactivation of the interest of the CCAR in
HUC amd are very desirous of (doing something) ...
There has been an incredible lack of success in
operating through established channels at the
school which is in part due to a fundamental
lack of respect for student opinion. There
must be some way to break the cycle of the
system now in operation.

In addition to the very penetrating thoughts of a constructive
nature that are noted on many of the questionnaires, one basic
thread that seems to weave itself throughout some of the students'
remarks is also a suspicion, sometimes implicit, sometimes quite
explicit, that the CCAR is poking into the HUC-JIR as a cover-up
for its own (CCAR) inadequacies.

Let us read directly from their comments:

    ... Though improvements must be made in the
school's curriculum and its whole attitude
toward the training of rabbis, of all the
organizations to endeavor to accomplish such
a revitalization of (HUC-JIR) and Reform
Judaism in general, the CCAR is institutionally-
speaking the one organization which should be
disbanded and reorganized. The authority its
leaders hold over rabbis seems much too great.
I personally resent these power-plays between
all the Reform institutions and thus feel that
these surveys are 'using' the Reform Jews and
the seminary students for the CCAR's own predetermined purposes. I hope this is not the
case.

    ... Also, while this study may indeed produce some
positive and valuable conclusions and perhaps results,
I personally feel it is a tragic comment on our lack
of sense of being a community which makes us turn to
professional agencies to help us see what we believe
and what our priorities are in Reform Judaism - to

say nothing of the pretty penny which could have
been used for far more important purposes, and
now will go to Theodore I. Lenn, PhD and Associates.
(A faculty member had also made a similar comment,
stating, "This (study) is a good example of the
misuse of good Jewish money.")

... What is needed is only a responsive faculty,
dedicated students, and a concerned laity. We
have only the foundations of all three, and we
need creative suggestions on how to build, not
more questionnaires.

In general, the entire survey strikes me as a
prejudiced set of inquiries designed to elicit
predetermined answers .... I can't help but
expect that the CCAR is attempting to confirm
some dispositions it has regarding the self-
image of the rabbi and the feelings of the
rabbinical student.
. . . .
It might have been instructive had the CCAR
questioned the students more about their
perception of the Conference rather than their
perceptions of the College. Personally, I resent the Conference's meddling in the affairs
of the College, posing as a concerned but objective 'parent' when one of the real problems
faced by the rabbinical student is not the
College but the autocratic nature of the
Conference and its attempts to gain inroads
into the power structure of the College. I
would honestly hope that the compilers of this
survey shall recommend that the Conference add
to this study a set of questions relevant to
the role perception of the seminarian vis-a-vis
the CCAR. There is a lot of improvement the
Conference should do before it seeks to remake
the College or the other institutions of Reform
Jewish life.
. . . .
Why did the Conference not seek to determine what
personal satisfactions the students might find at
HUC-JIR, outside of the formal organizational
structure? Could the Conference wish to avoid
hearing that the College, while in need of some re-
forms, is not such a bad institution? Or is there
a preconceived image of the College which must be
confirmed at vast expense?

University graduate students usually have little knowledge
of what goes on in the national or even regional professional
societies in the disciplines in which they are pursuing their
graduate or professional degrees. Many professional societies
have actually set up student memberships, at reduced dues, in
order to get the students involved.

It is unique that Reform rabbinical students are, or at least
claim to be, so intimately familiar with the policies and
procedures of their national professional society as to warrant
such devastatingly incisive assessments. One does wonder with
what attitudes the seminarians will be embarking as pulpit
rabbis vis-à-vis the Conference. To the seminarian who is
already disenchanted, it appears that the Conference has
already struck out, not twice, but out!

And yet, in terms of the total cultural context within which
our seminarians find themselves today, and particularly in
terms of the keen and perceptive ways in which younger people
today relate to the overall culture, an expression of alarm
is, very probably, out of order.

There are three obvious choices that are open to those seminarians
who are distressed:

1) They can try to change things.
2) The can drop out of the rabbinate.
3) They can accept their lot, but develop cynical personalities
   with all that this portends for their futures, and for the
   future of Reform Judaism.

5. Postscript: The Seminarian's Wife.

We shall devote a separate chapter in this study to the rabbi's
wife (Chapter 20), but a few words might be in order here about
the seminarian's wife. It was noted earlier that 57% of the
present sample of seminarians have already selected their future
rebbetzins. So for over half of our rebbetzins, the prelude to
the rabbinical world starts out as a student's wife. What
orientation does she receive for her future role as a rebbetzin?

No direct contact was made with seminarians' wives. All of our
data here come from young rebbetzins who had just recently "been
through the mill."

Actually, the rebbetzins were studied for the purpose of ascertaining their own positions, as rabbis' wives, as part of
our searching and probing for information regarding the rabbi's
world.

The real surprise came when several of the younger rebbetzins
(those who were married while their husbands were still in
seminary), started their comments with such phrases as, "I'm
still getting over our student days (at HUC-JIR) ....", or
"It's a lot better than it was (at HUC-JIR)..."

Following are excerpts from interviews with five young rebbetzins:

> I don't know what I can tell you as a rebbetzin (her husband
> had graduated within the past five years, and
> now was a rabbi of a small congregation), but it's much
> better than (at HUC-JIR). My experience there
> was not only bad, but demeaning. The wives (of
> seminarians) felt anger and frustration, especially

the wives who started having babies. The wives
who worked were better off.

... Fun it wasn't. We were far from our parents,
and it wasn't exactly easy to make friends. We
had our (marital) problems ... (of) early adjustment. There just wasn't anyone to talk to. Once
I was so depressed ... I called my parents ...
(and) was **ready to take** the next plane home. Later
that day I ran into Mrs. ____ (the wife of an HUC-
JIR faculty member), quite by accident. She noticed
something was wrong ... I broke down ... (and) she
was wonderful. I went to her home ... If it weren't
for Mrs. _____, I don't know if we would have made
it.

Being a rebbetzin isn't so bad. If anyone ever told
me (a few) years ago that I would say this to you
now, I wouldn't believe it. We really should have
waited (to get married) ... They (HUC-JIR students)
have too much pressure. It's dehumanizing and it
was dehumanizing for me. They should have a full-
time psychiatrist there, just for the students,
the married ones and the single too. We all
needed someone and there was no one. And one
or two of the professors could use some help too.

My parents spoke about it ... and I prepared myself, before I went to live with my husband. (HUC-
JIR student) ... that in addition to everything else,
my husband was studying to be a rabbi. I wasn't
just going to a (secular) university. My grandfather was a rabbi, and my father was wonderful,
trying to prepare me for the religious life,
and he really put it in a beautiful, almost
serene way. You can say he brain-washed me, but
I liked it. Well, what a surprise! At the College,
(HUC-JIR), you can't even be religious. We were
a joke when we had ... (two other married seminarian couples) over for Friday dinner and I
lit the candles and made the blessing. One of
the other students said something like, "Leave

that stuff for later on" (presumably after
ordination, or after her husband became a
rabbi). . . Hillel at _____ University provided me with more religion than my (few) years
at HUC-JIR. But now I'm on my own and we have
a religious home that even my grandfather would
be proud of . . . As I look back, they weren't
very beautiful days.

The type of thing you heard today (the writer
had been attending a rebbetzin's meeting at
a Regional conference, which was very ably
chaired by an experienced rebbetzin), that's
what would have helped us if we could have
had it (at HUC-JIR). I would recommend that
panel discussions with small groups of women
(rebbetzins) who have had all sorts of experiences should come to the College once or
twice a year and share what they know with us
(the seminarians' wives), so that we won't be
so apprehensive about everything. It's really
not such a deal. I love being a rebbetzin.
And I like to be called, "the rebbetzin" . . .
and although it was harrowing at times, maybe
it makes us enjoy a little more now.

So if some of our rabbis do not recall their seminarian days with
too much glee, neither do some of their helpmeets.

6. <u>Summary Highlights (Seminary Students: Choice of Rabbinate
as Career)</u>.

1) Seminarians (and rabbis) are most likely to mention <u>self-
fulfillment</u> and serving people as their chief motivations
for becoming rabbis. (Incidentally, so do physicians,
social workers, and politicians.)

2) Least mentioned (by seminarians and rabbis) is the power
component (i.e. seeing the rabbi as a powerful figure), as
a motive for becoming a rabbi.

3) The image of the rabbi seems to have shifted from the un-
approachable, deeply learned father-figure to more informal,
permissive, pastor type.

4) Almost 40% of seminarians view Jewish scholarship almost of
secondary importance for the modern rabbi.

5) "Religious teacher" is rated highest by seminarians (92%) as
the primary role for the rabbi; adult education teacher, 69%;
priestly roles (officiating at life-cycle rituals), 61%;
counselor, 59%; visitations, 54%.

6) The least important rabbinical roles, according to seminarians,
are: work with synagogue auxiliaries, 9%; synagogue administration,
9%; radio and television speaker, 4%; fund raiser, 0.

7) Less than half the seminarians intend to become pulpit rabbis
upon ordination; 19% indicate graduate studies; many hope to
go into full-time teaching; 15% plan to teach full-time immediately
upon ordination.

8) Over two-thirds of present seminarians feel the Union Prayer Book
needs revision; over half feel "man's moral responsibility for his
own destiny is omitted in much of the prayerbook."

9) Regarding a passage in the prayerbook that states, "We gratefully
acknowledge, O Lord our God, that Thou art our Creator and Preserver
. . .," only 17% of the seminarians say, "It moves me, represents
my faith in God."

10) Seminarians are not complacently satisfied with their seminary
training, but their most vociferous disparagement is aimed at
the CCAR. (Many view this study as an attempt on the part
of the CCAR to obtain data in order to criticize the HUC-JIR).

11) By and large, seminarians appear to be very cynical about
Judaism and about their own futures.

12) From interviews with young rebbetzins who were student-wives
just a few years back, it appears that life was not happy for
them or their husbands while they were still at the seminary.
They describe their experiences as "demeaning," "dehumanizing,"
"anger," "frustration," and "you can't even be religious (there)".

PART V

T E M P L E   Y O U T H

CHAPTER 19: SELECTED JEWISH ISSUES: SOME COMPARATIVE VIEWS
OF YOUTH, PARENTS, AND TOTAL CONGREGANT SAMPLE

1. Some Demographic Characteristics of Temple Youth.

This section is a report on the characteristics and attitudes of a
sample of 264 synagogue youth representing a 53% sample rate of
return. The data are derived from mail questionnaires that were
sent to all of the synagogues that were involved in our questionnaire
to congregations. Of these, returns were received from nine congregations. Additional data were obtained from various meetings
where Temple Youth were participating, particularly when they were
present at Regional activities.

So much for an overview of the sample from whom most of our information comes. The remainder of this chapter will be devoted to a
comparative assessment of selected Jewish issues. The comparative
response patterns will represent our youth sample, and our adult
congregant sample.

The reader is asked to keep in mind that the adults who constitute
our congregant sample are from the same synagogues from which our
youth responses come. While we make no claim that we thus have
specific parent and child responses to the same questions, it is
highly likely that many of the adults, if not the majority, are
indeed the actual parents of many of the youngsters who are the
respondents to our Temple Youth questionnaires.

Our respondents are primarily from among the older children enrolled
in the religious school of their respective congregations. Those
who responded consisted of 40% male, and 60% female. Only 10% are
younger than 13 (Figures 57, 58, and 59). Some 64% of those who
could have been Bar/Bas Mitzvah did not do so. This is exclusive
of those who belonged to synagogues where these rituals are
not a recognized practice. The Bar/Bas Mitzvah is not univer-
sally performed even when it can be. What about confirmation? More
than a fourth have already been confirmed, and of those who have not,
almost all (93%) plan to be. The confirmation ceremony, then, is
clearly the ritual of arrival into Jewish adulthood in our Reform

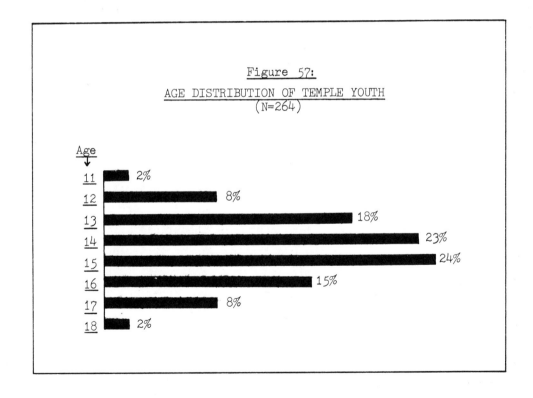

Figure 57:

AGE DISTRIBUTION OF TEMPLE YOUTH
(N=264)

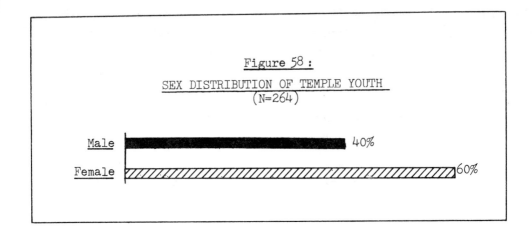

Figure 58:

SEX DISTRIBUTION OF TEMPLE YOUTH
(N=264)

Male 40%
Female 60%

congregations. Significantly, a little over 20% indicate that they
have no Bar/Bas Mitzvah ritual in their synagogue, but would like
to have it. *

It would be derelict to omit the fact that many of our youngsters
are not altogether happy with the Confirmation ritual. Some rabbis
speak against it as well. But the strongest discontent that was
evidenced during the course of this research was brought forth by
a large Regional Temple Youth Group. They had brought their
grievances to a UAHC Regional meeting. They wanted no more of the
Confirmation ritual. It was a time-consuming theatrical affair, they
said. Furthermore, they pointed out that it was of Protestant, not
Jewish, origin. Instead, they pleaded for a good religious school
program through high school graduation. It was a sober and fervent
statement. With the exception of one rabbi in the audience, no one
voiced any objections. The Youth Group spokesman received a strong
ovation.

---

* About 2% indicate this for Bar Mitzvah. Discrepancy in percentages
   due to fact that a far greater number of synagogues do not have
   Bas Mitzvah.

346

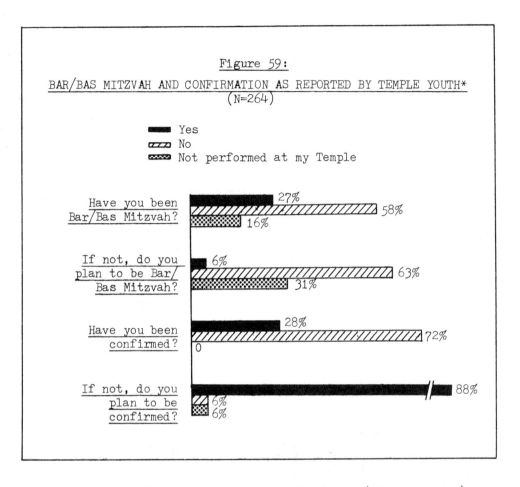

Figure 59:
BAR/BAS MITZVAH AND CONFIRMATION AS REPORTED BY TEMPLE YOUTH*
(N=264)

■ Yes
▨ No
▧ Not performed at my Temple

Have you been Bar/Bas Mitzvah? — 27% / 58% / 16%

If not, do you plan to be Bar/Bas Mitzvah? — 6% / 63% / 31%

Have you been confirmed? — 28% / 72% / 0

If not, do you plan to be confirmed? — 88% / 6% / 6%

Following is a pertinent excerpt from a five-page (single-spaced) statement of concern that was prepared by the aforementioned Regional Youth Group.

> We recommend the substitution of graduation at the conclusion of grade 12 in lieu of the present Reform practice of Confirmation. Confirmation after grades 9 or 10 is an inappropriate and premature conclusion to formal Jewish study. With increasing maturity during the adolescent

---

* While the youth in our sample had a very respectable return rate of 52%, it is quite probable that some of their responses might show some inconsistencies despite their interest.

years, more profound and meaningful education can
be effected. To insure that Reform Jewish Youths'
roots are sunk deeply into our tradition, culture,
and faith, we emphatically encourage the trans-
mission of as much knowledge as possible prior to
the departure of the student for college.
. . . .
Therefore, to pursue Jewish education on a meaningful and more mature level, we recommend the development of an intensive high school level.
. . . .
Further, wherever possible, existing religious institutions should combine and coordinate a joint
high school program for all their students, making
available increased financial support, better
qualified faculty, and continuous contact between
Jewish youth of high school age.

A rabbi, addressing a CCAR regional meeting earlier this year, voiced
his objections to Confirmation in a similar vein. Here are some of his
observations:

The Confirmation Class experience, so characteristic
of American Reform Judaism, does not seem to be working any more.
. . . .
. . . Extravagant pageants ill suit an age charac-
terized by the private search for basic values.
Ringing public affirmations ring false; for everyone knows that few of our young people have formulated their own personal religious styles by the
mid-teens. To force them to demonstrate a phony
commitment in a public ceremony deeply violates their
integrity and autonomy.

2. Zionism and the State of Israel.

When we ask our youngsters about the role of Zionism in their homes,
it tends to become reasonably clear that, while anti-Zionism has
virtually disappeared in Reform Jewish homes, it has largely been

replaced by apathy or indifference. Where 42% of the adults had claimed that they had never heard the matter discussed, this is currently true in the homes of 54% of the children, - according to the children's responses. This despite the fact that 72% of the congregants say that they support the right of Israel to exist as a Jewish state, and another 15% give it qualified support. This despite the fact that 45% of the congregants say that support of the State of Israel is "very important."

On the matter of Israel, there is a slight, but to some, an ominous shift on the part of some Reform youth in the direction of being anti-Israel. Small, but articulate numbers accord it the right to exist "but not as the Jewish homeland," or favor a Palestinian state that would replace the present one.

It comes as some surprise to read comments that are written on the questionnaires by some of our young people regarding some strong anti-Israeli feelings. They are sober and well-written comments, and the majority are of near college-level caliber in articulation. The concerns are not unlike those that were raised at a recent Reconstructionist University Fellowship Conference, where there were assembled "forty young men and women, many of whom had been turned off by the Jewish establishment and whose social action had been channeled into causes outside organized Jewish life."*

---

*Marian G. Greenberg, "Turning Off and On with Jewish Youth; A Reconstructionist Weekend," Reconstructionist, October 2, 1970, p. 24.

> Jewish college youth is on the firing line. Fur-
> ther questions confirmed the strength and often
> virulence of anti-Israel sentiment on campus. Why
> does the Israeli army blow up houses and permit
> Jewish settlers to occupy the West Bank? How can
> we defend retaliatory air strikes against Arab
> guerrilla camps when we oppose saturation bombing
> in Vietnam? Is it logical to demand American
> withdrawal from Southeast Asia while pressing for
> military aid to Israel? Are not the displaced
> Palestinians entitled to their own state.*

Parenthetically, it should be noted that the previous passage does
not stray too far from what a few Reform seminarians and a very
small number of Reform rabbis indicate on their respective questionnaires as well.

One wonders how many of our Temple Youth will be expressing themselves a few years hence, as does Tom Wartenberg, an Amherst
senior:

> My generation has become dissatisfied with the
> democratic process as a means of effecting change.
> We have, therefore, sought more forceful means
> to change things and, perhaps inevitably, violence
> has occurred. An increasing number of my peers
> are turning to violence because they see no other
> way. We implore you to prove us wrong. Show
> us that you are with us in spirit, that change can
> occur in our society, and we will join you.**

---

* Ibid, p. 30.

**Tom Wartenberg, "Ferment on Campus: Moral Revolution," Brotherhood
(National Federation of Temple Brotherhoods), September -
October 1970. (From a guest sermom delivered at a college
youth service at Temple Beth El, Great Neck, N.Y.)

Before we leave the subject of Israel, it is worth noting that 4%
of our youth sample have visited Israel, and the unusually high
number of 61% plan to do so in the future. One 15-year-old girl,
a very active Youth-Grouper put it as follows:

> I've learned more about Israel from one of my
> (high school) social studies classes and from mag-
> azines than from Temple . . . but we went to a
> Conclave (Temple Youth Group), and Rabbi _____
> (a UAHC Regional rabbi) was all excited about
> (Israel) . . . He really 'turned us on.' If my
> two friends will go with me, I'd like to go this
> summer. (The same rabbi) promised to help us
> with all the arrangements.

Finally, it might be noted that while two out of three have visited
or would like to visit and/or study in Israel, only 40% evidenced
any interest to work in Israel.

Now it can be argued that children live their own lives and do not
pay too close attention to parental attitudes and values. But that
is simply not so. To some extent, there are exceptions. But the
more unpleasant suspicion is the possibility that support for
Israel - while genuine - may be performed in a more or less per-
functory manner by some parents, so that little rubs off on the
children. This phenomenon is not limited to Israel and Zionism.
As we shall see in subsequent pages, it is just as visible in the
area of Jewish identity, religious behavior, and religious belief.

3. The Hebrew Language.

Despite the popular assumption that "religious schools don't hurt,
but they don't help either," it is clear that something does
happen. Possibly not enough, but something. Over one-third (36%)

of the youngsters say they can read prayer-book Hebrew at least
fairly well, and 16% claim to understand it at the same level. Of
course, some of the responses may be overstatements. Yet we know
from experience that questionnaire responses from young people
(where no identification is required), usually yield reasonably
accurate validity. More important to note, psychologically speaking, is the possibility that these young people imply by their
responses (assuming they are overstatements), that there is an
unconscious desire to be able to say yes to such a question.

4. Attendance at Worship Services.

Attendance at worship services by our youngsters seems to vary in
approximately the same way as it does among the adults.

As Figure 60 points out so well, the relationship between adult
and youth attendance at worship services invites the surmise that
children usually go when their parents do and stay home when their
elders do. (Indeed, access to the automobile may be sufficient
reason for this pattern.) One should also keep in mind that 55% of
our young respondents report that attendance at worship services is
required by their Religious School. Whether our youngsters are referring to regular adult services or to separate services of their
own is not ascertained by this study. At any rate, it suggests once
again that parents cannot hope for too much from their children if
they do not themselves become the kind of Jews they romantically
wish their children would be.

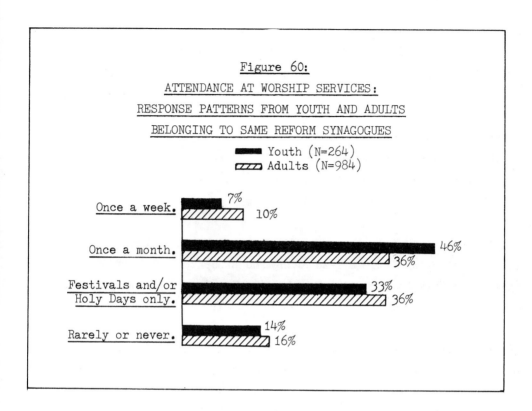

Figure 60:

ATTENDANCE AT WORSHIP SERVICES:

RESPONSE PATTERNS FROM YOUTH AND ADULTS

BELONGING TO SAME REFORM SYNAGOGUES

▬▬ Youth (N=264)
▨▨ Adults (N=984)

Once a week. — 7% / 10%

Once a month. — 46% / 36%

Festivals and/or Holy Days only. — 33% / 36%

Rarely or never. — 14% / 16%

5. Belief in God.

The question was asked:

> "How would you rate the following areas of Jewish
> concern in terms of their importance?"

1. Being an ethical person.
2. Belief in God.
3. Contributions to charity.
4. Jewish identification.
5. Jewish study
6. Social action in the community.
7. Support of the State of Israel.
8. Synagogue worship.

Mentioned most frequently by our Temple youth (58%) as **"very** important"
is "belief in God," followed next with "being an ethical person" (50%),
and third in importance, the "support of the State of Israel" (46%).
The adults, on the other hand, as their first choice overwhelmingly
endorse "being an ethical person" (89%), - a massive gap indeed
between the generations. The second theme most important to adults
(62%) is "Jewish identification." This is ranked fourth by our youth
(39%), - a 23% difference. These last data are summed up in Figure
61.

But the big finding is the one with which we began. There appears
to be relatively little spread among the students with respect to
what is important. In other words, our Temple youth are still
very much in the process of sorting out their values.

We have already commented on the relatively low level of religious
belief among members of Reform congregations. Compared to their
youngsters, however, they are positively devout. Or are our young
people more forthright?

Some 51% of our young people believe in a more or less traditional
version of God as against 66% of the adults. Some 12% of our youth
as compared with 8% of the adults have a rather radical view of God
(Figure 62).

Another 33% of our youth sample are agnostics as compared with 21%
of the adults. Finally, 4% of our young people say they are
atheists, and the same figure applies to the adults.

354

And at the same time, just as with rabbis, we find an interesting
correlation between a low level of traditional religious belief
and a relatively high level of private praying. "Doing their own

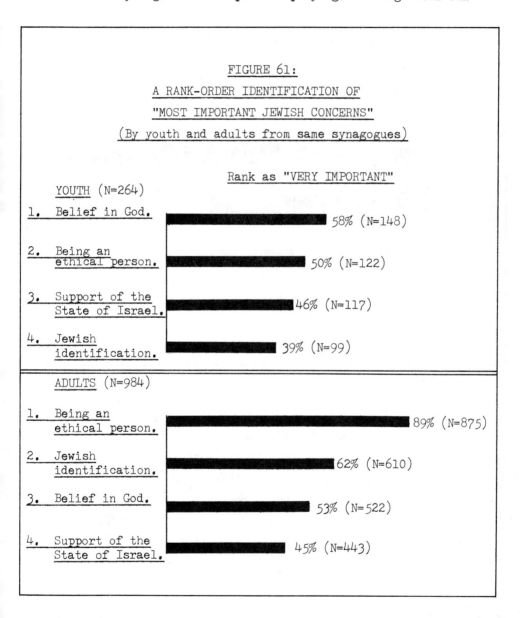

FIGURE 61:

A RANK-ORDER IDENTIFICATION OF

"MOST IMPORTANT JEWISH CONCERNS"

(By youth and adults from same synagogues)

Rank as "VERY IMPORTANT"

YOUTH (N=264)

1. Belief in God. — 58% (N=148)

2. Being an ethical person. — 50% (N=122)

3. Support of the State of Israel. — 46% (N=117)

4. Jewish identification. — 39% (N=99)

ADULTS (N=984)

1. Being an ethical person. — 89% (N=875)

2. Jewish identification. — 62% (N=610)

3. Belief in God. — 53% (N=522)

4. Support of the State of Israel. — 45% (N=443)

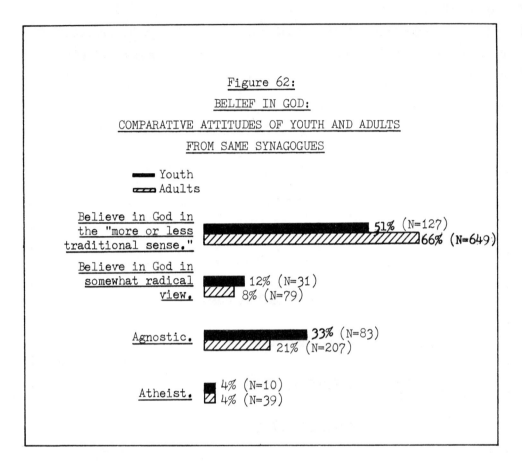

Figure 62:

BELIEF IN GOD:

COMPARATIVE ATTITUDES OF YOUTH AND ADULTS

FROM SAME SYNAGOGUES

━━ Youth
▭▭ Adults

Believe in God in the "more or less traditional sense."   51% (N=127)   66% (N=649)

Believe in God in somewhat radical view.   12% (N=31)   8% (N=79)

Agnostic.   33% (N=83)   21% (N=207)

Atheist.   4% (N=10)   4% (N=39)

thing!" Some 27% of the youngsters report that they pray privately at least several times a week. This finding is somewhat puzzling, and definitely needs to be studied carefully in subsequent research. One possibility is that what is meant by private prayer more often resembles the kind of meditative and "consciousness-expanding" exercises that are part of the Code of Action for so many young people these days. We seriously need to know if this phenomena of prayer is, in Buber's language, an "I-It" or an "I-Thou" relationship

Table 50:

RABBI AND SYNAGOGUE:

COMPARATIVE ATTITUDES OF REFORM YOUTH AND ADULTS

FROM SAME SYNAGOGUES

	Youth	Adults
	("STRONGLY AGREE")	
	%	%
The Union Prayer Book bores me.	28 (N=258)	12 (N=926)
As I get older, I become less and less satisfied with my synagogue services.	20 (N=257)	9 (N=938)
The rabbi is intensely interested in the school and gives it the maximum attention that he can.	19 (N=258)	36 (N=937)
It is easy for young people to approach and talk with our rabbi.	13 (N=258)	(not asked)
Generally speaking, we have a good religious school.	10 (N=257)	14 (N=927)
The Sabbath Service inspires me.	4 (N=258)	9 (N=930)
The sermon is the highlight of the service.	3 (N=256)	15 (N=942)

that our youngsters are having with God. It makes a big difference.

6. Religious School, the Rabbi, Worship Services, and the Prayer Book.

How do young people feel about religious school, their rabbis, and about their worship services? Table 50 tells us not only their own

feelings, but also the feelings of our adult congregants. What
does this comparative view tell us?

It becomes strongly clear that the youngsters think less of the
rabbi than their parents do. Their grounds may not be sound, but
this is how they feel. It is to be noted, especially, that only
a small number of youth report that they feel "comfortable" with
their rabbi. Neither adults nor children are very impressed with
their Religious School. Indeed, it can be said that over half of our
youthful respondents are possibly depressed. Significantly, some 15%
report having done some religious school teaching, of whom 5% do not
plan to continue. Some 16% have not yet taught, but hope to do so
in the future. Over two-thirds (69%) say, "Never!"

And if the young people are "turned off" by the Religious School, they
are even harsher in their criticism of their synagogue's worship
services.

It is the same story, and a consistent one. Young people in the Reform
Movement, and perhaps young people everywhere, are simply not being
effectively reached or touched by what is going on inside of the
syngogue. Much of this is little different, if at all different,
from the way things were for many during the Talmund Torah days of
earlier generations. Indeed, this may alway have been so. When we
speak of religion we normally mean adult religion, - or better, - the
religion of adults. If we look at what goes on among the youngsters
and within the youngsters themselves, we may have a different view
of the matter.

Table 51:

THE TEMPLE YOUTH GROUP:

COMPARATIVE ATTITUDES OF REFORM YOUTH AND ADULTS

FROM SAME SYNAGOGUES

The Youth Group is:	Youth	Adults
	Percent reporting AGREEMENT:	
A very active and successful activity for most young people.	51% (N=253)	43% (N=937)
Primarily monopolized by a small number of young people, and the rest are really not "with it."	35% (N=253)	24% (N=875)
An activity that calls for professional direction and not by the parents who come and go.	23% (N=244)	51% (N=862)
Usually supervised by parents whose children happen to be the officers.	18% (N=254)	15% (N=871)
Not as involved as it should be when it comes to UAHC summer camp activities.	13% (N=253)	16% (N=879)

7. The Temple Youth Group.

When it comes to the Temple Youth Group, the young people are somewhat more positive about things. When they are asked a few questions regarding the Temple Youth Group affairs (Table 51), they are more likely than the adults to say that the Temple Youth Group is doing a good job.

<u>More than the adults,they see the need for professional direction!</u>
More than the adults, they view positively UAHC summer camp. On the
other hand, they are more critical than the adults of the way things
are actually run. The implication is that young people like to be in
control of their own show, that they do <u>not</u> want outside "interference."
And here again, there is nothing new or surprising.

This study makes no attempt to assess Temple Youth Groups, but only
to identify some pertinent views of a sample of young Reform congregants in order to assess attitudes. We have identified that substantial numbers belong to Temple Youth Groups. We have not identified
what specific Jewish content takes place, for instance, nor has this
been our objective. Temple Youth Group members report that 38% of them
have participated in <u>Jewish camping</u>. Another 18% are hoping to do so
in the future. Most have glowing remarks about their camping experiences. When the writer approached a small group of youngsters who
were attending a UAHC Regional meeting to tell about Jewish camping,
the large majority seemed enthusiastic and many indicated they
couldn't wait to go again.

<u>8. Jewish Identity: Skeptical, Yes; Alienated, No</u>.

The question of Jewish identity is something that has interested
Jewish scholars for at least the last hundred years. In what follows
we will look at the ingredients of Jewish identity from the standpoint
of the young people themselves, and we will follow it up with their
perception of their parents' views of the matter, and finally we will
see how the adult congregants themselves (most of whom are parents of
these same young people) answer the same questions.

The proposition that was put to our youngsters is as follows:

"A FEELING OF JEWISH IDENTITY CAN COME TO A PERSON
IN A VARIETY OF WAYS."

A. Which <u>one</u> of the following is most important in
    <u>your</u> case?
B. Which one is - <u>in your opinion</u> - most important
    in your <u>father's</u> case?
C. Which one is - <u>in your opinion</u> - most important
    in your <u>mother's</u> case?

A list of ten identity items was then presented for their consideration. Table 52 presents these items along with the complete response
patterns and also includes the response pattern of the adults since
the latter, too, had been asked the same question as it applies
to themselves.

The first thing to be noted (Table 52) is that, while many young
people disregarded the instructions and listed more than one thing
as being most important to them, <u>28% and 26% respectively did not
answer the question with respect to their parents.</u> Is this some
cause to believe that in many homes the whole question just never
comes up? What is "Jewish identity" to our young people? The "most
important" to most respondents is Jewish moral and ethical traditions
(31%), followed closely by "association primarily with other Jews (15%)."
As to the first, the young people see themselves as being pretty much
in agreement with their parents.

With regard to attendance at worship services, the adults and youth
seem to agree. Only 5% and 2%, respectively, mention this as the
most important ingredient of Jewish identity.

Our youth do <u>not</u> see a difference between themselves and their parents
with respect to synagogue attendance, and here their perception is
most accurate. The congregants are completely in agreement with their

Table 52:

JEWISH IDENTITY:

COMPARATIVE ATTITUDES OF YOUTH AND ADULTS

FROM SAME SYNAGOGUES

Percent reporting "MOST IMPORTANT:"

Components of Jewish identity:	Youth speaking for themselves (N=264) %	Youth speaking for father (N=191) %	Youth speaking for mother (N=196) %	Congregants speaking for themselves (N=960) %
My Jewish moral and ethical traditions.	31	29	29	57
Associating primarily with other Jews.	15	12	14	5
Don't subscribe to the "Jewish identity" concept.	14	6	4	13
Observance of holy days and/or festivals.	13	20	20	5
My commitment to God and Torah.	12	8	8	10
Attendance at religious school.	7	8	8	3
Contribute to Jewish charities.	3	4	5	2
Reasonably good weekly Temple attendance.	2	7	3	5
Stress the rejection of intermarriage.	2	5	5	0
Sabbath candles kindled.	1	1	6	1

children's view of the role that attendance plays for the adults.
Exactly the same situation pertains in the matter of kindling the
Sabbath candles.

In one case, the observance of the Holy Days and the Festivals, our
youth see their parents as far more concerned with this factor as a
component of Jewish identity than they are themselves. Some 13%
say that attendance at the Holy Day and Festival services is the
"most important" item of Jewish identity. The same young people
view it as "most important" for 20% of their parents. The parents
do not share this view. In fact only 5% indicate such attendances
as "most important," one-fourth as much as their children indicate
for them.

Finally the big surprise. Only a handful of our young people stress
the fact that contributing to Jewish charities is an important
ingredient or source of Jewish identity, and they see their parents
in the same way. Instead, our congregants agree with the youth,
only 2% point to charity as a "most important" component for Jewish
identity.

But what is really going on? Do the data suggest a well-nigh complete breakdown in communication between parents and children on
some of the basic values that comprise Judaism? Not really. At any
rate, such breakdowns may occur in the most completely integrated
and solidary settings. That much must be said. Of course it
is one thing when the children know what their parents stand for
and disagree with them. It is another when children do not know
what their parents stand for. This usually happens only when
the Jewish atmosphere at home is ephemeral and unimportant.
At least this is the verdict of one eminently qualified

behavior scientist who served as a consultant to this study.
The gentleman who made this evaluation put it this way: "Would the
kids have been more or less knowledgeable if the questions had been:
'What is your father's political preference? Which is his favorite
baseball team?' We leave it to the reader to ponder.

9. Jews, Judaism, and Jewish Survival: What Meaning for Jewish Youth?

> No generation ever talked so much about "commitment,"
> yet seemed so unwilling to commit itself to one man
> or woman, or one useful job of work. None has talked so
> much about the great political and social issues of
> the age, or written so badly about them. Seldom has
> so much physical and intellectual energy been
> combined, often in the same persons, with so much
> physical and intellectual slackness and even lazi-
> ness.
>
> They (today's youngsters) talk about "participatory
> democracy," but most of them do not participate
> in the democratic process. They complain about
> the loss of "individualism," but run in packs.
> They condemn the welfare state but lean on it,
> and praise the good life and personal happiness,
> but for all their activity, often seem bored
> and singularly joyless.*

As we can see in Tables 53 and 54, adult congregants are not only more
aroused by "threats" than are the children, they are more worried
about threats to survival than by the intrinsic attractions of
Judaism and Jewishness.

---

*James Reston, "A Generation Gap or Regeneration?," (Washington:
   New York Times Wire), Hartford, Connecticut, The Hartford
   Courant, 1970, p. 12.

Table 53:

JEWS AND JUDAISM:

COMPARATIVE ATTITUDES OF YOUTH AND ADULTS

FROM SAME SYNAGOGUES

	Youth	Adults
	Expression of "AGREEMENT:	
	%	%
I really see no meaning to "Jewish community" in my life. I am an American with my basic commitment to my country. I may or may not have more to do with Jewish people, but even if I do, I don't see where this makes us any separate "Jewish community."	41% (N=254)	34% (N=947)
I feel that any attempt to identify ourselves with and as a "Jewish community" is undesirable and does us more harm than good, inasmuch as we don't live in isolated solidarity, and are subject to the same authority as the general society.	36% (N=250)	28% (N=947)
The most exciting things happening in religion are happening outside the synagogue and outside the church.	53% (N=251)	31% (N=928)
When you get right down to it, the differences among the three major religions are not very great. I remain a Jew because it is simply the most convenient thing to do.	15% (N=252)	11% (N=940)
It's not important which religion you belong to, just as long as you maintain membership in one of the faiths.	17% (N=253)	25% (N=934)
People who think that American Jews are primarily Americans are mistaken. Basically, Jews are different from other Americans and Judaism is different from other religions.	28% (N=250)	28% (N=935)

Table 54:

JEWISH SURVIVAL:

COMPARATIVE ATTITUDES OF YOUTH AND ADULTS

FROM SAME SYNAGOGUES

	Youth	Adults
	Expression of "STRONG THREAT:"	
Anti-semitism.	37% (N=244)	30% (N=940)
Intermarriage (without conversion).	16% (N=243)	20% (N=924)
Generally weak religious school education.	10% (N=244)	29% (N=923)
Black militancy.	9% (N=236)	22% (N=913)
Jewish "new-Leftism."	8% (N=231)	22% (N=969)
Changes in traditional Jewish family structure.	5% (N=246)	22% (N=923)

Even at this writing, which is less than a year since the raw data
were collected, there is evidence of some change in youth patterns.
The campuses have quieted down considerably, and the Woodstocks have
diminished to a mere ghost of their previous frenzy of just a year ago.

Jewish "new-Leftism" is changing along with all the other patterns.
The class of 1971-1972 Jewish Freshman is not manifesting pro-Arab or
anti-Jewish sentiments in degree or in amount, compared with those

Jewish students who had preceded them by only one year. And even
the older Jewish students, who had demonstrated their "new-Leftism"
with much vigor a year ago seem to have subsided as of this writing.
These comments are based on personal observation, and on the basis
of information from some dozen Jewish college administrators and/or
faculty. The latter are all from the Eastern part of the country.

One Jewish college administrator expressed himself as follows:

> This (Jewish new-Leftism) is changing . . . New
> students coming to (my institution) - and other
> schools - are not as pro-Arab or as anti-Jewish
> in many, many ways . . .

A Jewish faculty member from a previously troubled university tells it
this way:

> It's almost amazing how things have turned this
> year (1971). Students have almost become meek.
> A few individual voices are heard, but no longer
> in the classroom. They're actually fighting for
> grades. They don't want Pass-Fail grades. They
> know this won't do them any good for admission
> to graduate or professional schools.

10. Summary Highlights (Temple Youth).

1) Confirmation, more than Bar/Bas Mitzvah is the major ritual
   for young people in Reform congregations; 20% report there
   is no Bas Mitzvah ritual in their congregation and 2% report
   no Bar Mitzvah; 63% do not intend to be Bar/Bas Mitzvah
   although it is available to them.

2) There is some marked discontent with Confirmation as a
   necessary ritual on the part of some Reform youth groups.
   Some prefer a good high-school department instead. They
   view Confirmation as a time-consuming, and non-Jewish ritual.

3) Two-thirds of our youth are pro-Israel; 14% accord it the right to exist, "but not as the Jewish homeland"; 5% favor replacing it with a Palestinian state; some strong anti-Israeli written comments are to be noted on approximately 10% of the questionnaires returned by the young people.

4) Despite any of the above (#3), 4% have visited Israel; 61% plan to do so, 36% of whom plan to work there for a period of time.

5) About one-third of Reform youth say they can read prayerbook Hebrew fairly well; 16% claim to understand it.

6) Youth attendance at services seem to be reasonably similar to adult attendance, but 55% report such attendance as a requirement of religious school.

7) Items of "Jewish concern", as rated by Reform youth (in rank order) are: belief in God, 58%; being an ethical person, 50%; support of State of Israel, 46%. These are quite different from adult congregant ratings.

8) Some 27% of Reform youth pray privately at least several times a week.

9) Some 51% of Reform youth believe in God in the "more or less traditional sense"; 12% in a somewhat radical view; 32% are agnostic; 4% are atheists.

10) Some 28% of Reform youth are bored with the Union Prayer Book; 20% say they are less satisfied with their worship services as they get older; only 19% say their rabbis are "intensely

interested in the religious school . . ."; only 10% consider
their religious school to be good; 4% are inspired by
Sabbath services; 3% say the sermon is the highlight of the
Sabbath services.

11) Reform youth view UAHC camping in a very positive manner, but
they criticize (more than adults do), the way things are
run at these camps.

12) The Temple Youth Group, according to 23% of youth respondents,
needs professional direction; 35% say it is monopolized by a
small number of young people in their respective Temples;
51% report it to be active and successful in their Temples.

13) Approximately one-fourth of Reform youth see the "moral and
ethical traditions" and "Temple attendance" as their most
important considerations of Jewish identity.

14) Anti-semitism is viewed by one-third of Reform youth as a
threat to Jewish survival; all other factors that many adults
view as threats (e.g., mixed marriage, black militancy,
break-down in Jewish family structure, Jewish new-Leftism),
are not regarded as threats by any significant number
of Reform youth.

15) Over 50% of Reform youth feel that the most exciting things
happening in religion are happening outside the synagogue
and outside the church.

PART VI

T H E   R A B B I ' S   W I F E

The rebbetzin, like any minister's wife, has an unusually difficult
role to play. In this brief section we will be taking a look at how
she regards her role, to what extent she helps her husband in his
work and in general how she feels about being a rabbi's wife. The
findings are based on the responses from 238 out of 471 who were
sent questionnaires.

CHAPTER 20: REBBETZINS ARE AMBIVALENT ABOUT THE RABBINICAL WORLD.

1. Ambivalence Shows in Several Ways.

Rebbetzins are clearly ambivalent about the rabbinical world, and
this comes out in a number of ways (Figure 63). First, only 53% of
them express a preference that they would like their husbands to
choose the rabbinate if they had it to do over again (the comparable
figure for the rabbis themselves, it will be recalled, is 53%).
However, where 12% of the rabbis would rather have become professors,
their wives voted for the academic life in 32% of the cases. While
most rebbetzins would approve of their daughter marrying a Reform
rabbi if that was what the daughter wanted, only 4% of the rebbetzins
preferred a Reform rabbi, and only another 2% preferred any rabbi as
the ideal mate. And while it is true that 58% expressed no preference
for a future son-in-law's occupation, 26% did prefer a physician or
other professional person. In short, among rebbetzins who have a
preference as to a son-in-law, it's doctors by better than four to
one.

From this we may conclude that the rebbetzin does not think very highly
of the rabbi's career as an occupation. Although, psychologically
speaking, this may reflect the rebbetzins' own dissatisfactions in
terms of their own dependency needs, their reaction is an expression
that is not different from most women who are devoted wives and mothers
who are in similar situations. Nevertheless, a manifestation of dependency needs on the part of many rebbetzins is a very real possible
diagnosis here. The feelings appear to be extended to their daughters.
The 26% who indicate they would "prefer a physician or other professional person" instead of a rabbi as a future son-in-law, may actually
be projecting a need to safeguard the future dependency needs of their
daughters, thus actually giving expression to their own unconscious
needs for fulfillment.

One is hard pressed to assess the full meaning of the response of 32%
who would prefer the academic life for their husbands. Some, possibly
the better educated, might be expressing a greater need for intellectual

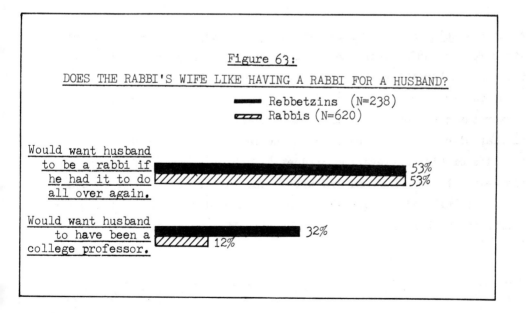

Figure 63:

DOES THE RABBI'S WIFE LIKE HAVING A RABBI FOR A HUSBAND?

Rebbetzins (N=238)
Rabbis (N=620)

Would want husband to be a rabbi if he had it to do all over again.
53%
53%

Would want husband to have been a college professor.
32%
12%

stimulation for themselves, thus seeking a closer bond with their
husbands. Others might wish to see their husbands in what they perceive to be less demanding and more fulfilling careers.

To the extent that a wife does not think very highly of her husband's
career as an occupation, to that extent one might infer that the overall situation does not provide an adequate source of gratification for
her own needs.

2. Perception of Husband's Performance.

This does not, of course, conflict with her perception of how her
husband sees his job. Some 94% of our "rabbinical wives" say, for
example, that he is generally appreciated by most who know him.
Another 89% think that he enjoys his work as a rabbi. Only 16% think
that he would prefer working in another field. Clearly, then, there
is a difference of opinions here, and that is not difficult to understand.

As to how well their husbands are doing, 19% say that their husbands
are more successful than they (the wives) would have expected. Exactly
the same number think the opposite. Some 43% think he is doing just
about par for the course. An interesting 20% could not or would not
answer the question. Does this suggest the possibility that these particular wives are less involved in the rabbi's world, particularly in
the life of his congregation, or does a lack of communication and perception exist between husband and wife? The latter question is raised because the rebbetzin apparently sees her husband's career as being more
fulfilling to him, actually, then he himself expresses.

3. The Rebbetzin's Role: A Self-Evaluation.

Let us look at how our rebbetzins view their own roles. In Figure 64
the respondents were allowed to check as many answers as they wished.
There is clearly considerable dissatisfaction and even some occasional
antipathy to the role of rebbetzin. Is it the marriage or the job,
or what? There seems to be some role confusion here.

It is at this point that one might raise a question as to whether this
situation is due to what goes on between husband and wife, or to the
situation on the outside? The answer appears to be "the outside."
Some 63% rate their marriages as "excellent," and another 28% pronounce them "good." An overall 91% positive response concerning
marital compatibility for any family sample is exceedingly high.
Moreover, in response to specific questions about the rabbi's relations with his wife, rebbetzins uniformly praise their spouses.
From these data, we might conclude, then, that it is what goes on
outside the home that accounts for the ambivalent responses we
have just looked at. Except for one thing,- Figure 64. Can we really
view one's marriage as "good" or "excellent" and still describe it
as "lonely" (35% do). Although we are not saying that the data
are to be considered contradictory, it would appear, however,
that the rebbetzins are telling us that whereas the overall situation is generally satisfactory or even good, there are still
problems. It is altogether possible to responde one way as the
wife of a man, and in a different way as the wife of a rabbi.

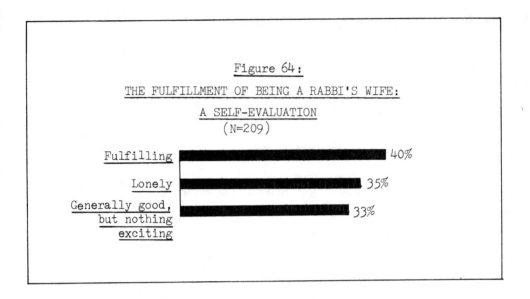

Figure 64:

THE FULFILLMENT OF BEING A RABBI'S WIFE:

A SELF-EVALUATION
(N=209)

Fulfilling	40%
Lonely	35%
Generally good, but nothing exciting	33%

4. Personal Friendships.

Take the matter of personal friendships. Only half (51%) have personal
friendships mostly within the congregation. Of the half that do not,
it is the opinion of 14% that they do not have friends within the congregation because of their role as rabbi's wife. Another 5% do not
choose to have friends within their congregation precisely because
they are rebbetzins. And 30% find most of their friends outside. Now
one could argue that in a well-integrated structure a whole network of
social relations should develop such that in one way or another every
person finds a place, and presumably is content with his life. If a
third of the rebbetzins go somewhere else for their friends, is it to
be concluded that the social networks involving Reform congregations
are not very well developed, and that this may account for some of the
indifference and apathy we see reported? The de-emphasized ritual in
Reform may hold some explanation here, not only for the rebbetzin, but
for the average congregant as well.

Here are three overview comments from rebbetzins:

> A Rabbi and his wife cannot have friends inside the
> congregation - it must be friendly but impersonal.

> My experience has taught me to be nice to everyone,
> but not too close to anyone.

> No confidants - never!

5. "Reasonably Active, - Not Overly Involved."

What does the rebbetzin actually do as a rabbi's wife? Three out of
four almost always attend Sabbath (Friday evening), Festival, and
special services, and another 15% do so as often as possible. Only a
handful (4%) rarely attend. As we note in Figure 65, the rebbetzins
are reasonably active, but not overly involved.

Of course, nine out of ten accompany their husbands to congregational
social affairs. And why not? Would many have much opportunity to go
out with their husbands otherwise? Some 75% attend synagogue services.
Considering the fact that many rebbetzins have younger children, this
must be truly a difficult task. Over half attend Bar/Bas Mitzvah
dinners. When their husbands officiate at weddings, some 43% are in
attendance. So much for the simchas. Some 22% of our rabbis' ladies
are also there when their husbands make their condolence calls, and
another 14% are there when their husbands recite the Kaddish at the
funeral service.

But that isn't all. There are often many other things going on in
the synagogue that are of concern to the Rabbi's wife, and not
necessarily because she is the Rabbi's wife. She is a member of the

375

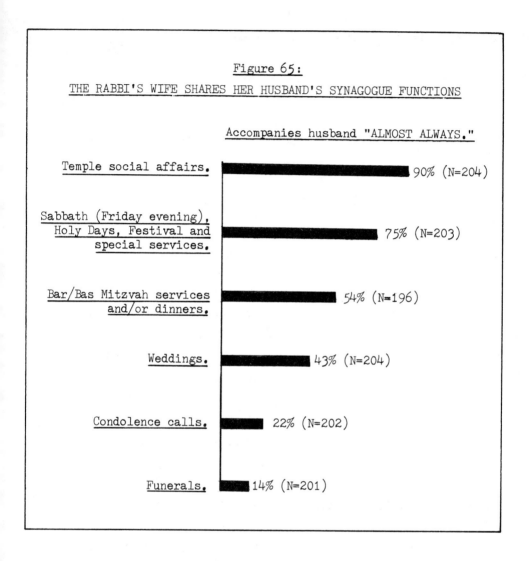

Figure 65:

THE RABBI'S WIFE SHARES HER HUSBAND'S SYNAGOGUE FUNCTIONS

Accompanies husband "ALMOST ALWAYS."

Temple social affairs. 90% (N=204)

Sabbath (Friday evening), Holy Days, Festival and special services. 75% (N=203)

Bar/Bas Mitzvah services and/or dinners. 54% (N=196)

Weddings. 43% (N=204)

Condolence calls. 22% (N=202)

Funerals. 14% (N=201)

congregation, and as such, there are such things as Sisterhood, Young
Couples Club, lectures, adult education programs, and many other
happenings. Some 84% claim to be "reasonably active" in Temple affairs.
Virtually all, but not all (94%), hold membership in Sisterhood.
"Reasonably active" in Jewish community affairs are 65%. Some 48% say
they are "reasonably active" in the general community.

6. Advising the Rabbi.

To be sure, most rebbetzins have a say as to what their husbands are
doing, but this is apparently done in privacy. More than half indeed,
(54%), volunteer their opinions whenever they feel it necessary,
while another 43% give advice only when it is requested. Only a
handful have nothing to say. Clearly, then, the rebbetzin, in order
to be able to comment, must know a lot about what is going on, but
she usually tries to keep herself in the background. Safely effective.

Furthermore, there is no evidence that they would have it otherwise. When asked about the importance of hob-nobbing with board
members or playing an influential role, rebbetzins are cool to the
idea. Only 15% endorse the hob-nobbing, and a mere 7% are in favor of
playing an influential role in the synagogue. Similarly, only 12%
think that a qualified rebbetzin should teach in the religious school.
As a matter of fact, 14% actually do teach in their religious schools.

So the rebbetzin is no frustrated meddler. She speaks up when she
wants to, but voluntarily refrains from getting overly involved in her
husband's domain.

Of course, one of the reasons why most rebbetzins don't become overly
involved in synagogue affairs might be because of their 'inside' view
of things which might at times be a little threatening to the rank
and file membership.

From a few rabbis, not from the rebbetzin, comes this version of why
some rebbetzins may not be overly involved:

> Interviewer: Rabbi, does your wife participate much
> in synagogue affairs?
>
> Rabbi: Not too much, no.
>
> Interviewer: How does that sit with the congregation?
>
> Rabbi: They're used to it by now. She withdrew very
> much from synagogue affairs. Unfortunately she's
> extremely efficient and too well-organized for the
> congregation - for me too - and they took it as a
> form of bossism . . . and there was a jealousy
> factor in there as well. My predecessor's wife was
> (very active in) the Sisterhood just prior to our
> coming here, and it was a very unhappy experience
> for the congregation, and the hangover remains.

Of course, the above mentioned rabbi's comments concerning his wife's
accomodation to the situation may be viewed psychologically as a manifestation of the rabbi's discontentment with his own role. Possibly
it is not dominant enough, as he sees it. Nevertheless, it sheds light
on why over-involvement doesn't work for some rebbetzins.

7. The Rebbetzin Is a Woman.

Hence, being a rabbi's wife is neither a source of torment nor torture.
Only 19% feel that being married to a rabbi is "like li ing in a glass
house." And while 18% say that it is easier to make friends outside
the congregation, that leaves a much larger number who have fewer or
no reservations on that score. Finally, only 13% report that the
congregation makes more demands on them than they wish to meet. The
rebbetzins questioned seem to run the gamut from one who states that

her role as rebbetzin is "shortening my life and turning me against
the human race," all the way to one who reports "I am myself first,
my husband's wife second, a mother third - and a rebbetzin about
29th."

What is left to say, then? One thing. The rebbetzin is a woman.
Almost half (47%) feel "the need for developing (their) potentialities
outside of home and synagogue," and another 26% are "somewhat in
agreement" on this score. Yet only 14% actually have full-time jobs,
and another 27% are similarly employed on a part-time basis (outside
of religious school teaching). To be sure, as we have already reported, a good many are active in community affairs at one level or
another, but there appears to be a rather large gap between what
rebbetzins would like to do with their lives and what they are actually
doing.

But the questionnaire did not probe the inner feelings of the rebbetzin
as a woman in her own right. Nor could it, without making it a major
study unto itself. However, some individual interviews filled this
gap a little. And some of the gap was also filled by sitting in at
meetings of the rebbetzins (they were always most gracious to the
interviewer), and finally by informal conversational probing here and
there.

So let's listen a little to some of our rebbetzins:

> After eight years of college and graduate school, I
> didn't come to listen to Sisterhood's deliberations
> regarding rummage sales, drapes for the library, and
> who's on first.

> . . . I married a man, not a rabbi. And I'm basically
> a woman, not a rebbetzin. If my husband gives me what
> I need as a woman, then O.K. What he does as a rabbi
> is his business. What he does for me as a woman is my
> business . . . Like I said, if business is good, I'm
> happy.

> My contact is mostly with young wives who also have
> all school-age children. Sisterhood is for senior
> citizens. It's boring. The younger women aren't
> joining Sisterhood. Maybe they pay dues . . . (but)
> they're not 'with it.'

> For the first ten years I was miserable (being a
> rabbi's wife). But now I think I wouldn't trade
> it for anything else in the world. My husband and
> I have an enviable position in our community . . .
> And we hold it with dignity. Being a rabbi is our
> job, not just my husband's job. In this way it's not
> a job at all. It's a way of life for both of us and
> for our son. I hope he decides to be a rabbi.

Although rabbis were rarely asked directly if they felt that their

wives were doing well or poorly in their roles as rebbetzins, several

rabbis volunteered their thoughts. By far the majority identified

their wives as having made a very admirable adjustment to their

rebbetzin's world.

One rabbi provides a framework within which he sees the rebbetzin as

a woman, and simultaneously expressed enhancement of his role through

his wife:

> My wife has helped me tremendously, and it's not so
> much what she does. Strange as it seems, and even
> more important, it's what she doesn't do to get me
> into trouble. You know a lawyer's wife or a merchant's
> wife can speak freely of what she thinks . . . (about
> people and things) in and out of a congregation. This
> is when a rabbi's wife learns early in the game that in
> addition to her many jobs as a wife and mother that all
> married women have, she also carries the burden of
> always acting, not just being, just a cut above her
> friends. I know my wife is doing the right thing.
> I feel it . . .

This comment is, of course, a good example of how a wife reflects her husband's contentment with his work.

A few rabbis are not so lucky, apparently. They have other comments, to wit:

> HUC-JIR should concentrate on preparing the rabbi's wife for the rabbinate. What I fell into,- Gottenue!

> At present, my wife and I are consulting a psychiatrist once a week. She is a fine person but not strongly committed to Judaism and the Synagogue. We have an internal power struggle between us, aggravated by a lack of confidence and sure purpose. She finds it difficult to accept being "the Rabbi's wife" in the typical sense. I thought she would be perfect but our experience is otherwise. She often resents my congregational involvement and interests. We hope to resolve this and other problems.

> I don't know what she (wife) wants,- me? the Temple? or what? She's a humanist, maybe even an agnostic or atheist. Who knows? I don't know what to do . . . When we were at school (they were married at HUC-JIR) we thought it was school (and that things would be better) . . . after I was ordained. It's even worse now.

It might be interesting to note that another contemporary study of clergymen also touches briefly on the role of the wife.* The author's chief finding regarding ministry and marriage is that there is a "powerful, reciprocal relationship between marriage and ministerial career." As one minister who had recently left his church put it, "I found it hard to take the guff. For her, it was impossible."

---

*Josiah R. Bartlett, Report of Unitarian Universalist Shifts Study, Berkeley, California, 1969.

Three wives of ministers who had shifted to other non-ministerial careers, put it this way:

> We would have had a much pleasanter social life if he hadn't had to be all church oriented.

> We're so much happier now. The strain was showing its effects on our relationship.

> Our marriage seemed 'secondary' because of our basic struggle of survival to reach a 'successful' and 'impressionable' status in the ministry and denomination. (divorcee, now re-married to same minister.)

8. Summary Highlights (The Rabbi's Wife).

1) Rebbetzins are ambivalent regarding their roles; they are married women with all that this entails; they are married to rabbis with all that this entails.

2) Some 53% would want their husbands to be rabbis if they were to start all over again (53% of the rabbis say this for themselves).

3) Some 32% would want their husbands to have been a college professor (12% of the rabbis say they want this for themselves; 12% of the congregants feel their rabbis should be professors.)

4) Only 6% of the rebbetzins would prefer that a daughter marry a rabbi; 26% prefer a physician or other professional person; 58% express no preference.

5) Some 19% say their husbands are <u>more</u> successful than they
   (the wives) would have expected; 43% think he is performing
   in line with the wife's expectation. Many chose not to
   express themselves on this point.

6) Rebbetzins express some role-confusion in terms of their own
   self-image; some limitations in perception and communication
   appear to exist between rabbis and rebbetzins inasmuch as
   the latter ascribe more fulfillment accruing to their
   husbands than the rabbis are claiming for themselves from
   their careers.

7) Much less than half the rebbetzins (40%) say their lives
   <u>as</u> <u>rebbetzins</u> are "fulfilling"; 35% say they are "lonely";
   33% say life is "generally good, but nothing exciting."

8) Yet nine out of ten rebbetzins say their marriage is
   "excellent" or at least "good." (There appears to be some
   contradiction between this statement and #7, above, and #14,
   below.)

9) Only half the rebbetzins make their personal friendships
   mostly <u>within</u> the congregation.

10) Most rebbetzins are reasonably active but not overly involved
    in their congregational world; 90% almost always attend Templ
    social affairs; 75% are at Sabbath services; over half are
    at the rabbi's side at Bar/Bas Mitzvah dinners; 43% at
    weddings; 22% accompany their husbands on condolence calls,
    and 14% attend the funerals of their congregants.

11) Some 65% are "reasonably active" in Jewish community affairs; 48% in general community affairs.

12) More than half the rebbetzins volunteer advice to their husbands on congregational matters if they feel it necessary; 43% do so only if the rabbi asks them for it.

13) Some 14% of the rebbetzins teach in the religious school.

14) As women, almost half the rebbetzins feel "the need for developing (their) potentialities outside the home and synagogue;" another 26% are "somewhat in agreement" with this position; only 14% have full-time jobs, and 27% have part-time jobs (not including religious school teaching).

15) The unhappiness that exists in the lives of some of the rebbetzins may go back to their days when they were "student-wives" at HUC-JIR. (See Chapter 18, Section 5, pp. 338-40.)

CHAPTER 21:   THE END IS WHERE WE START FROM. . .

Judaism may be perennial, but its work changes according to the cultural conditions in which the rabbis and their congregants live
and think. And the cultural conditions, spurred by the rapid growth
of the secular city, the piercing strides of modern technology,
and suburbanization, have wrought their havoc on all our social
institutions, including religion.

> Ever since the Age of Enlightenment there has been a
> tension between the traditional religions of the West -
> Judaism and Christianity - and the secular world then
> beginning to merge: its science, technology, econo-
> mics, politics, and, in general, its attitude toward
> life. And since the modern-secular world would not
> go away and could not be wished away, its effect on
> orthodox belief was one of crisis - whether orthodox
> belief declared itself under total siege, ventured
> the odd sortie, or even undertook a wholesale assault
> on the alien territory and in so doing became itself
> transformed. By now, this crisis has existed for so
> long that it has become a permanent condition of re-
> ligious belief in the modern world; and most of the
> recent talk about a brand-new religious crisis in
> our own age merely reflects the permeation of the
> old crisis into nearly all parts of modern society.*

The findings of the present study concur with Fachenheim that if there
is a crisis in religion (particularly the religion of Reform Judaism),
it is a crisis more by definition than by fact. By _fact_, it is
simply a component of continuum.

---

*Emil L. Fachenheim, "On the Self-Exposure of Faith to the Modern-
    Secular World: Philosophical Reflections in the Light of
    Jewish Experience," _Daedalus_ (Journal of the American Aca-
    demy of Arts and Sciences), Winter, 1967, p. 193.

Religion, like philosophy, is first and foremost a mental discipline.
The cultural lag theory tells us that what usually ails a modern
culture is that the material accomplishments of man move ahead too
fast for the non-material accomplishments to keep pace. An example
would be to look at our atomic and nuclear accomplishments. We have
created powerful forces, but as of now we have employed them mostly
in ways that threaten our very existence as a human race. Our
mental capacities have not yet worked out ways for living in a
manner that would include the harnessing of these forces for human
betterment.

So much for the cultural lag theory as it pertains to the overall
situation. Let us extract religion from our mass society, just
to examine it in terms of a further problem. As a mental discipline,
with no empirical underpinnings to support it in the eyes of the
pragmatist, it suffers even more than other "non-material" bodies
of knowledge, such as art or literature. From the latter we expect
no required rules of human conduct, only ideas. But with religion,
we deal with ideas and rules for living. The ideas aren't so much
what is giving us trouble. We either accept, partially or completely,
or we don't. The rules are the troublemakers. The problem is akin
to what philosophy started to confront many decades ago.

> It is not merely that the cultural aggrandizement of
> the investigative or phenomenological sciences has
> gradually threatened the very existence of philosophy
> and has progressively worked to dispossess it of its
> ancient home; worse, and in consequence, the preva-
> lence of positivism today requires the philosopher to
> face an audience radically skeptical of anything he
> may say, doubtful even that he can say anything worth
> listening to it all.*

---

*Mortimer J. Adler, A Dialectic of Morals, University of Notre Dame
  Press, 1941, p. 3

But now we confront the white-hot core of the problem. Not only does
religion "face an audience radically skeptical of anything (it)
may say," but a good deal of this same skepticism abounds within
the very ranks of organized religion itself.

Let us examine some specifics. At a CCAR Regional meeting, a
prominent HUC-JIR rabbi-professor was invited to address the assembled
members of the rabbinate. The speaker began his presentation by
asking his audience of rabbis what they would want him to speak on
and what they would want to discuss with him. The first question
that the group put forth was "What is our position on God?"

Only 10% of the total rabbinate are able to agree categorically with
the statement, "I believe in God in the more or less traditional
Judaic sense." It is to be noted immediately that another 62% can
agree with the statement once we add to it "as modified in terms
of my own views of what God is, what he stands for, etc." This means
that 28% of our rabbinate can be described as skeptical to say the
least. If a rabbi is a teacher and preacher of an overall pattern
of human behavior whose watchword is "Hear O Israel, the Lord Our
God the Lord is One," how can it be done if he does not accept the
very existence of the one God?

At another rabbinical meeting, a former CCAR president made this
statement: "We (the Reform rabbinate) still have a long way to go
in establishing a theology that would be acceptable to the Reform
Movement." Throughout the study, this same concern was expressed
over and over again. A Reform Shulchan Aruch does not exist.

If a Reform Shulchan Aruch does not exist, then what is the code of
law that prescribes the pattern of behavior that the Reform rabbi
teaches and preaches? And what would a Reform Shulchan Aruch mean

to the 28% who express skepticism about God? If a rabbi cannot or
will not accept God and the role He plays in Jewish heritage, will
he accept a Shulchan Aruch? And if not, what steps is the CCAR
prepared to take to invoke sanctions? At the present time, there
is at least one Reform rabbi who a few years ago, publicly renounced
God. He continues to remain a member in good standing in the CCAR.

To be sure, it is an easy sociological exercise to explain faltering
societal stability in terms of the social disorganization that has
been brought about by suburbanization, assimilation, secularization,
and occupational and residential mobility. But if we press too
hard, are we not overlooking the fact that societies are and always
have been dynamic? The changes of the past were of different
variety, but constant change there has always been. There is not now,
and there never was a static society. So it might not be altogether
fair to explain things in terms of the aforementioned sociological
phenomena. Instead of explaining and understanding the situation, we
may simply be explaining the situation away. As time moves along, we
continue to make our adjustments in terms of the social change that
confronts us. Our mass adjustment mechanisms are always in process.

But whatever the changes in the mass society, where does the rabbi qua
rabbi stand? What is his focus? What is his function? It is the rabbi,
not the congregant who spells out what Reform Judaism is, and to date
it has never yet been spelled out. Although each individual rabbi may
spell out his interpretation of Reform Judaism to his congregation, a
systematic code for the Movement does not appear to exist. Without a
uniform prayerbook, would there be any rallying point at all? As for
the congregations themselves, we seem to have a Shulchan Aruch in
reverse, viz., complete congregational autonomy. The Constitution
and By-Laws of the UAHC makes this explicity clear:

Nothing contained in this Constitution or the By-Laws
shall be construed so as to interfere in any manner
whatsoever with the mode of worship, the school, the
freedom of expression and opinion, or any of the
congregational activities of the constitutent congregations of the Union.

It would appear, therefore, that <u>unless Reform Judaism is a rabbinical
responsibility, it is no one's.</u> The whole Movement then, revolves
around the person of the rabbi. If it is a strong, viable Movement,
the rabbis have made it so. If it is a faltering Movement, if there
is a crisis, the rabbis have made it so. If there <u>is</u> a crisis, and
if this crisis is to be overcome, the rabbis will do that too.

In terms of what this study tells us about our contemporary American
Reform rabbinate, it is not easy to say in what direction change might
be expected. It is quite possible that <u>directions</u>, rather than any
single direction, might be a more accurate view of what the future
holds in store for Reform Judaism.

Let us look at what confronts us. Concerning the present study,
here is how two rabbis reacted to it after they were first informed
of its objectives:

> The major areas of inquiry to be studied ... leave me
> rather dismayed. Here we already have the answers.
> (What we need are answers to the following:)
>   1) Has the rabbinate a future?
>   2) Is religion disappearing?
>   3) Should the synagogue survive?

The second rabbi put it this way:

> If we think about it soberly, there is no question
> that Judaism will survive. Entrenched as integral
> parts of Judaism are the rabbi and the synagogue.
> We (the rabbis) and our synagogues will therefore
> also survive. But what does survival mean? This
> is where we need to take stock of ourselves. We
> must know what we are doing and where we are at,
> or we dare not talk about what is yet to be done.
> I look forward to this study to serve us as a
> mirror. Without this mirror - which should reflect
> honest answers from all of us - we can only rely
> on what we are telling ourselves. We must see
> ourselves as we are.

We see, then, where to one rabbi there is serious concern that perhaps
all is about to crumble. Emotion abounds. To the other rabbi,
such mass disintegration isn't even questioned. For him, it is
a matter of rational self-evaluation. For the first rabbi, a
crystal ball is needed. The second calls for a body of knowledge
(a mirror).

One of the big questions in the minds of some rabbis is, "What does
the congregation expect of me?" One experienced Reform rabbi attacks
this as an improper question. He states as follows:

> We must be leaders, not followers, and no small part
> of the rabbi's mission is educating the congregations
> not to expect the impossible. Actually . . . the
> question should be . . . "What does the congregation
> have a right to expect of the rabbi?"

Again we see how there seem to be two completely different sides
to the same coin. To some rabbis there is an earnest desire for
the congregation to tell them what to do. To other rabbis, it is
the rabbi who should do the telling (or possibly be told off).

Much of what is happening to the Synagogue today is little
different from what started to happen to the University a few
years ago. Chancellor Samuel B. Gould of the State University
of New York described the situation as follows:

> I want to talk about only one thing today: the
> step-by-step elimination of reason or rationality
> from the education scene and perhaps from our
> whole society. This is a phenomenon evident for
> some time but only now beginning to be understood
> as it should be. It represents the single most
> fundamental value change of our time. Some pople
> find it exhilarating and liberating; some find it
> disquieting and even frightening; all find it fas-
> cinating both as to its present and its future. To
> me it is a fearful sort of fascination.*

Throughout his address, Dr. Gould tells us that faculty as well as
students are equal contributors to this retreat from reason. Could
this be what is happening in some of our Reform Synagogues? It
appears to be so.

Since the objective was to identify the malaise, if any, that now
exists in the Reform Movement, let us highlight some attitudes and
behaviors of Reform constituencies that may be identified as such
by some, perhaps not by others.

Concerning the Rabbinate

  1) There is dissatisfaction in the whole area of rabbinical
     economics:

---

* "Retreat from Reason," Commencement Address, University of
     Pittsburgh, April 26, 1970.

1. Salaries
2. Increments
3. Vacations
4. Insurance benefits
5. Tenure
6. Pension benefits
7. Sabbaticals

Not only do many rabbis not understand what is going on. they aren't even clear what should be going on. Here the UAHC and/or the CCAR is clearly unclear, or possibly remiss. It is the system, the arrangements, the procedures that distress the rabbis more than the actual dollars involved.

2) Rabbis are discontent with what they call the non-rabbinical demands that congregations are making of them.

3) There are many rabbis who enter the seminary who come from comparatively uninvolved Jewish backgrounds.

4) Rabbis, especially the more recently ordained, appear to be oriented in increasing numbers to the secular as opposed to the Jewish academic world.

5) Less than half the rabbis say they are "fully satisfied" with their careers.

6) Less than a third of our rabbinate look upon "presiding over ritual and worship" as a "most satisfying" component of their professional activities.

7) Only 53% of the rabbis say they would choose the rabbinate again if they had the chance.

8) There is an extremely high and positive relationship between lack of commitment to career and one's dissatisfaction with it.

9) Despite the fact that only a comparatively small number of rabbis complain strongly about their own careers, 42% say there is a crisis in the Reform rabbinate.

10) Over one-fourth of Reform rabbis do not believe in God in "the traditional Judaic sense" or as modified "in terms of my own views of what God is and what He stands for."

11) In terms of religiosity, Reform rabbis can be categorized as 10% traditionalists, 62% moderates, and 28% radicals.

12) Some 41% of Reform rabbis officiate at mixed marriages (no prior conversion). Of those who do not, over half refer couples to rabbis who do.

13) The biggest single complaint that Reform rabbis have against their congregations is the "Jewish distance" between rabbi and congregation.

14) The majority of Reform rabbis feel that the use of the chuppa and the breaking of the glass in the wedding ritual should be at the discretion of the bride and groom.

15) Almost half the rabbinate agree with the statement, "The CCAR promulgates the values of success and competitiveness among its members to the point that it pits one man against another." The younger rabbis are more often those who register the most vitriolic complaints against their parent organization.

16) There are no marked uniformities to describe any majority
complaints against the CCAR. Many individual objections are
expressed by many different rabbis, but the objections differ
from rabbi to rabbi. The CCAR often seems to serve as an
overall scapegoat for most of its detractors.

17) Reform rabbis are asking for effectively functional CCAR
Regional organizations. They ask of these Regional mechanisms
opportunities for study and sociability, as well as guidance
and assistance with their business and administrative needs
vis-à-vis their respective congregations.

18) Reform rabbis do not feel that the UAHC Regions are structur-
ally or functionally suited to meet the individual rabbi's
needs vis-à-vis his congregation.

19) Reform rabbis from all age groups express mild to harsh
criticism concerning the performance of HUC-JIR as a rabbinical seminary. The criticisms are often that the seminary
1) does not produce or even motivate Jewish scholarship
2) does not adequately prepare for the pulpit rabbinate, and
3) does not provide sufficient personalized assistance and
guidance to its students and their needs (especially the
married ones).

20) Reform rabbis are suggesting that HUC-JIR ought to develop
cooperative programs with other academic institutions. Some
69% of the rabbis and 85% of the seminarians would like to
see the seminaries located in major academic centers.

21) The overwhelming majority of rabbis and seminarians agree that a Reform multi-university comprehending several different schools, in addition to a rabbinical seminary, would provide for a more enriched preparation in rabbinics, as well as a course of study in Jewish scholarship for those who do not seek ordination.

22) Less than one-fifth of Reform rabbis identify a crisis concerning themselves or their congregations, but some 42% say that it applies to the rest of the entire rabbinate. Almost two-thirds say it applies to most Reform congregations.

23) Reform rabbis, while they prefer to go it alone, are showing an increasingly receptive attitude toward a merger with the Conservative Movement with the understanding that this means becoming more traditional in the process.

24) Over half of Reform rabbis oppose the idea of a community team rabbinate (involving a combined structure with Conservative and Orthodox personnel), but those who favor such an innovation are very articulate in their position.

25) Regarding any merger procedures, on national and/or local levels, it appears that those rabbis who perceive Reform to be in crisis are those who are most willing to do something, although in one case it involves greater separation from the rest of Judaism, and in the other it involves greater cooperation.

Concerning Reform Congregants:

1) More than one in three congregants, ages 20 to 24, is now married to a spouse who was born non-Jewish. One in four of this age group is married to a spouse who has not converted.

2) Reform congregants rate "being an ethical person," and "Jewish identification" above "belief in God" as basic components of their Jewish consciousness.

3) Two-thirds of Reform congregants say, "I remain a Jew because it is simply the most convenient thing to do."

4) Over half of Reform congregants are strongly universalistic; 10% are strongly particularistic.

5) Less than one-fifth of Reform congregants believe in God "in the more or less traditional Judaic sense." Another 50% add "as modified in terms of my own views of what God is, and what he stands for."

6) Based on response patterns regarding "belief in God" and "being an ethical person," 48% of Reform congregants can be identified as religious, and 28% as non-religious.

7) It is the parents who are least religious who tend to be most critical of the rabbi's role in the religious school, and are also most critical of the rabbi's leadership of youth group activities.

8) Reform congregants who are married to converts are themselves
more religious than those married to fellow-Jews. Based on
our small sample, those whose spouses are not converted tend to
be even more religious than those with converted spouses.

9) Of those congregants identified in this study as religious,
most come from Orthodox-affiliated backgrounds, the second
largest group comes from Reform-affiliated homes, next in
number are those from Conservative-affiliated homes, and
almost a third come from "other" backgrounds.

10) Generally speaking, there seems to be a negative relationship
among congregants between religiosity and income, and between
religiosity and formal secular education.

11) Most congregants affiliate with synagogues when the time
comes to enroll children in the religious school.

12) The vast majority of Reform congregants do not consider themselves religious.

13) A little over one-tenth of Reform congregants are (or have
been), active leaders in their congregations. They are
usually fathers, and the more affluent but not the highest
formally educated. Most often they are from either Orthodox
or Reform backgrounds.

14) The most active lay synagogue leaders are those who usually
blame poor rabbinical leadership for what is wrong with
Reform Judaism.

15) The most active lay synagogue leaders tend to be much more concerned with Jewish affairs, the Jewish community, the general community, and with Israel than the rest of the Reform membership.

16) More than anything else, reform congregants expect their rabbis to be a good <u>pastor</u> (counseling, visitations, officiating at life-cycle events). The performances of most rabbis in this field tends to <u>exceed</u> their congregants' expectations.

17) Those congregants who are usually least satisfied with their rabbis are the ones who report that their rabbis do <u>more</u> than they expect of him.

18) In terms of general platitudes, congregants <u>say</u> they like their rabbis. In answer to specific questions, all sorts of qualifications are voiced.

<u>Concerning the Seminary Student</u>:

1) Many seminarians are disenchanted with many aspects of Reform Judaism. The CCAR is their chief target. They are reticent in revealing their sources of information. Many particularly suspect this study as a CCAR device to undermine the HUC-JIR. On the other hand, many vehemently criticize their seminary.

2) Some 44% of Reform seminarians identify themselves as agnostic. This is more than twice as many as amongst those who have been ordained since 1967. (For rabbis as a whole, the figure is 13%).

3) Only 4% of seminarians believe in God "in the more or less traditional Judaic sense." Belief in a qualified version of God is much lower than for rabbis, much lower even than among rabbis who were ordained in the last five years.

4) Of many reasons given for choosing the rabbinate as a career less than half say that it is because of "my intense belief in God and in Judaism and my desire to continue one of its major traditions, - to be a teacher unto my people." (Rabbis scored this same reason somewhat lower than the seminarians.)

5) Of several reasons given for choosing the rabbinate as a career, the largest number of seminarians (74%) say it is because "as an occupation it offered me the most opportunity to 'do my thing' in terms of my interests, needs, and general fulfillment."

6) Less than half our present seminary students plan to enter the pulpit rabbinate. Some 17% plan to enter teaching immediately after ordination. Another 20% intend to pursue graduate studies.

8) Seminarians tend to be more critical of the Union Prayer Book than are the rabbis.

9) Many wives of seminarians (based on interviews with wives of most recently ordained rabbis), indicate displeasure with HUC-JIR because of the latter's disregard for their welfare during their "student days." Some brand-new rebbetzins describe their days at the seminary with such words as "demeaning" and "dehumanizing."

Concerning Reform Youth:

1) Although virtually all Reform youth (97%) have been or plan to be confirmed, there is much displeasure with this ritual. Many are asking for a good religious high school program instead.

2) Over half of Reform youth say they never hear Zionism as a subject of discussion in their homes, despite the fact that 66% say that contributing to the United Jewish Appeal is the most important element in establishing their Jewish identities.

3) Only two out of three Reform youngsters are solidly pro-Israel. Many express strong anti-Israeli positions.

4) One-third of Reform youth attend services for Festivals and/or Holy Days only; 14% say they rarely or never attend services.

5) Some 50% of Reform youth believe in God "in the more or less traditional sense;" 32% are agnostics, and 4% are atheists.

6) One-fifth of Reform youth indicate the older they get they "become less and less satisfied with synagogue services."

7) Less than one-fifth of Reform youth feel that their "rabbi is intensely interested in the school and gives it the maximum attention that he can."

8) Only 13% of Reform youth say "it is easy for young people to approach and talk with our rabbi."

9) Reform youth feel that their Temple Youth Group should have professional leaders, not parents as leaders.

10) Reform youth view positively UAHC summer camp, but are critical of the ways things are run at these camps.

11) With regard to various components of Jewish identity, many Reform youth do not seem to know what their parents stand for.

12) On every issue of Jewish identity on which they were queried, Reform youth seem to be more detached from Judaism and Jewishness than their parents.

13) Only in anti-semitism do a number of Reform youth (37%) see a possible threat to Jewish survival. Issues such as mixed marriage and weak religious education are seen as threats by small numbers of Reform youngsters.

Concerning the Rebbetzins:

1) Rebbetzins tend to be ambivalent about the rabbinical way of
   life. Only 41% would want their husbands to be rabbis if
   they had it to do all over again. Some 21% would want them
   to be professors instead.

2) Only about 40% of the rebbetzins would say that they are
   living "fulfilling" lives; about one-third say they are
   "lonely," another one-third say it's been "generally good,
   but nothing exciting."

3) About half the rebbetzins feel "the need for developing
   (their) potentialities outside of home and synagogue."

4) While most rebbetzins would approve of their daughter
   marrying a Reform rabbi if that was what the daughter
   wanted, only 4% of the rebbitzins preferred such a choice
   for their child. Only 2% preferred any rabbi as the ideal
   mate for their daughter.

So much for some of the more blatant highlights concerning potential
crisis, even if viewed by the most traditional criteria. Let us now
use a medical model to identify crisis. This provides conceptual
as well as empirical insights.

Psychosomatic medicine identifies an ulcer as a psychosomatic
illness. This means that the psyche (mind) had been exposed to
such stress and strain that it had gone beyond a certain threshold
of endurance at which point the psyche then "takes it out" on the
soma (body). To argue that "it's all in the patient's mind," is
folly. The psyche may still be in a stressful condition, but

the psyche is compensating by its new outlet. The body is now
carrying some of the burden of pain. And now the pain isn't just
in the person's head. It is now based on <u>organic</u>, <u>physical</u> malfunc-
tion.

But the best medical tests may reveal <u>no</u> ulcer. The <u>patient</u> may be
convinced he has an ulcer. The empirical diagnosis reveals <u>no</u> ulcer.
This is <u>hypochondria</u>. But the patient <u>is</u> ill. However, the diagnosis
calls for treating <u>anxiety</u>, a <u>mental</u> condition, not an ulcer, which is
an <u>organic</u> illness.

The <u>medical</u> definition of crisis is as follows:

> The point in the course of a serious disease at which
> a decisive change occurs, leading either to recovery or
> death.

Without arguing whether we are in a true state of crisis or merely
in an anxiety state, there is no question Reform Judaism is in a
state of some <u>malaise</u>. If so, we have problems, but <u>all</u> forms of
illness are not automatically to be labelled as crises. Not if
diagnostic data are to be used honestly and responsibly.

Based on the overall findings from this study, Reform Judaism is
not in a <u>seriously painful and malfunctioning state</u>. This statement
is not made on the basis of an evaluation of all the <u>positive</u> things
that are happening in Reform Judaism. On the contrary, the statement
is made on the basis of an intensive quantitative and qualitative inquiry into the <u>aches and pains</u> of the patient, a sample of which has
just been noted.

Aches and pains there are. The stresses and strains <u>are</u> diagnosable.
Are they hypochondria or organic breakdown? It is very possible, however,

that without treatment, <u>the Movement may have within it the potential for organic breakdown.</u>

But what is the case history of the patient? We mean here the whole organism, - the whole of Judaism. Based on the social change that is now evidencing itself throughout the whole of Judaism, and throughout Reform Judaism in particular, does the case history project a diagnosis of death? The most important thing is the diagnosis. What <u>has been</u> the case history? What is it now?

The case history:

1) Judaism is a case history of Inquisitions, Pogroms, Holocausts, and chronic anti-Semitism even under the best of socio-cultural conditions, and it <u>lives.</u>

2) With all its desecrations from without, with all its self-hatred from within, it <u>lives.</u>

3) From <u>within</u>, we have moved from the Pharisees/Sadducees/Essenes to Orthodox/Conservative/Reform. The case history is a history of argumentation and debate, and Judaism <u>lives.</u>

4) From <u>without</u>, we have confronted an Ethical Culture Society, an American Council on Judaism, and the Bahai and the Unitarians. Judaism <u>lives.</u>

<u>It is a case history of argumentation and debate.</u> Possibly there have been somatic-type stresses and strains that <u>could have</u> produced organic breakdown that <u>might have</u> led to demise. But it didn't!

In a moribund state we never were, and we are not now.

Are we in a seriously painful state? At times very seriously painful.
And we may still have before us more painful days and years of our
lives. But we continue "to be fruitful and to multiply."

Our "adjustment mechanisms" have taken us through years of wandering
to years in Ghettos to Diaspora to the Secular City, Suburbia, and
to Statehood, and the mind and the body have stayed alive, - still
arguing, still debating, and thriving.

Nowhere has the writer seen it expressed more beautifully and with
such poignant realism than in a sermon by Rabbi Abraham J. Feldman,
Rabbi Emeritus, Temple Beth Israel, West Hartford, Connecticut:

> Ours is the romance of a people inspired ... of a people
> whose soul is on fire with the flame which played
> about the crags of Sinai as Moses proclaimed the moral
> law! Ours is a soul on fire with the charge and fervor
> of the prophets! Ours is a soul that harbors the flame
> that consumed the Temple but spared the Torah! Ours
> is a soul purified in the flames of the Inquisition, a
> soul undaunted by the brutalities of nations and ages
> ... Ours is a soul which in spite of all that it has
> witnessed and endured ... still dares to face the
> future with hope and confidence and trust... Ours is
> the romance of a people convenanted with God ...
> Individuals among us ... have failed to grasp the
> significance of the ... ideal glory of our Jewishness.
> There are dead branches on every tree ... but the
> trunk is sturdy.
> ... and even whilst we suffer ... Hamans go and
> Hitlers come--and go, (and) the Jew opens his book
> and reads his (own) tale. Tears glisten in his eyes
> ...*

So much for the case history. There simply is no hard evidence of

---

*Rabbi Abraham J. Feldman, "The Romance of a People," Sources
    of Jewish Inspiration, 1934, pp. 206-209.

any state or condition ever having existed, when Judaism, the
whole corpus, was in the throes of a life and death crisis period.

Are we now in crisis, or are we at another time in the continuum
of history where once again a crescendo of argumentation and
debate is causing some of us to press the panic button?

First of all, even if Reform Judaism, as an organized Movement
were to close its doors, there is no hard evidence that Judaism,
the totality, would die. And what of Reform Judaism? This
study has certainly revealed evidences of stress and strain. Can
these stresses and strains be diagnosed as being psychosomatically
conducive to subsequent organic breakdown? Yes and no. Very
possibly yes, if the aches and pains, and the infections, if any,
are allowed to fester without self-examination, without honest
diagnostic acceptance of what is. Possibly yes, if no treatment or
remedial processes are honestly formulated, honestly invoked, and
honestly pursued.

Can these stresses and strains be diagnosed as hypochondria? To the
extent that there are rabbis, congregants, and rabbinical students,
whose emotional needs (regarding their own personal and/or professional lives), are lacking fulfillment, so that they consciously
or unconsciously project their own discomfort on the system as a
whole, and label the system as sick and dying (sic crisis), - to
that extent there is a state of hypochondria. Can mass hypochondria
lead to mass hysteria to mass organic breakdown? Nothing in the
history of social systems of this ever happening is known to us.
An example is the counter-culture movement in America today. But
the culture lives, and by its very being makes possible the existence of the counter-culture. We are simply in a state of cultural
change.

The heart of the whole question is this: What are the <u>actual</u>
changes that are now taking place in Reform Judaism, and what are the
<u>assumed</u> changes that many believe are taking place? An assumption,
no matter how honestly perceived, may still be only an assumption,
and not a fact. If an unverified assumption is then used <u>as though</u>
<u>it were a fact</u>, the results may bring forth many unwarranted
"conclusions." Such "conclusions" may induce subsequent behavior
that may or may not be justified. Furthermore, such a situation
may actually bring forth rejection of <u>all</u> problems.

Here is how one Board member at a UAHC Regional Biennial Convention
reacted to the question of crisis when the interviewer discussed
the matter with him:

> I think our rabbis are building up anxiety in us.
> Look at this (pointing to the program): Five of the
> six topics listed . . . we're told they are all
> crisis . . . Look at this . . . (He read the follow-
> ing titles:)
>
> 1) The Social Justice Crisis . . .
> 2) The Crisis in Reform Jewish Worship.
> 3) The Crisis in Reform Jewish Education.
> 4) The Crisis in Reform Jewish Youth . . .
> 5) The Crisis in Temple Budgeting.
>
> To me, all this is demoralizing. You know, you can
> always make a crisis. I used to have a foreman
> who always made a crisis of everything. I had to
> let him go. Now we don't have a crisis every
> day. Sure, things go wrong, - all the time . . .
> (but) you make changes . . . adjustments.

To the extent that the rabbinate itself, individually, in small
groups, and in convention assembled will examine the data meticulously, to that extent will they unravel their own structure and

process. A thorough-going diagnosis may be 90% of the "solution."
Honest and knowledgeable confrontation with any problem is the
minimum requirement for dealing with it constructively and
effectively.

The findings that have been presented in this study provide data
for diagnostic purposes.

And thus comes the end to this study, but as the poet T.S. Elliot
put it so plaintively,

        " - the end is where we start from . . ."

APPENDIX

A Multi-University Model

This is a rather unusual question. It will require considerable thought on your part. The question revolves around a hypothetical model of an all-comprehensive school that is designed to provide for all types of religious workers in the total Jewish community (rabbis, researchers, academicians, religious school administrators and teachers, social service workers, community agency personnel, temple administrators, cantors and allied musical personnel, youth camp personnel, etc., etc.).

The hypothetical model is based primarily on the recommendations and comments that have been made by many of your colleagues, and by some rabbinical students. (Possibly you will see some of your own ideas used here.)

The model is not a recommendation: the model was designed for research purposes only. It is being used here as a research technique to eliminate hundreds of questions with hundreds of accompanying explanations that would otherwise have to be asked.

The model (including variations), reflects a joint gathering of ideas to promote comment, and to elicit YOUR ideas, YOUR thoughts, YOUR knowledge, and YOUR recommendations.

The question consists of four parts:

A. Underlying assumptions.

B. The hypothetical model of an all-comprehensive HUC-JIR.

C. Footnotes.

D. Questions for you to answer regarding the assumptions and the model.

A. UNDERLYING ASSUMPTIONS:

1. The four reform training institutions would be reorganized into separate universities, preferably under separate governing bodies, or possibly into one overall university system under one governing body.

2. Each institution would be called the same name, but renamed THE UNIVERSITY OF REFORM JUDAISM or THE UNIVERSITY OF JUDAISM, or JEWISH UNIVERSITY OF AMERICA or similar title, wherein the city of location will be part of the name (such as the California system, e.g., The University of California at Berkeley.)

3. The chief priority would be to train pulpit rabbis. Other priorities, however, would be open, e.g., academic, Jewish social agency, and other occupational areas with focus on Jewish life.

4. A School of Basic Studies (two years) would be prerequisite for all students who wish to enter any of the other undergraduate Schools in the university. However, one could enroll for graduate studies on the basis of earned degrees elsewhere, including the School for Rabbinical Studies.

5. An overall administrator for academic affairs would insure the development of a variety of interdisciplinary majors and minors, and also set up smooth arrangement for students to have resource to an elective system that would make available to them courses from all schools other than the one in which he is enrolled. Thus a student might major in liturgical music in the School of Sacred Music, and might take elective courses in liturgy in The School of Judaica and Cognate Studies, or related courses in The School of Rabbinical Studies. Or a student might major in anthropology in the School of Arts and Humanities, and take appropriate courses in biblical archeology etc. in the other schools.

B. THE UNIVERSITY DESIGN:

		Prerequisite for degrees	Degrees
1.	SCHOOL OF BASIC STUDIES	2 years	A.A. (a)*
2.	SCHOOL OF ARTS AND HUMANITIES	A.A. + 2 years Bachelor's + 1 year M.A. + 2 years	B.A. (b) M.A. Ph.D.
3.	SCHOOL OF SACRED MUSIC	A.A. + 2 years Bachelor's + 1 year M. Mus. + 2 years	B. Mus. (c) M. Mus. D. Mus.
4.	SCHOOL OF RELIGIOUS EDUCATION	A.A. + 2 years Bachelor's + 1 year M.S. + 2 years	B.S. (d) M.S. (e) Ed.D.
5.	SCHOOL OF JUDAICA AND COGNATE STUDIES	A.A. + 2 years Bachelor's + 1 year M.A. + 2 years	B.A. M.A. Ph.D. (f)
6.	SCHOOL OF SOCIAL WELFARE AND COMMUNITY STUDIES	A.A. + 2 years Bachelor's + 2 years M.S.W. + 2 years	B.S. M.S.W. (g) D.S.W.:Ph.D.
7.	SCHOOL OF RABBINICAL STUDIES	**Plan 1** Bachelor's + 2 years (incl. 1 yr. in Israel) M.H.L. + 2 years D.H.L. + 1 yr. (ORDINATION) 5 yrs.	 M.H.L. D.H.L. Ph.D.
		or	
		Plan 2 Bachelor's + 1 yr. in Israel B.H.L. + 1 year M.H.L. + 3 yrs.(ORDINATION) 5 yrs. D.H.L. + 1 year	 B.H.L. M.H.L. D.H.L. Ph.D.
		or	
		Plan 3 Bachelor's + 1 yr. in Israel B.H.L. + 1 year M.H.L. + 3 yrs.(ORDINATION) 5 yrs.	 B.H.L. M.H.L. Ph.D.
		or	
		Plan 4 Bachelor's + 1 yr. in Israel M.H.L. + 2 years D.H.L. + 3 yrs.(ORDINATION) 6 yrs.	 M.H.L. D.H.L. Ph.D. (h)

*Footnotes on following page.

C. <u>FOOTNOTES</u>:

(a) Similar to community college or junior college, but basically liberal arts. Strong <u>survey</u> and <u>orientation</u> courses in such areas as Jewish history, literature, and philosophy; some Hebrew language; comparative religions, human relations. A course or two in education might be taken. Enrollees might be right out of high school or adults. Preparation provides for teacher aides for religious schools, UAHC camp counselors, administrative assistants in Jewish agencies. Primary purpose would be to prepare for upper divisions of the other Schools in the university system. Some graduates, because of precollegiate background, might be eligible to be teachers in synagogue religious schools.

(b) Basically a liberal arts college. Strong majors in comparative religions, comparative religious philosophies, behavioral and social sciences of religion, e.g., psychology of religion, sociology of religion, archeology, linguistics, etc. Strong interdisciplinary programs in conjunction with other Schools of the university system.

(c) Certification for Music Teacher in Religious School. Education courses would be completed in the <u>School of Religious Education</u>. May also provide certification for Cantors.

(d) Certification as Religious School Teacher.

(e) Certification as Religious School Director or Principal.

(f) Primarily for scholars who do not seek ordination.

(g) Same requirements as for American Association of Schools of Social Work.

(h) Several considerations are given to <u>The School of Rabbinical Studies</u> and requirements for ordination:

1) B.H.L. may be granted after one year of study in Israel by Israeli institution, or by American institution in which student is matriculated.

2) Ordination is provided for on the basis of four possible plans, either after five years or six years beyond bacherlor's degree. (There are many other variations.)

3) Ordination may be attained by acquiring the D.H.L. <u>or</u> the Ph.D., or <u>both</u>.

4) <u>Extraordinary flexibility</u> is possible for each student in terms of two conditions:

i) He may continue with a fixed goal from the day he enters the university at any level, or he may shift his goal in terms of his interests and aptitudes as he proceeds, and as these develop.

ii) Requirements of all degrees can be adjusted in terms of
varied educational background and proficiencies that
student possesses at any stage and level in his studies.
Flexibility permits, for example, for a student who has
earned his A.A. and B.A. (the latter from The School of
Judaica and Cognate Studies), and has excellent Hebrew
language facility to bypass some of the later requirements for D.H.L. and Ph.D. programs, thus possibly earn-
ing a doctorate and ordination a year or so earlier than
usual.